Madame est trop belle; comédie en trois actes par Eugene labiche & Alfred Duru

Eugène Labiche, Alfred Duru

MADAME EST TROP BELLE

Poissy. — Typ. S. Lejay et Cie.

MADAME EST TROP BELLE

COMÉDIE EN TROIS ACTES

PAR

MM. EUGÈNE LABICHE & ALFRED DURU

Représentée pour la première fois, à Paris, sur le théâtre du Gymnase,
le 30 mars 1874.

PARIS

E. DENTU, ÉDITEUR

LIBRAIRIE DE LA SOCIÉTÉ DES AUTEURS ET COMPOSITEURS DRAMATIQUES

ET DE LA SOCIÉTÉ DES GENS DE LETTRES

PALAIS-ROYAL, 17 ET 19, GALERIE D'ORLÉANS

1874

PERSONNAGES

MONTGISCAR...............................	MM.	RAVEL.
CHAMBRELAN...		PRADEAU.
JULES DE CLERCY.................	{	LANDROL.
		PUJOL.
DE GOBERVILLE......		FRANCÈS.
ERNEST MONTGISCAR		F. ACHARD.
OCTAVE BLANDAR...		ANDRIEU.
MOULINOT.........		BLAISOT.
UN GARDIEN DU MUSÉE DES ANTIQUES...		PLET.
HECTOR GRANDIN....		· LENORMANT.
JUSTIN, domestique...		MEY.
JEANNE, fille de Chambrelan..."	Mmes {	ANGELO.
		JULIETTE.
HÉLOISE DE GOBERVILLE...		SPÉLIERS.
HERMANCE...............		TESSIER.

INVITÉS DES DEUX SEXES.

UNE FAMILLE ANGLAISE.

La scène à Paris, de nos jours.

MADAME EST TROP BELLE

ACTE PREMIER

Une salle au musée des Antiques, au Louvre. — Contre les murs des bas-reliefs, des têtes d'empereurs romains sur des socles. — Au milieu, sur un piédestal, la statue de Pollux. — Galeries à droite et à gauche, deuxième plan.

SCÈNE PREMIÈRE

LE GARDIEN, puis OCTAVE.

Au lever du rideau le gardien a le manteau vert pardessus son uniforme ; il se promène un instant sans parler, puis il s'arrête devant le public et bâille.

LE GARDIEN.

Mon Dieu ! que c'est ennuyeux d'être gardien au musée des Antiques On ne voit jamais personne... en haut, à la peinture, ils ont de la chance. . c'est plein de dames qui peignent sur des échelles. mais ici pas un chat !.. Ça finit par rendre mélancolique. (Apercevant Octave au fond venant de droite. — A part.) Tiens ! un monsieur !... ça doit

1.

être un étranger. (s'avançant d'un air aimable vers Octave.) Monsieur... *

OCTAVE.

Brrou!... Il ne fait pas chaud dans votre musée des Antiques.

LE GARDIEN.

On n'y allume jamais de feu... on dit que c'est contraire aux statues.

OCTAVE.

Je comprends... ça leur fait monter le sang à la tête.

LE GARDIEN, riant par complaisance.

Ah! ah!... monsieur est Anglais?

OCTAVE.

Moi, pourquoi voulez-vous que je sois Anglais?

LE GARDIEN.

Dame!... nous voyons si peu de Français.

OCTAVE, ouvrant un album.

Non... je suis statuaire, je viens dessiner... prendre des mouvements.

LE GARDIEN, heureux.

Ah!... alors Monsieur viendra tous les jours.

OCTAVE.

Peut-être. (A part.) Il m'ennuie, j'ai un rendez-vous avec une dame. (Il se met à dessiner la statue de Pollux.)

LE GARDIEN, familier.

Et qu'est-ce qu'on dit de nouveau?... avons-nous un ministère?

OCTAVE.

Pardon... je ne peux pas travailler quand on me parle.

LE GARDIEN.

Tiens!

OCTAVE.

Ni quand on me regarde... vous comprenez.

* Octave, le Gardien.

LE GARDIEN, s'en allant.

Très-bien... très-bien... (A part.) C'est un paresseux!
(Il disparaît à droite.)

OCTAVE, seul, fermant son album

J'ai cru qu'il ne s'en irait pas. (Tirant sa montre.) Je suis
en avance... Madame de Goberville ne tardera pas à arriver... charmante femme!... seulement, elle vous donne
des rendez-vous, dans des endroits... mal chauffés...
brou!... Puisque je suis en avance, je vais marcher un
peu... il fait ici un froid de Sibérie. (Il sort par la gauche
au moment où le gardien reparaît du côté opposé.)

SCÈNE II

LE GARDIEN, puis DE CLERCY.

LE GARDIEN, se promène un instant avec mélancolie, baillant.

Mon Dieu, que je m'ennuie! (Apercevant de Clercy qui entre
à droite.) Ah! encore un monsieur! (Le saluant d'un air très-
aimable.) Monsieur cherche quelque chose?*

DE CLERCY.

Oui... la statue de Pollux, s'il vous plaît?

LE GARDIEN, désignant la statue.

La voici. (Récitant.) Telle qu'elle a été trouvée en 1821
dans les jardins de la villa Palmiéri et expédiée par les
soins de M. le consul de France

DE CLERCY, l'arrêtant.

Ne vous fatiguez pas... ça m'est complètement égal...
ce n'est pas pour ça que je viens. **

LE GARDIEN.

Ah!... alors monsieur vient?...

* De Clercy, le Gardien.
** Le Gardien, de Clercy.

DE CLERCY, avec intention.

Chercher la solitude.

LE GARDIEN.

Monsieur ne peut pas trouver un meilleur endroit. (Changeant de ton.) Eh bien! quoi de nouveau? avons-nous un ministère?

DE CLERCY.

Et la solitude, consiste à rester seul... ainsi ne vous gênez pas pour moi... surveillez vos statues, je vous en prie.

LE GARDIEN.

Monsieur est bien bon. (A part et s'en allant.) C'est un Anglais qui a le spleen. (Il disparaît à gauche.)

DE CLERCY, seul.

Deux heures... j'espère que M. Montgiscar, mon oncle, ne me fera pas attendre. C'est un banquier, très-occupé... mais exact. Il a mis dans sa tête de me marier... il a peut-être raison, j'ai passé l'âge des fantaisies... et si la demoiselle me plaît, ma foi!... Notre entrevue doit avoir lieu ici... par hasard... au pied de la statue de Pollux... une idée de mon oncle... Ah! ça, mais il est en retard, pourvu que le côté de la demoiselle n'arrive pas avant lui... je serais obligé de me présenter moi-même. Ah! le voici!

SCÈNE III

MONTGISCAR, DE CLERCY, puis LE GARDIEN.

MONTGISCAR, entrant de droite, sa montre à la main, il porte un parapluie.

Deux heures à la Bourse... tu es en avance, c'est de l'inexactitude... (Lui serrant la main.) Du reste, ça va bien?

DE CLERCY.

Aussi bien que possible dans ma position.

MONTGISCAR.

Quelle position?

DE CLERCY.

D'homme à marier... j'ai mal dormi... j'ai rêvé que ça réussissait...

MONTGISCAR.

Mon ami, je te préviens que les plaisanteries sur le mariage sont très-usées... Je suis ton oncle, j'ai été ton tuteur, c'est moi qui t'ai élevé, par conséquent tu dois avoir confiance en moi.

DE CLERCY.

Oh! ça!

MONTGISCAR.

Eh bien, marie-toi... il n'est que temps!

DE CLERCY.

Comment!

MONTGISCAR.

Tu te déplumes sur les tempes, tu as quelques fils d'argent dans les cheveux, et enfin les femmes commencent à avoir confiance en toi... c'est un symptôme...

DE CLERCY.

Cependant, mon oncle...

MONTGISCAR.

Mon Dieu, tu fais encore prime, mais dans deux ans tu seras au-dessous du pair...

DE CLERCY.

Merci bien!

MONTGISCAR.

Voyons... je suis très-pressé... je suis dans les affaires, causons de notre entrevue. Chambrelan va venir avec sa fille... elle ne sait rien... toi, de ton côté, tu es censé ne rien savoir, moi non plus... nous nous rencontrerons par hasard... je te présenterai comme un de mes correspondants de Roubaix. . non, de Bordeaux, c'est plus gai.

DE CLERCY.

Comme vous voudrez.

MONTGISCAR.

Maintenant, quelques renseignements sur la famille dans laquelle tu vas entrer.

DE CLERCY.

Ah ! permettez... pas si vite !

MONTGISCAR.

Le père, M. Chambrelan, est un brave homme; pas instruit, pas spirituel... mais qui a gagné une grosse fortune à fabriquer des poignées de sabre, dans la ville de Saumur.

DE CLERCY.

Des poignées de sabre ?

MONTGISCAR.

Oui, les uns fabriquent la lame, les autres, la poignée... on fait ce qu'on peut... Quant à la demoiselle...

DE CLERCY.

Est-elle jolie ?

MONTGISCAR.

Jolie, ce n'est pas assez... C'est une beauté exceptionnelle... une de ces beautés qui font faire : ah !

DE CLERCY.

Diable ! mon oncle, vous allez m'effrayer... j'ai peur maintenant de la trouver trop belle.

MONTGISCAR *.

Allons donc ! est-ce que la mariée est jamais trop belle ! Tu ne connais pas les avantages qu'il y a à épouser une jolie femme... je ne parle pas du tête-à-tête qui a pourtant son mérite... D'abord, quand on possède une jolie femme, on ne court pas après celle des autres... généralement.

* De Clercy, Montgiscar.

DE CLERCY.

Ce n'est pas toujours une raison.

MONTGISCAR.

Aussi ai-je dit : généralement... Ensuite une jolie femme... honnête, bien entendu, c'est une puissance, c'est une force pour un mari. S'il a du goût pour le monde, tous les salons s'ouvrent devant lui; s'il est ambitieux, les protections, les influences, les recommandations viennent à sa rencontre; s'il aime la table, ça s'est vu, les invitations pleuvent sur son estomac... enfin sa femme est un talisman ; comme dans les féeries, il n'a que la peine de la montrer et de souhaiter.

DE CLERCY.

Oui, mais il y a le revers de la médaille, le danger...

MONTGISGAR.

Quel danger ?

DE CLERCY.

Dame ! une jolie femme est plus attaquée qu'une autre...

MONTGISCAR.

Si elle est plus attaquée, elle est plus habituée à se défendre...

DE CLERCY.

Quand elle a de l'esprit, mais mademoiselle Chambrelan a-t-elle de l'esprit ? Voilà la question

MONTGISCAR.

Mon ami, on ne sait jamais si une jolie fille a de l'esprit... la beauté est un manteau tellement éblouissant qu'on n'en peut distinguer l'étoffe... Une niaiserie qui tombe d'une jolie bouche, devient tout du suite une perle... Ainsi, je connais une femme, adorablement belle; à tout ce qu'on lui dit, elle répond : « C'est splendide ! c'est splendide ! » Ce n'est pas grand chose, eh bien ! c'est délicieux !

DE CLERCY.

Diable ! vous n'êtes pas rassurant.

MONTGISCAR.

Mais au contraire, tout ce que je souhaite à mon fils Ernest, c'est de trouver une femme pareille à celle que je te propose.

DE CLERCY.

Eh bien ! mais, mon oncle, il n'y a encore rien de fait ; je ne connais pas mademoiselle Chambrelan, ainsi ne vous gênez pas.

MONTGISCAR.

Non... je te remercie, mon ami... mais elle n'est pas assez riche pour ton cousin.

DE CLERCY.

Ah !

MONTGISCAR.

Moi, je donne cinq cent mille francs, elle n'en a que deux cent mille... Je rêve pour Ernest la fille de la maison Burnett, Baring et Cie... crédit de premier ordre.

DE CLERCY.

Elle est jolie ?

MONTGISCAR.

Jolie... elle a une beauté personnelle qui n'est pas celle de tout le monde... Ernest est à Vienne, il revient dans un mois, et en attendant, je couve l'affaire.

DE CLERCY.

Brrou ! ne trouvez-vous pas qu'il fait ici un froid de loup ? (Il remonte.)

MONTGISCAR *.

Oui, mais on n'y est bien tranquille. (Tirant sa montre.) Deux heures et demie, est-ce qu'il y aurait malentendu avec Chambrelan ?

_____

* Montgiscar, de Clercy.

DE CLERCY.

Si nous cherchions dans les autres salles, ça nous échaufferait.

MONTGISCAR, apercevant le gardien qui se promène *.

Attends!... (Au gardien.) Pardon, mon ami...

LE GARDIEN, s'approchant avec empressement.

Monsieur?

MONTGISCAR.

Est-ce qu'il n'y aurait pas par hasard deux statues de Pollux?

LE GARDIEN.

Non monsieur... mais nous avons là-bas un magnifique Castor... il ne reste plus que le torse (Récitant.) Il a été trouvé en 1824 dans les jardins de la villa Palmieri et expédié par les soins de M. le consul de France.

MONTGISCAR, l'interrompant.**

Merci! merci! (A part.) Si on le laissait faire il nous réciterait le livret. (A de Clercy.) Ils auront peut-être confondu Castor avec Pollux... Allons voir.

DE CLERCY. ***

Allons!

LE GARDIEN, récitant.

Ce morceau est justement regardé comme un des modèles les plus purs... il a été trouvé...

MONTGISCAR, au gardien, l'interrompant.

Merci, mon ami, merci... (Ils sortent tous deux par la gauche.)

* Montgiscar. le Gardien, de Clercy.
** Le Gardien, Montgiscar, de Clercy.
*** De Clercy, Montgiscar, le Gardien.

SCÈNE IV

LE GARDIEN, puis CHAMBRELAN et JEANNE.

LE GARDIEN, seul.

Ce ne sont pas là de vrais savants... (Apercevant Chambrelan et Jeanne qui entrent par la droite*.)Encore deux! Que de monde aujourd'hui! Est-ce qu'il peut?

CHAMBRELAN, au gardien.

Pardon... Pourriez-vous m'indiquer la statue de Pollux?

LE GARDIEN.

La voici. (récitant.) Telle qu'elle a été trouvée en 1821, dans les jardins...

CHAMBRELAN, l'interrompant.

Ça, ça m'est égal! (à part.) C'est drôle, je ne vois pas Montgiscar...

LE GARDIEN, à part.

Ils demandent tous la statue de Pollux, et ils ne veulent écouter aucun détail.

CHAMBRELAN, au gardien.

Mon ami, est-ce qu'il n'y aurait pas deux statues de Pollux?

LE GARDIEN.

Non, monsieur, mais nous avons là-bas un magnifique Castor.

CHAMBRELAN.

Ah! c'est un animal bien laborieux... l'emblème du travail!

LE GARDIEN.

Mais non, monsieur... Castor, c'est l'ami de Pollux... une autre statue...

CHAMBRELAN

Ah! très bien... très bien...

* Le Gardien, Chambrelan, Jeanne.

LE GARDIEN, à part.

Ce n'est pas encore un vrai savant celui-là...

CHAMBRELAN, à Jeanne.

Attendons!

JEANNE.

Attendons... quoi?

CHAMBRELAN.

Tu le sauras tout à l'heure.

LE GARDIEN, à Chambrelan, avec familiarité.

Eh bien, monsieur... quoi de nouveau?... avons-nous un ministère?

CHAMBRELAN.

Un ministère? (à part) Il veut me faire parler politique (haut.) Pourquoi un ministère? Je le trouve très bon le ministère!.. Et celui qui viendra après, et tous les autres aussi!

LE GARDIEN.

Ne vous fâchez pas.

CHAMBRELAN.

Pardon, j'ai à causer avec ma fille; je crois qu'on vous appelle par là!

LE GARDIEN.

J'y vais. (à part.) C'est un homme qui n'a pas d'opinions.

(Il sort par la gauche.)

SCENE V

CHAMBRELAN, JEANNE.

JEANNE.

Voyons papa, maintenant que nous sommes seuls.. pourquoi m'as-tu amenée dans ce musée?... Tu as mis une cravate blanche, il y a quelque chose?

CHAMBRELAN.

Eh bien oui, il y a quelque chose... il s'agit d'une entre-vue pour toi.

JEANNE.

Oh! que je vais avoir peur!...

CHAMBRELAN.

Mais non! puisque le jeune homme ne sait rien... tu es censée ne rien savoir... mi, non plus .. personne ne sait rien .. c'est une rencontre fortuite. — Tiens! vous voilà! — Ah! si je m'attendais à vous rencontrer! De cette façon, vous vous verrez, vous vous examinerez, et si vous vous convenez... nous donnerons suite à nos projets...

JEANNE.

Et... est-il bien, ce jeune homme?

CHAMBRELAN.

Physiquement, je ne le connais pas... c'est le neveu de monsieur Montgiscar, un banquier des mes amis... pas très spirituel, mais très riche... son neveu est un ancien élève de l'école Polytechnique... ingénieur des ponts-et chaussées...

JEANNE.

Qu'est-ce que c'est que ça, ingénieur des ponts-et-chaussées?

CHAMBRELAN.

Ces sont des jeunes gens auxquels le gouvernement apprend les mathématiques .. pour leur faire faire des ponts... On vient! Ce sont eux! ayons l'air de nous pro-mener.

(Ils remontent en se promenant.)

SCÈNE VI

LES MÊMES, MONTGISCAR, DE CLERCY.

MONTGISCAR, bas à de Clercy.

Les voici ! ayons l'air de nous promener. (Haut à Chambrelan*.) Monsieur Chambrelan ! je ne me trompe pas ?

CHAMBRELAN.

Monsieur Montgiscar ! ah ! si je m'attendais à vous rencontrer !

MONTGISCAR.

On se serait donné rendez-vous...

CHAMBRELAN.

Le fait est que c'est un hasard. (Désignant Jeanne). Je vous
présente ma fille...

MONTGISCAR, saluant.

Mademoiselle... et moi, monsieur Jules de Clercy... un
de mes correspondants de Roub... (Se reprenant.) De Bordeaux !... que je viens de rencontrer aussi... par hasard.

DE CLERCY, saluant Chambrelan et sa fille.

Monsieur... Mademoiselle... (a part.) Charmante !...

MONTGISCAR.

Est-ce extraordinaire ? Je vous croyais à Saumur.

CHAMBRELAN.

Non... nous habitons Paris maintenant... depuis deux,
mois !

MONTGISCAR, bas à de Clercy.

Dis quelque chose !

DE CLERCY, bas.

Oui...** (à Chambrelan.) Ah ! monsieur connaît Saumur !
charmante ville... que j'ai visitée en détail.

* Jeanne, Chambrelan, Montgiscar, de Cercy.
** Jeanne, Chambrelan, de Clercy, Montgiscar.

JEANNE.

Il y   un bien beau pont...

CHAMBRELAN.

Superbe! le pont de Saumur est renommé! Il est moins bien que celui de Bordeaux... parce que dame! le pont de Bordeaux!...

MONTGISCAR.

Oh! oui' le pont de Bordeaux!...

DE CLERCY

Sans doute... le pont de Bordeaux... (à part.) Qu'est-ce qu'ils ont donc à me parler de pont? — (Haut à Jeanne.) Vous aimez les voyages, mademoiselle?

JEANNE.

Oh! beaucoup... avec mon père, nous avons déjà visité, Florence, Rome, Naples, et tout le midi de la France.

CHAMBRELAN.

Moi, ce qui m'a le plus étonné, c'est le Colisée... à Rome...

DE CLERCY

Je crois bien, le Colisée!...

CHAMBRELAN.

Il y a là un écho!... Quand on fait : hum! c'est répété quinze fois... merveilleux! merveilleux!

DE CLERCY.

Et vous, mademoiselle, qu'est-ce qui vous a le plus frappé?

JEANNE.

Dame!... je ne sais pas... (Tout à coup.) C'est le pont du Gard!

CHAMBRELAN.

Oh! le pont du Gard'!... Quel pont!

MONTGISCAR.

Oh! oui! le pont du Gard! Quel pont!

DE CLERCY, à part.

Ah! nous recommençons.

MONTGISCAR, bas à de Clercy

L'as-tu assez vue?

DE CLERCY, bas.

Non... jamais assez!... elle est ravissante!

CHAMBRELAN, bas à sa fille.

Examine-le bien... je vais le faire causer- (Haut à Mont giscar.) Quel temps! quel temps! vous avez bien fait de prendre un parapluie.

MONTGISCAR.

Oui, mon baromètre baissait.

CHAMBRELAN*.

Tiens! le mien montait... comment est-il fait votre baromètre?

MONGISCAR.

C'est un tube... avec du mercure...

CHAMBRELAN.

Comme celui de l'ingénieur Chevalier, sur le Pont-Neuf. (A de Clercy.) Voilà encore un beau pont!

MONTGISCAR.

Ah! oui! le Pont-Neuf!

DE CLERCY.

Certainement... le Pont-Neuf. (A part.) C'est un tic!

CHAMBRELAN.

Eh bien! moi, mon baromètre est construit sur un tout autre système.

DE CLERCY, à part.

Allons! les baromètres maintenant!

CHAMBRELAN.

C'est un grand cadran, avec des aiguilles... on tape dessus, c'est très-gai (A de Clercy). Et vous, Monsieur... comment est-il votre baromètre?

DE CLERCY.

Moi? mais, je n'en ai pas.

* Jeanne, Chambrelan, Montgiscar, de Clercy.

CHAMBRELAN, s'oubliant.

Il faudra en acheter un, c'est très-commode dans un
ménage.

MONTGISCAR, toussant pour l'avertir.

Hum !

JEANNE, bas.

Papa !

CHAMBRELAN, vivement.

Dans un ménage de garçon, s'entend ! (Bas à Montgiscar.)
Dites donc... je crois s'ils se sont assez vus ?...

MONTGISCAR, bas.

Dame ! s'ils ne se connaissent pas maintenant !

CHAMBRELAN bas.

Laissez-moi seul avec ma fille, je vais l'interroger.

MONTGISCAR, bas.

De mon côté, je vais questionner mon neveu.

CHAMBRELAN, bas.

Revenez dans cinq minutes... par hasard.

MONTGISCAR, bas.

Oui, je vais perdre un gant... ça nous fera une rentrée. (Haut.) Nous allons continuer notre promenade.
(Saluant.) Cher Monsieur... Mademoiselle.

DE CLERCY, saluant aussi.

Monsieur... Mademoiselle !

CHAMBRELAN.

Enchanté !... charmé !...

MONTGISCAR.

Nous allons voir un sarcophage de Théodose qu'on dit
extrèmement curieux *. (Il laisse tomber son gant, bas à Chambrelan.) Le gant !

CHAMBRELAN, à part.

Il est très fin !

* De Clercy, Montgiscar. Chambrelan, Jeanne.

MONTGISCAR, sortant, à de Clercy.

Eh bien ?

DE CLERCY.

Elle est charmante ! mais le père ne m'a pas l'air fort.

MONTGISCAR.

Oh ! le père !... Il faisait très-bien les poignées de sabre. (Il disparaît, avec de Clercy, par la gauche.)

SCÈNE VII

CHAMBRELAN, JEANNE.

CHAMBRELAN.

Voyons, comment le trouves-tu ? Tu as eu le temps de l'étudier...

JEANNE.

Dame ! papa, il me paraît comme il faut.

CHAMBRELAN.

Oui, il est distingué.

JEANNE.

Seulement, il parle trop souvent de ses ponts.

CHAMBRELAN.

Qu'est-ce que tu veux ? il a l'amour de sa profession... après ça... s'il ne te convient pas... ne te gêne pas...

JEANNE.

Je ne dis pas ça...

CHAMBRELAN.

Avec ta beauté, tu peux choisir...

JEANNE.

Vous me parlez toujours de ma beauté, mais tout le monde n'est peut-être pas de votre avis ?

CHAMBRELAN.

C'est impossible ! Comme père, je ne dois pas te faire de

compliments, je le sais... mais je ne puis m'empêcher de reconnaître qu'à la perfection du visage, tu joins la grâce. le charme...

JEANNE.

Oh ! papa !

CHAMBRELAN.

Est-ce la vérité ? Dans la rue, dans les promenades, tu fais sensation ; on nous suit, j'entends murmurer les propos les plus flatteurs... Et dame ! je ne le cache pas, ça me fait plaisir.

JEANNE.

Ah bien ! moi, ça ne m'amuse pas !... ces messieurs qui vous regardent sous le nez.

CHAMBRELAN.

Ce n'est pas leur faute... ils ne peuvent pas s'en empêcher.., dis-toi : ils ne peuvent pas s'en empêcher !... Il faut t'habituer de bonne heure, ma chère enfant, à recevoir les hommages qui te sont dûs... Ta mère, qui était belle aussi, voyait tomber toute la ville de Saumur à ses pieds, sans en être émue .. Elle cueillait les cœurs sur son passage, comme on cueille des roses, dans un jardin qui vous appartient. Fais comme elle, mon enfant, la nature t'a comblée... marche dans ton triomphe.

JEANNE.

Mais papa...

CHAMBRELAN.

Maintenant, nous disons que cet ingénieur ne te plaît pas... très-bien !

JEANNE, vivement

Mais je n'ai pas dit un mot de cela.

CHAMBRELAN

Alors il te plaît. . très-bien !

JEANNE.

Mais..

CHAMBRELAN.

Avec ta beauté, tu peux choisir... si tu le veux, il sera ton mari...

JEANNE.

Ce n'est pas si pressé... Quand le reverrez-vous ?

CHAMBRELAN.

Tout de suite !

JEANNE.

Mais il est parti.

CHAMBRELAN.

Chut !... l'oncle a laissé tomber son gant... le voilà !... Tu es censée ne pas le savoir... moi non plus.

SCÈNE VIII

LES MÊMES, MONTGISCAR, DE CLERCY *.

MONTGISCAR.

C'est encore nous... Je viens de m'apercevoir que j'ai perdu un de mes gants.

CHAMBRELAN.

Vraiment ?... nous ne l'avons pas vu !

MONTGISCAR, ayant l'air de chercher.

Où diable peut-il être ! (Le trouvant) Ah ! le voici !... le voici !

CHAMBRELAN.

Ah ! bien !... on peut appeler ça de la chance !

DE CLERCY, à part.

Ils sont d'une finesse !

CHAMBRELAN, bas à Montgiscar.

Eh bien ! que dit votre neveu ?

* De Clercy, Montgiscar, Chambrelan, Jeanne

MONTGISCAR, bas.

Il est enthousiasmé! c'est du délire.

CHAMBRELAN, bas à sa fille.

Il est enthousiasmé! c'est du délire.

MONTGISCAR, bas à Chambrelan.

Et votre fille? son sentiment?

CHAMBRELAN, bas.

Il n'a pas déplu.

MONTGISCAR, bas à son neveu.

Tu n'as pas déplu!

DE CLERCY.

Bravo! (Bas à Montgiscar) Alors vite, mon oncle, faites la demande!

MONTGISCAR, bas.

' La demande... ici?

DE CLERCY.

Puisque nous sommes réunis... il faut battre le fer...

MONTGISCAR.

C'est juste... D'ailleurs, je suis pressé. (Bas à Chambrelan) Dites donc, nous allons vous faire la demande.

CHAMBRELAN, bas.

Comment! au musée...

MONTGISCAR.

C'est de l'empressement .. il n'y a personne... nous serons aussi bien là que dans votre salon.

CHAMBRELAN.

Cependant les convenances ..

MONTGISCAR.

Vous savez, moi, je suis dans les affaires... je n'ai pas une minute à perdre.

CHAMBRELAN, bas.

Je comprends... je comprends.. Allons préparez-vous... (Bas à Jeanne) Il va me faire la demande...

JEANNE, à part.

Comment ! mais je ne suis pas en toilette !

MONTGISCAR, se posant cérémonieusement.

M. Chambrelan... oncle de mon neveu... j'ai reçu ses confidences... il aime !...

CHAMBRELAN.

C'est fatal !

MONTGISCAR, continuant.

Une minute a suffi pour le fixer... il cherchait une jeune fille accomplie... il a trouvé un ange.

CHAMBRELAN, approuvant.

Très bien !

MONTGISCAR.

J'ai donc l'honneur de vous demander pour mon neveu la main de mademoiselle Chambrelan. (Bas à Chambrelan). A vous !...

CHAMBRELAN, se posant.

M. Montgiscar... père de ma fille, je crois être son interprète... et le mien, en vous disant que votre recherche nous honore, autant qu'elle nous flatte... (A de Clercy) M. de Clercy, je vous considère, à partir d'aujourd'hui comme le fiancé de ma fille... et je vous autorise à donner cours à l'admiration légitime qu'elle est en droit de vous inspirer.

DE CLERCY, avec joie, allant à Jeanne *.

Ah ! monsieur ! mademoiselle !... que je suis heureux.

MONTGISCAR.

Voilà qui est fait. (Tirant sa montre) 22 minutes.

DE CLERCY.

Que vous êtes bonne, mademoiselle, d'avoir bien voulu m'agréer.

* Montgiscar, Chambrelan, de Clercy, Jeanne.

JEANNE.

Du moment, monsieur, que vous étiez présenté par mon père...

DE CLERCY.

Je vous promets l'affection la plus profonde, la plus dévouée, la plus tendre...

MONTGISCAR, bas à Chambrelan.

Les voilà partis ! j'ai été comme ça ! Le jour où j'ai été accepté, dans ma joie, j'ai cassé un globe de pendule.

CHAMBRELAN.

Comment ça ?

MONTGISCAR.

J'avais ma canne à la main... et en me jetant dans les bras de ma belle-mère... (Il lève violemment son parapluie, attrape un des bras de la statue de Pollux et le casse) Oh ! saperlotte !

TOUS.

Cassé !

CHAMBRELAN.

Un antique !

MONTGISCAR, ramassant le bras.

C'est donc en sucre ces machines là ?

CHAMBRELAN.

Le gardien ! (Montgiscar fourre vivement le bras dans sa poche, le gardien passe nonchalamment au fond).

MONTGISCAR, à Chambrelan.

Il est parti ?

CHAMBRELAN, à de Clercy.

Il est parti ?

DE CLERCY.

Il est parti !

JEANNE *.

Parti !

* Montgiscar, Chambrelan, Jeanne, Clercy.

MONTGISCAR.

Nous voilà bien !... Ce bras est au gouvernement, et c'est le droit. Le bras droit du gouvernement !... Que faire ?

CHAMBRELAN.

Cachez-le... et sauvons nous !

MONTGISCAR.

Oh ! non !... on pourrait croire que je veux dévaliser le musée. (Tirant le bras de sa poche) Si je pouvais le remettre adroitement.

CHAMBRELAN.

J'ai votre affaire... j'ai vu une boutique, en face le guichet du Louvre, où l'on vend une composition appelée : Mastic d'Athènes.

MONTGISCAR.

Qu'est-ce que c'est que ça ?

CHAMBRELAN.

C'est une espèce de gélatine liquide, en bouteille .. il paraît que ça recolle pour l'éternité... à ce que dit le prospectus.

MONTGISCAR.

Vous me sauvez .. (Il fourre le bras dans la poche de son paletot.) Jules !

DE CLERCY.

Mon oncle.

MONTGISCAR.

Va me chercher une bouteille de ce mastic d'Athènes, en face le guichet du Louvre.

DE CLERCY.

Moi, à votre place, j'aimerais mieux déclarer l'accident.

MONTGISCAR.

Merci, pour qu'on me fasse payer la statue entière !.. va, dépêche toi !...

* Chambrelan, Jeanne, Montgiscar, de Clercy.

DE CLERCY.

Vous le voulez?... J'y vais!... (Il sort vivement par la droite.)

SCÈNE IX

JEANNE, CHAMBRELAN, MONTGISCAR.

MONTGISCAR, à Chambrelan.

Nous allons recoller ça à nous deux... vous avez fabriqué des poignées de sabre... vous ne devez pas être embarrassé. (Le gardien passe au fond.)

CHAMBRELAN.

Non... je ne suis pas maladroit... mais il faudrait occuper le gardien *.

MONTGISCAR.

Rien de plus facile... il aime à causer... Mademoiselle Jeanne, ma nièce, va se faire expliquer le sarcophage de Théodose... Il y en a pour trois bons quarts d'heure.

CHAMBRELAN.

Très-bien... (A sa fille.) Tu entends... le sarcophage de Théodose... écoute-le avec avidité... prends même quelques notes...

JEANNE.

Je comprends... soyez tranquilles... (Elle sort par la gauche avec le gardien.)

LE GARDIEN, en sortant, à Jeanne.

Il a été trouvé en 1821...

(Le gardien et Jeanne disparaissent par la gauche.)

* Chambrelan, Jeanne, Montgiscar.

SCÈNE X

MONTGISCAR, CHAMBRELAN.

MONTGISCAR.

Jules est bien long à revenir.

CHAMBRELAN.

Un peu de patience... sapristi! qu'il fait froid. (Éternuant.) Je m'enrhume.

MONTGISCAR.

Moi, j'ai les pieds à la glace... marchons un peu..., et ne cassons rien! (Ils se promènent un moment.)

CHAMBRELAN.

En attendant votre neveu, si nous causions un peu du contrat.

MONTGISCAR.

Je veux bien... ça nous échauffera... de notre part tout est clair, net et liquide. (Il éternue.) Tiens! je m'enrhume aussi... (Reprenant.) Nous apportons quinze mille livres de rentes, représentées par une maison, sise rue Amelot.

CHAMBRELAN.

Des boutiques?

MONTGISCAR.

Quoi?

CHAMBRELAN.

Avez-vous des boutiques?

MONTGISCAR.

Une seule..., un boulanger.

CHAMBRELAN.

Ça met le feu.

MONTGISCAR.

Nous sommes assurés... d'ailleurs ne disons pas de mal du feu.

2

CHAMBRELAN, relevant son collet.

Oh! non! ici surtout.

MONTGISCAR.

Quant à vous, vous m'avez annoncé deux cent mille francs.

CHAMBRELAN.

C'est exact

MONTGISCAR.

Qui se composent?

CHAMBRELAN.

Cent mille, en cinq pour cent libéré

MONTGISCAR.

Bon!

CHAMBRELAN,

75 mille, en obligations de l'Ouest.

MONTGISCAR.

Bon!

CHAMBRELAN, hésitant.

Et 50 actions des mines de phosphore des Asturies.

MONTGISCAR.

Aïe!... aie!...

CHAMBRELAN, vivement.

Oui... mais c'est une valeur qui rebondira.

MONTGISCAR.

A quel taux les comptez-vous vos phosphores?

CHAMBRELAN.

Mais... au cours d'émission... à 500 francs.

MONTGISCAR.

Ah! non! il ne faut pas me la faire! à moi, un banquier!

CHAMBRELAN.

Quoi?

MONTGISCAR.

Je ne connais que la cote... 47 francs... et offert... et offert!... nous ne pouvons pas accepter ça pour 25,000.

CHAMBRELAN.

Laissez-moi vous expliquer... j'ai acheté ces valeurs pour le compte de ma fille, avec le bien de sa mère... si elles montent, tant mieux... si elles baissent, c'est un malheur.

MONTGISCAR.

Ça ne nous regarde pas... vous annoncez 200 mille francs... il en manque 22 mille...

CHAMBRELAN

Mais je n'ai pas envie de les perdre... (s'attendrissant.) Je perds déjà ma fille... une ange!

MONTGISCAR, l'imitant.

Et moi, je perds mon neveu .. un autre ange!

CHAMBRELAN.

Alors, monsieur, vous marchandez mon enfant !

MONTGISCAR.

Non... je marchande vos phosphores .. vous voulez nous colloquer pour 500 francs ce qui en vaut 47 . je trouve ça un peu... ficelle, comme on dit à la Bourse.

CHAMBRELAN, irrité.

Ficelle ! ficelle ! monsieur, retirez le mot !

MONTGISCAR.

Jamais de la vie !

CHAMBRELAN.

Eh bien ! il n'y a rien de fait !

MONTGISCAR.

Comme vous voudrez !

CHAMBRELAN.

Ma fille avec sa beauté hors ligne ne sera pas embarrassée pour... (Il éternue.)

MONTGISCAR.

Que Dieu vous bénisse !

CHAMBRELAN.

Merci !

MONTGISCAR.

Et fasse remonter les phosphores.

CHAMBRELAN, sèchement.

Serviteur! (Sortant.) Ficelle! (Appelant.) Jeanne! Jeanne!
(Il disparaît par la gauche.).

SCÈNE XI

MONTGISCAR, puis DE CLERCY.

MONTGISCAR.

Dame!... les affaires sont les affaires!... je ne peux pas
me laisser rouler comme ça... (Changeant de ton.) Sapristi!
que ce bras me gêne. (Il tire le bras de la statue de sa poche
de droite et la change de côté.) Mon neveu ne revient pas...
(L'apercevant.) Ah!... enfin!...

DE CLERCY, entrant par la droite.

Mon oncle, voilà votre affaire... (Lui donnant une petite
bouteille.)Mastic liquide d'Athènes, avec la manière de s'en
servir.

MONTGISCAR.

Très-bien... tu vas m'aider.,.

DE CLERCY.

Volontiers. (Regardant autour de lui.) Mais je ne vois plus
M. Chambrelan et sa fille.

MONTGISCAR, lui montrant la gauche.

Ils viennent de partir.

DE CLERCY.

Comment... partir!

MONTGISCAR

Les négociations sont rompues.

* Montgiscar, de Clercy.
* De Clercy, Montgiscar.

DE CLERCY.

Rompues ?

MONTGISCAR.

Oui, ce papa Chambrelan est l'indélicatesse même...
figure-toi qu'il voulait me faufiler dans la dot des phosphores à 500 francs... au pair.

DE CLERCY.

Eh bien ?... qu'est-ce que ça fait ?

MONTGISCAR.

Ça fait une différence de 22,000 francs... Il s'est en-
têté... moi aussi... et il est parti, c'est rompu.

DE CLERCY.

Comment, rompu ! Mais vous ne voyez donc pas que je
suis amoureux !...

MONTGISCAR.

C'est un tort. . On ne doit être amoureux que lorsque
tout est bien convenu.

DE CLERCY.

C'est possible !... mais c'est fait... j'aime la demoiselle,
j'en suis fou !... je prends les phosphores au pair... et je
l'épouse !

MONTGISCAR.

Comme tuteur, je proteste !

DE CLERCY.

Ça m'est égal... je cours après eux, je leur fais des
excuses et je les ramène !...

MONTGISCAR.

Mais malheureux...

DE CLERCY.

Pourvu que je les retrouve... Ah ! mon oncle !. . mon
oncle !... (Il sort en courant par la gauche.)

SCÈNE XII

MONTGISCAR, puis MADAME DE GOBERVILLE, puis OCTAVE.

MONTGISCAR.

Ce garçon là ne fera jamais un financier... (Regardant autour de lui.) Personne!... racommodons Pollux. (Lisant l'instruction collée sur la bouteille.) *Etendre une legère couche sur la partie fracturée. — Nota : L'effet de ce mastic est tellement puissant que si l'opérateur en laissait couler quelques gouttes entre ses doigts, il ne pourrait plus les ouvrir.* (Incrédule.) Oh! oh! quelle farce! (Lisant.) *Il devrait alors plonger immédiatement sa main dans l'eau bouillante!* (Changeant de ton.) Ah! diable!... il ne faut pas jouer avec ça. (Il tire le bras de sa poche et s'approche de la statue.) Voyons .. il s'agit de recoller ça artistement. (Il approche un escabeau.)

MADAME DE GOBERVILLE, entrant par la droite, à part*.

Il doit m'attendre ici... en dessinant... (Apercevant Montgiscar de dos.) Ah! c'est lui... **

MONTGISCAR.

Oh! quelqu'un? (Il cache vivement le bras derrière son dos.)

MADAME DE GOBERVILLE.

M. Montgiscar!

MONTGISCAR.

Madame de Goberville! (A part.) Que le diable l'emporte!

MADAME DE GOBERVILLE, a part.

Quel contretemps!

---

* Montgiscar, Mme de Goberville.
** Mme de Goberville, Montgiscar.

MONTGISCAR, gracieux.

Ah! quelle charmante rencontre!

MADAME DE GOBERVILLE, du même ton.

En effet... je ne m'attendais pas...

MONTGISCAR.

J'adore les statues... et dès que j'ai un moment à moi, j'accours au musée des Antiques.

MADAME DE GOBERVILLE.

C'est comme moi... j'aime l'art grec... (Elle remonte.)

MONTGISCAR*.

Il n'y a que celui-là! (Fourrant le bras dans la poche de son paletot.) Comment se porte votre cher mari, M. de Goberville?

MADAME DE GOBERVILLE.

Très bien, fort occupé... son chemin de fer, *le grand Occidental*, dont il est administrateur, l'absorbe complètement.

MONTGISCAR, avec galanterie.

Complètement... en vous voyant.. je ne puis le croire.

MADAME DE GOBERVILLE, minaudant.

Ah! M. Montgiscar!... vous êtes galant...

MONTGISCAR.

Je le dis comme je le pense, madame, comme je le pense! (A part) Elle est bien gênante!

MADAME DE GOBERVILLE, à part.

Est-ce qu'il ne va pas s'en aller? (Apercevant Octave qui entre par la gauche.) Oh!

OCTAVE, s'avançant vers elle.

Madame, je...**

MADAME DE GOBERVILLE, bas et vivement.

Chut! Nous ne nous connaissons pas!

* Montgiscar, Mme de Goberville.
** Montgiscar, Octave, Mme de Goberville.

OCTAVE, apercevant Mongiscar.

Ah! (Il ouvre son album et se prépare à dessiner en fredonnant)
Tu, tu, tu, tu!

MONTGISCAR, à part.

En voilà un autre à présent!

MADAME DE GOBERVILLE, à Montgiscar.

Adieu, cher monsieur.

MONTGISCAR, saluant.

Madame... mes hommages à M. de Goberville.

MADAME DE GOBERVILLE, passant près d'Octave qui s'est
assis sur l'escabeau, et bas.

Dans un quart d'heure au musée d'artillerie. (Elle sort
par la droite.)

MONTGISCAR, regardant Octave qui taille son crayon,
à part.

C'est celui-là qui me gêne maintenant... il m'a l'air
d'un piocheur.

OCTAVE, regardant la statue et poussant un cri.

Ah!

MONTGISCAR.

Quoi?

OCTAVE, se levant.

Il lui manque un bras!

MONTGISCAR, vivement.

Non, je l'ai toujours vue comme ça.

OCTAVE.

Pardon, je l'ai dessiné ce matin. (Montrant son album.)
Le voilà!

MONTGISCAR, jouant l'étonnement.

Tiens! c'est ma foi vrai, il y en a deux! Mais qu'est-ce
que l'autre a pu devenir? Il est sans doute en répara-
tion.

OCTAVE, regardant la fenêtre.

Ah! décidément le jour est détestable... (Fermant son
album.) Je reviendrai demain. (Saluant) Monsieur...

MONTGISCAR, saluant.

Monsieur... (Octave sort par la droite.)

SCÈNE XIII

MONTGISCAR, seul.

Parti! enfin! (Il tire le bras de sa poche et s'approche de la statue.) Dépêchons-nous. (Il monte sur l'escabeau, débouche la petite bouteille et en verse le contenu sur la cassure.) Là!... un peu de ce baume de fier-à-bras, sur l'endroit malade... et prenons garde de m'en verser sur les doigts... (Il replace le bras de la statue et le consolide.) Ça tient!... ça tient tout seul!... c'est même mieux qu'auparavant.

SCÈNE XIV

DE CLERCY, CHAMBRELAN, JEANNE, MONTGISCAR,
puis LE GARDIEN.

DE CLERCY, ramenant Chambrelan et Jeanne.

Mais puisque j'accepte vos phosphores, c'est une valeur excellente...

CHAMBRELAN.

Qui rebondira... Mais monsieur votre oncle...

MONTGISCAR, en haut de l'escabeau.

Moi, j'ai fait mes observations, comme tuteur... mais puisque ça convient à mon neveu... (Descendant de l'escabeau.) Tout est arrangé.

CHAMBRELAN, regardant la statue.

Tiens, le bras aussi! vous l'avez replacé. Il est très bien.

MONTGISCAR.

Oui, je crois que comme restauration... c'est assez bien venu.

DE CLERCY, regardant la statue.

Mais, Dieu me pardonne! vous l'avez recollé à l'envers

MONTGISCAR, même jeu.

Comment ! à l'envers ?

JEANNE, de même.

C'est positif !

CHAMBRELAN, de même.

C'est ma foi vrai !

MONTGISCAR.

Allons, bon ! il va falloir le recasser.

DE CLERCY, bas et vivement.

Chut !... le gardien.

CHAMBRELAN.

Il est capable de s'en apercevoir... Filons !

MONTGISCAR.

Allons causer de nos derniers arrangements.

CHAMBRELAN.

Où ça ?

MONTGISCAR.

Au musée d'artillerie

CHAMBRELAN.

Pourquoi au musée d'artillerie ?

MONTGISCAR.

C'est plein de poignées de sabre... et on est chauffé.

CHAMBRELAN.

Évitons le gardien. (Ils remontent a gauche. Au moment où ils se disposent à sortir, le gardien entre suivi d'une famille anglaise, portant des guides des voyageurs. Le père prend des notes. Pendant que le gardien parle, de Clercy et Jeanne sortent en courant par la droite, puis Chambrelan, puis Montgiscar.)

LE GARDIEN, récitant.

Yes, mylord. La statue de Pollux... telle qu'elle a été trouvée en 1821 dans les jardins de la villa Palmieri... et expédiée par les soins du consul de France...

FIN DU PREMIER ACTE.

ACTE DEUXIÈME

Un salon chez Montgiscar — Au fond, au milieu, une glace sans tain. — Portes de chaque côte de la cheminée, ouvrant sur d'autres salons. — Portes latérales au premier plan. — Chaises, fauteuils, à droite, un canapé.

SCÈNE PREMIÈRE

MONTGISCAR, INVITÉS, INVITÉES au fond ; puis CHAMBRELAN, puis MOULINOT.

Au lever du rideau, musique à l'orchestre == On danse dans les salons du fond.

MONTGISCAR, seul, venant d'un des salons du fond.

Allons, mon bal est très-réussi... (S'essuyant le front.) On s'étouffe déjà... et il n'est que dix heures! (Apercevant Chambrelan qui entre par la gauche.) Ah! voilà Chambrelan !

CHAMBRELAN *.

Bonjour, cher ami...

MONTGISCAR.

Comment ! vous êtes seul? Eh bien! et nos jeunes mariés de huit jours ?

CHAMBRELAN.

Vous les verrez tout à l'heure... je viens en éclaireur.

---

* Chambrelan, Montgiscar.

Il faut vous dire, qu'à la maison nous sommes bien em-
barrassés... Ma fille a deux coiffures... une avec des fleurs,
l'autre avec des fruits... laquelle mettre ?

MONTGISCAR.

Diable ! c'est grave.

CHAMBRELAN.

Je crois bien que c'est grave... c'est son début dans le
monde, aussi je suis d'une émotion !... Alors j'ai pris un
grand parti... je me suis jeté dans un fiacre et je suis
venu pour inspecter les coiffures... Si c'est le fruit qui do
mine, nous mettrons les fleurs ; si ce sont les fleurs, nous
mettrons le fruit.

MONTGISCAR.

Naturellement! (A part.) C'est une modiste que ce père-
là ! (Haut.) Et le ménage, comment va-t-il ?

CHAMBRELAN.

Ah ! mon ami... depuis huit jours qu'il est marié, votre
neveu ne cesse pas de regarder sa femme !... Je dois dire
pour l'excuser, que ma fille a encore embelli... si c'est
possible... Hier, nous avons eu un succès !... nous étions
a l'Opéra... toutes les lorgnettes nous dévoraient, elles
nous mangeaient. . et nous n'avions pourtant qu'une
pauvre petite coiffure de lilas blanc ! Je vais passer mon
inspection et je me sauve. (Il sort par le fond à gauche.)

MOULINOT, entrant timidement par la gauche.

Tenue de bal râpée, saluant*.

Monsieur Montgiscar...

MONTGISCAR.

Ah ! c'est mon teneur de livres... J'y suis très attaché...
Bonjour, Moulinot.

MOULINOT.

Je voulais remercier monsieur, de l'honneur qu'il m'a
fait en m'invitant...

_____

* Moulinot, Montgiscar.

MONTGISCAR.

Il n'y a pas de quoi, mon ami; entrez dans le bal, promenez-vous, prenez des rafraîchissements; comme tout le monde, vous m'entendez, absolument comme tout le monde...

MOULINOT, prenant une glace sur un plateau que promène un domestique et saluant humblement.

Vous êtes trop bon... mille fois trop bon. (Il entre dans le bal au fond a gauche en faisant des courbettes.)

MONTGISCAR, seul.

C'est un employé laborieux, exact, honnête... et 1,800 fr. d'appointements.

CHAMBRELAN*, revenant du fond à gauche.

Décidément, nous mettrons des fleurs.

MONTGISCAR.

Dites donc, je vous présenterai mon fils... il est arrivé de Vienne, ce soir à 5 heures... il s'habille.

CHAMBRELAN.

Je ferai sa connaissance avec plaisir... on le dit très beau cavalier.

MONTGISCAR.

Il est superbe... élégant... distingué... il est en homme, ce que votre fille est en femme... peut être mieux.

CHAMBRELAN, incredule.

Oh! ça! (a part.) Mon Dieu, qu'il y a des pères ridicules!

MONTGISCAR.

Entre nous, ce bal cache. .

CHAMBRELAN, vivement.

Vous me conterez ça tantôt, on m'attend, (Il sort en courant par la gauche.)

MONTGISCAR, seul.

Ernest est bien long à sa toilette... Ah! le voilà!

* Chambrelan, Montgiscar.

3

SCÈNE II

MONTGISCAR, ERNEST.

ERNEST, entrant par la droite.

Papa, me voilà prêt. (Examinant le salon.) Superbe ton bal!... des fleurs, des bougies... des jolies femmes!...

MONTGISCAR*: l'admirant.

Qu'il est beau! Il est plus grand que moi! tu es plus grand que moi! (Il l'embrasse.) Dis donc, si tu valses, prends bien garde de te refroidir .. et au besoin va changer, ne te gêne pas!

ERNEST, riant et s'asseyant sur le canapé.

C'est ça... entre chaque quadrille... voyons, parle-moi un peu du mariage de mon cousin... sa femme est-elle jolie?

MONTGISCAR.

Charmante! remarquable même...

ERNEST.

Ah! ah! tu me présenteras.

MONTGISCAR, s'asseyant à côté de lui.

Oui, mais ne va pas t'aviser de porter le trouble par là.

ERNEST.

Oh! sois tranquille'... la famille, c'est sacré!... cependant j'aurais peut-être le droit d'exercer quelques représailles...

MONTGISCAR.

Pourquoi?

ERNEST.

Mon cher cousin m'a soufflé il y a cinq mois une... petite relation.

* Montgiscar, Ernest.

MONTGISCAR, incrédule.

Allons donc! il y a une femme qui a pu le préférer à toi?...

ERNEST, se levant.

Absolument.

MONTGISCAR, vexé.

Je ne la connais pas... mais j'ai une pauvre opinion de cette dame. (Changeant de ton et se levant) Allons, voilà ton gilet qui grimace... (Le lui arrangeant.) Tu n'es pourtant pas difficile à habiller, toi...

ERNEST.

Mais tu t'inquiète de ma toilette, comme si j'étais une demoiselle à marier.

MONTGISCAR, riant.

Eh! eh! tu n'es peut être pas loin de la vérité.

ERNEST.

Un mariage! Je retourne à Vienne*.

MONTGISCAR..

Il s'agit d'un de ces mariages!... la fille de la maison Burnett, Baring et Cie... Ça dit tout.

ERNEST.

Je ne la connais pas...

MONTGISCAR.

Comment? Burnett...

ERNEST.

Est-elle bien ?...

MONTGISCAR.

Quatre langues !... elle parle quatre langues.

ERNEST.

Oui, mais son extérieur?

MONTGISCAR.

Parfait !... Ce n'est pas un de ces petits minois chiffon-

* Ernest, Montgiscar.

nés et rétrécis!.. elle a de grands yeux, un grand nez, une grande bouche... elle a été taillée en plein drap.

ERNEST.

Et les pieds ?

MONTGISCAR.

Les pieds aussi!... seulement elle a fait une saison aux bains de mer cet été, et elle en a rapporté quelques petites taches de rousseur... qui du reste égaient sa physionomie-

ERNEST.

Je n'aime pas cette gaîté là.

MONTGISCAR.

Ça s'en va.

ERNEST.

Et ça revient.

MONTGISCAR.

Ah! ça, je te trouve froid, triste...

ERNEST.

Dame! franchement je ne songe pas du tout à me marier.

MONTGISCAR.

Ah! (l'examinant.) Alors, il y a quelque anguille sous roche. Voyons, sois franc!... Je ne suis pas homme à contraindre les inclinations... tu aimes une autre femme?

ERNEST.

Eh bien! oui, c'est vrai!

MONTGISCAR.

Qui ça ?

ERNEST.

Une adorable jeune fille, que j'ai rencontrée en Italie, voyageant avec son père... nous avons passé douze heures ensemble dans la grotte d'azur.

MONTGISCAR.

Dans la grotte d'azur... une nymphe alors?

ERNEST.

Tout ce que je sais, c'est qu'elle est admirablement
jolie.

MONTGISCAR.

Douze heures sous le même toit !... c'est donc une
auberge cette grotte d'azur ?...

ERNEST.

C'est une excavation que la mer a creusée dans le
rocher... on n'y pénètre qu'en bateau ; et comme l'orifice
en est très-bas, lorsque la mer devient forte, il est impossible d'en sortir.

MONTGISCAR.

Eh bien ?

ERNEST.

Eh bien ! nous nous sommes trouvés bloqués tout une
nuit, le père, la fille et moi.

MONTGISCAR.

Heureusement que le père était là...

ERNEST.

Il s'est endormi.

MONTGISCAR.

Bien !

ERNEST.

Après avoir constaté avec chagrin que la grotte n'avait
pas d'écho.

MONTGISCAR.

Eh bien ! et toi ? qu'est-ce que tu as fait ?

ERNEST.

J'avais heureusement dans ma poche une boîte d'allu-
mettes-bougies. (Faisant le geste d'allumer) Alors toute la
nuit... frrit ! (Avec sentiment) pour la voir.

MONTGISCAR, l'imitant.

C'est touchant ! frrit !

ERNEST.

Oh! quel esprit! quelle grâce! nous avons causé de tout et de rien, de la mer, des étoiles, de l'infini... de l'opéra! car elle est musicienne... Nous avons fait aussi un peu de musique...

MONTGISCAR.

Il y avait donc un piano dans ton aquarium?

ERNEST.

Non, nous avons chanté.

MONTGISCAR.

Ça a du réveiller le père.

ERNEST.

Pas le moins du monde... c'est un homme qui dort fortement. Au petit jour, nous fûmes délivrés... je les reconduisis à leur hôtel...

MONTGISCAR.

Et tu y retournas le lendemain?

ERNEST.

Comment, le lendemain!... au bout de dix minutes!... trop tard encore!... ils venaient de partir sans laisser leurs noms, sans dire où ils allaient.

MONTGISCAR.

Eh bien, alors...

ERNEST.

Alors je me mis à parcourir toutes les villes de l'Italie, les musées, les théâtres .. rien!... impossible de la retrouver!...

MONTGISCAR.

A ta place, je n'y penserais plus.

ERNEST *.

Ah! c'est plus fort que moi... cette jeune fille... ou plutôt ce rêve, cette apparition, me poursuit partout. Je ne puis l'arracher de mon cœur.

Montgiscar, Ernest.

MONTGISCAR.

N'arrachons pas... guérissons... je suis de l'avis des
dentistes, guérissons.

ERNEST.

Me guérir.. mais comment ?

MONTGISCAR.

En épousant la petite Burnett, Baring et C\ie.

ERNEST.

Allons donc !

MONTGISCAR.

Regarde la ! je ne te demandes que ça! fais la danser,
elle est dans le second salon, près de la cheminée... entourée de sa famille... neuf tantes, dont quatre fruc-
tueuses... je les ai mises à part, à droite... tu peux sourire
à la gauche, mais sois délicieux avec la droite... va... je
t'en prie.

ERNEST.

Soit... mais c'est saus conviction... pour te faire plaisir.
(Il sort par le fond a gauche).

MONTGISCAR, seul.

Il y viendra... je ne prends pas au sérieux ce petit
roman maritime.

SCÈNE III

MONTGISCAR, Invités des deux sexes, MOULINOT,
HECTOR, HERMANCE, puis DE GOBERVILLE,
MADAME DE GOBERVILLE, OCTAVE, puis DE
CLERCY, JEANNE et CHAMBRELAN.

MONTGISCAR.

Ah ! la valse est finie... (Des invités entrent par le fond et
chaque cavalier reconduit sa danseuse à sa place, deux domestiques
offrent des rafraîchissements)

HECTOR, à Montgiscar[*].

Votre fête est charmante...

MONTGISCAR, mystérieusement.

Entre nous... c'est presqu'un bal de fiançailles... je suis sur le point de marier mon fils... mais n'en parlez pas !... c'est encore un secret.

HECTOR.

Oh ! soyez tranquille.

MONTGISCAR, aux domestiques [**].

Offrez ! offrez à ces messieurs... (A Moulinot) Vous aussi, comme tout le monde ! comme tout le monde ! (Il va s'asseoir près d'Hermance sur le canapé et cause à voix basse).

MOULINOT, à part prenant sur le plateau.

C'est la quatrième glace que je prends... est-ce bien prudent ?

MONTGISCAR, aux personnes qui l'entourent.

N'en parlez à personne... c'est encore un secret.

UN INVITÉ, derrière le canapé.

Soyez tranquille, nous serons muets.

UN AUTRE INVITÉ.

Tous muets.

JUSTIN, annonçant à gauche.

Monsieur et madame de Goberville ! monsieur Octave Blandar ! (De Goberville entre en donnant le bras à sa femme, il porte des lunettes d'or. Octave suit madame de Goberville dont il tient le flacon et l'éventail).

MONTGISCAR, se levant et allant à eux.

Ah ! comme vous venez tard. (Madame de Goberville va s'asseoir près d'Hermance sur le canapé) [***].

[*] Hector, Montgiscar.
[**] Invités, Domestique, Moulinot, Montgiscar, Invites.
[***] Invités, Octave, Goberville, Montgiscar, Mme de Goberville, Invités.

DE GOBERVILLE.

Vous savez, la toilette des dames... Permettez-moi de vous présenter M. Octave Blandar, un de mes amis.

MONTGISCAR, saluant.

Monsieur...

OCTAVE, de même.

Monsieur...

DE GOBERVILLE.

Sculpteur de beaucoup de talent.. il a déjà fait mon buste... oui... il a la bonté de trouver que j'ai une tête de penseur... maintenant il fait celui de ma femme... c'est beaucoup plus long...

MONTGISCAR, allant à Octave *.

Mais si je ne me trompe, j'ai déjà eu le plaisir de rencontrer monsieur au musée des Antiques...

MADAME DE GOBERVILLE, toussant.

Hum !

OCTAVE.

En effet... en effet !...

MONTGISCAR.

Puis le même jour au musée d'artillerie.

OCTAVE.

En effet... en effet !...

MONTGISCAR.

Et par une coïncidence, que je ne me lasse pas de bénir, j'ai fait également la rencontre de...

MADAME DE GOBERVILLE, lui coupant la parole.

Pardon... cher monsieur, vous n'auriez pas une table de whist à offrir à mon mari !

MONTGISCAR.

Si ! par là. (Il indique la droite.)

---

* Octave, Montgiscar, de Goberville, Mme de Goberville et Hermance assises sur le canapé.

3.

DE GOBERVILLE*.

Oh! je ne suis pas pressé.

MONTGISCAR.

Un homme grave!... le bal manque de charme pour vous...

DE GOBERVILLe.

Il y a le coup-d'œil.

MONTGISCAR.

Non! entrez là... on vous attend. (Il le conduit à droite.)

DE GOBERVILLE, à part.

Je reviendrai. (Il sort.)

OCTAVE, à Montgiscar.

Ah! Monsieur Montgiscar, mon compliment.. votre bal est un bouquet de jolies femmes.

MONGISCAR, s'oubliant

Oh! ce n'est rien encore! (Les femmes font un mouvement.) Vous allez en voir une tout à l'heure, près de laquelle les autres ne sont que...

TOUTES LES FEMMES.

Hein?

MONTGISCAR, se reprenant.

Non! ce n'est pas ce que je voulais dire! (A part.) Sapristi! qu'est-ce que j'ai fait?

MADAME DE GOBERVILLE, d'un air pincé.

Et quand verrons nous cette beauté merveilleuse?

MONTGISCAR.

Oh! merveilleuse... (A part.) Réparons! (Haut) Elle est jeune... la beauté du diable... voilà tout.

JUSTIN, annonçant.

Monsieur et Madame de Clercy!

MONTGISCAR.

La voici!

* Octave, Goberville, Montgiscar, Mme de Goberville.

JUSTIN, à Chambrelan.

Le nom de monsieur ?

CHAMBRELAN.

Je suis le papa.

JUSTIN, annonçant.

Monsieur Lepapa ! (Mouvement général de curiosité, murmure flatteur partant des groupes des hommes.)

UN INVITÉ, à son voisin, à gauche.

Elle est charmante !

DEUXIÈME INVITÉ.

Adorable !

TROISIÈME INVITÉ, à droite.

Elle sera le succès de la saison.

DEUXIÈME INVITÉ.

Je la ferai danser.

PREMIER INVITÉ.

Après moi.

DEUXIÈME INVITÉ.

C'est ce que nous verrons.

CHAMBRELAN, bas à de Clercy *.

Entendez-vous le murmure flatteur !... la glace est rompue !

DE CLERCY, bas.

Je ne le cache pas... ça me fera plaisir !

CHAMBRELAN.

Et à moi donc !

MADAME DE GOBERVILLE, toujours assise, aux dames qui l'entourent.

Je ne lui trouve rien d'extraordinaire.

HERMANCE.

Moi non plus ! (On entend la ritournelle de l'orchestre.)

Invités, Jeanne, Montgiscar, Chambrelan, de Clercy.

MONTGISCAR.

Messieurs, c'est un quadrille. (Tous les jeunes gens se pressent autour de Jeanne pour l'inviter*)

MADAME DE GOBERVILLE, se levant et arrêtant Octave, bas.

Je vous défends de danser avec elle!

OCTAVE.

Je n'y songeais pas ..

CHAMBRELAN, un carnet de bal à la main, aux jeunes gens.

De l'ordre! Messieurs, de l'ordre! je vais vous inscrire. (Bas à de Clercy.) Hein! quel effet! (Il sort avec Jeanne, entouré de jeunes gens dont il inscrit les noms. Octave a offert son bras à madame de Goberville. Plusieurs dames restent seules.)

HERMANCE.

Eh bien, et nous?... (A une dame, en riant.) Madame veut-elle me faire l'honneur... (Elles sortent se donnant le bras suivies des autres dames.)

SCENE IV

DE CLERCY, MONTGISCAR, puis DE-GOBERVILLE.

MONTGISCAR**.

Eh bien! j'espère que voilà un succès!

DE CLERCY.

Ah! mon bon oncle, que vous avez bien fait de me marier! Si vous saviez comme Jeanne est douce, et bonne et gracieuse... et elle m'aime!.. hier, elle m'a dit. Je ne connais pas d'homme plus beau que toi, si ce n'est mon père!

* Montgiscar, Jeanne entourée de jeunes gens, Octave, Mme de Goberville, Chambrelan, de Clercy.
** Montgiscar, de Clercy.

MONTGISCAR.

C'est d'une fille bien élevée!... maintenant veux-tu un conseil pratique?

DE CLERCY.

Lequel!

MONTGISCAR.

Cherche une occupation... cela t'empêchera d'user ton bonheur trop vite.

DE CLERCY.

J'y ai déjà songé... mais à quoi suis je bon?

MONTGISCAR.

D'abord, tu es ingénieur... ensuite tu as écrit un livre... compact, sur les chemins de fer : *Des tarifs différentiels, proportionnels et spéciaux!*

DE CLERCY.

Vous l'avez lu?

MONTGISCAR.

Ah! non! coupé seulement... comme oncle! mais il y a ici, un homme qui doit l'avoir lu... Monsieur de Goberville...

DE CLERCY.

Le directeur du *Grand-Occidental.*

MONTGISCAR.

C'est un de mes vieux amis... je vais te présenter et tu lui adresseras ta demande.

DE GOBERVILLE, entrant et parlant à la cantonade.

Merci... je ne joue plus.

MONTGISCAR *.

Le voici... (A de Goberville.) Eh bien, avez-vous gagné?

DE GOBERVILLE.

Non.. je perds quatre louis

* De Clercy, Montgiscar. de Goberville.

MONTGISCAR, bas à de Clercy.

Nous l'abordons dans de mauvaises conditions... mais ça ne fait rien. (Haut.) Mon cher de Goberville, permettez-moi de vous présenter mon neveu, M. Jules de Clercy.

DE GOBERVILLE, aimable.

Monsieur...

MONTGISCAR.

Ingénieur.. qui a fait des chemins de fer, une étude de toute sa vie.

DE GOBERVILLE, très-froid.

Enchanté..

MONTGISCAR.

Il a une petite requête à vous adresser... je vous laisse... * (A part.) Je vais voir comment se comporte mon fils au milieu de ses neuf tantes. (Il entre dans le bal.)

SCÈNE V

DE CLERCY, DE GOBERVILLE, puis JEANNE.

DE GOBERVILLE, très-froid

Je vous écoute, monsieur.

DE CLERCY.

Voici ce dont il s'agit, en deux mots... je viens de me marier, la vie oisive me déplaît, je suis ingénieur et je désirerais, si cela était possible, obtenir un emploi dans la compagnie que vous dirigez.

DE GOBERVILLE.

Monsieur, j'ai une devise immuable : respect aux droits acquis ! jamais de passe-droits !

DE CLERCY.

J'ai peut-être quelques titres, j'ai fait un livre sur les chemins de fer...

* Montgiscar, de Clercy, de Goberville.

DE GOBERVILLE.

Eh ! monsieur ! qui est-ce qui n'écrit pas sur les chemins de fer ? Comment s'appelle-t-il votre livre ?

DE CLERCY.

Des tarifs différentiels, proportionnels et spéciaux...

DE GOBERVILLE.

Vaste matière ! mais il y en a quatorze sur ce sujet-là.

DE CLERCY.

Je n'insiste pas Monsieur... il me reste le regret de vous avoir importuné.

JEANNE, entrant par la porte du fond, à gauche,

Mon ami, mon père vous demande tout de suite.

DE CLERCY.

J'y vais. (Les présentant l'un à l'autre.) Monsieur de Goberville... Madame de Clercy. (Il sort)

SCÈNE VI

JEANNE, DE GOBERVILLE, puis CHAMBRELAN.

DE GOBERVILLE, à part.

Sa femme ! jolie comme un ange. (Il ôte ses lunettes, regarde s'il n'y a personne et s'approche de Jeanne qui se disposait à sortir*.) Monsieur votre mari est un homme charmant.

JEANNE.

Oh ! Monsieur, vous êtes peut-être indulgent.

DE GOBERVILLE.

Moins que vous sans doute... car étant mariée depuis peu.

JEANNE.

Depuis huit jours seulement.

DE GOBERVILLE, à part.

Huit jours !... Écoutez-moi, mon enfant... votre cher

* Jeanne, de Goberville.

mari me parlait à l'instant de ses projets d'avenir,.. il voudrait... il désirerait s'occuper...

JEANNE.

En effet, Monsieur.

DE GOBERVILLE.

Il m'a fait entendre qu'il ne serait pas éloigné d'accepter une place dans notre administration...

JEANNE.

Me permettez-vous d'appuyer sa demande ?

DE GOBERVILLE, lui prenant la main.

Elle ne peut être apostillée par une main plus charmante.

JEANNE, retirant la main.

Ah ! Monsieur !

DE GOBERVILLE, lui reprenant la main.

Écoutez-moi, mon enfant... nous aurons quelques difficultés à surmonter pour arriver à notre but...

JEANNE.

Ah ! il y a des obstacles ?

DE GOBERVILLE.

Oui, mais nous les vaincrons... car vous m'intéressez. (Lui caressant la main.) Votre mari aussi... beaucoup... beaucoup... beaucoup...

CHAMBRELAN, paraissant à une porte du fond, à droite, tenant un carnet à la main*, à Jeanne, très-haut.

Septième marzourka, ton danseur t'attend !

JEANNE, qui a retiré sa main.

Tout de suite !

CHAMBRELAN, à Goberville.

Mille excuses ! mais le devoir avant tout !

(Il disparaît par la gauche.

*Jeanne, de Goberville, Chambrelan.

JEANNE, à Goberville.

Vous permettez... (Elle remonte un peu.)

GOBERVILLE, la retenant et à demi-voix.

Le conseil d'administration se réunit demain à trois heures, si vous voulez passer à quatre à mon cabinet, j'espère vous donner une bonne réponse.

JEANNE.

Ah! que vous êtes bon!

DE GOBERVILLE.

A quatre heures!

JEANNE, à part avant de sortir.

Il a l'air d'un bien brave homme. (Elle disparaît par le fond à gauche.)

SCÈNE VII

DE GOBERVILLE, puis DE CLERCY.

DE GOBERVILLE, essuyant ses lunettes avec son mouchoir.

Jolie comme un ange!.. C'est un vrai bouton de rose... et une candeur... une naïveté... que l'on trouve bien rarement chez les femmes des employés de mon administration... (Il remet ses lunettes.) J'ai été un peu dur avec le mari... C'est un homme de talent après tout... ingénieur .. sorti de l'école polytechnique... Il a des titres.

DE CLERCY, entrant [*].

Pardon... ma femme n'est plus ici?

DE GOBERVILLE, à part.

Lui! (Haut.) On est venu la chercher pour danser. (Très-aimable.) Je suis bien aise de vous revoir, mon cher Monsieur de Clercy.

[*] De Goberville, de Clercy.

DE CLERCY, etonné.

Moi, Monsieur !...

DE GOBERVILLE.

J'ai à causer avec vous... j'ai lu votre livre... remarquable! très remarquable!

DE CLERCY, à part.

Est-ce qu'il l'a lu pendant le bal?

DE GOBERVILLE.

Vous avez porté la lumière dans une question ténébreuse... vous avez comblé une lacune... la science vous en remercie.

DE CLERCY.

Vraiment, Monsieur, je suis confus...

DE GOBERVILLE.

D'ailleurs vous avez d'autres titres...

DE CLERCY.

Ah! lesquels?

DE GOBERVILLE.

Ne vous appelez-vous pas de Clercy! et Mathieu de Clercy est un des initiateurs des lignes ferrées, en France.

DE CLERCY.

Nous n'étions pas parents...

DE GOBERVILLE, vivement.

Ça ne fait rien, vous portez le même nom.

DE CLERCY.

C'est juste !

DE GOBERVILLE,

Mon jeune ami... permettez-moi de vous donner ce titre!

DE CLERCY.

Comment donc!

DE GOBERVILLE.

J'aime les travailleurs .. respect aux droits acquis, pas de passe-droits!... voilà ma devise!... et tout me fait espérer pour vous un heureux et prompt résultat.

DE CLERCY.

Ah! monsieur! je ne sais comment vous remercier.

DE GOBERVILLÉ.

Votre main, jeune homme. (Ils se serrent la main.) J'aime les travailleurs!.. nous nous reverrons. (A part.) Je vais la voir danser. (Il remonte au fond à gauche. Haut à de Clercy.) Nous nous reverrons. (Il entre dans le bal.)

SCÈNE VIII

DE CLERCY, puis MONTGISCAR, puis CHAMBRELAN.

DE CLERCY.

Changement à vue! Qu'est-ce ça signifie?

MONTGISCAR, entrant par le côté gauche et à la cantonade *.

Surtout ne faites pas de bruit... ne le réveillez pas!

DE CLERCY.

Qui donc?

MONTGISCAR.

Ton cousin. Je le cherchais partout. Il dort dans le vestiaire... le pauvre enfant a passé trois nuits en chemin de fer..

DE CLERCY.

Il ferait mieux de se coucher... il va attraper du froid.

MONTGISCAR.

Je lui ai mis cinq pelisses de dames sur le dos; en le regardant dormir, je ne pouvais pas m'empêcher de l'admirer... Mon Dieu! que cet enfant là est réussi!

CHAMBRELAN, paraissant au fond à gauche, entouré d'un groupe de danseurs **.

De l'ordre! de l'ordre! (Inscrivant sur son carnet.) Vous

* Montgiscar, de Clercy.
** Montgiscar, Chambrelan, de Clercy.

aurez votre tour! (Les jeunes gens se disperent. Chambrelan descend en scène.) Quel succès!... je suis en nage!... Tout à l'heure elle a laissé tomber son mouchoir par mégarde... vingt bras se sont jetés à genoux! c'était un beau coup d'œil!

MONTGISCAR, à part.

Il est un peu ennuyeux avec sa fille. (Il remonte sur la pointe des pieds et disparaît dans le bal.)

CHAMBRELAN, à de Clercy.

Notre carnet est plein.

DE CLERCY.

Eh bien ! beau-père... et moi ?

CHAMBRELAN.

Quoi ?

DE CLERCY.

Je ne serais pas fâché de danser un peu avec ma femme.

CHAMBRELAN.

Très-bien... je vais vous inscrire. (Consultant son carnet.) Vous êtes le quarante-neuvième.

DE CLERCY.

Ah! permettez... comme mari...

CHAMBRELAN.

Ah ! pas de faveurs ! respect aux droits acquis... à l'ancienneté... voilà ma devise.

DE CLERCY.

Tiens!... comme M. de Goberville... A propos, vous savez qu'il m'a presque promis cette place que je désire... et qu'il m'avait refusé d'abord.

CHAMBBELAN.

Parbleu ! il n'avait pas encore vu votre femme.

DE CLEBCY.

Mais qu'est-ce que ma femme a à faire là-dedans ?

CHAMBRFLAN.

Tout, mon ami, tout!

DE CLERCY.

Comment ?

CHAMBRELAN.

Ah ça! est-ce que vous croyez bonnement que ces pré-
venances, ces égards, ces petits soins dont vous êtes
l'objet, s'adressent à vos beaux yeux?

DE CLERCY.

Mais... (On entend l'orchestre,)

CHAMBRELAN.

Une valse! Je vous quitte... il faut que je remplisse mes
fonctions. (Sortant son carnet à la main et appelant.) Numéro 18... numéro 18... (Il disparaît par le fond.)

SCÈNE IX

DE CLERCY, puis OCTAVE, puis UN DOMESTIQUE.

DE CLERCY, seul

Le bonhomme radote... cependant ce qu'il vient de me
dire me trouble... m'inquiète...

OCTAVE, entrant, à part *.

Le mari! (Haut.) Ah! on respire un peu ici!

DE CLERCY.

En effet, il fait par là une chaleur étouffante.

OCTAVE, avec complaisance.

Ah! c'est bien le mot... étouffante! monsieur a trouvé
le mot... Monsieur ne danse pas?

DE CLERCY.

Non, monsieur.

OCTAVE.

Moi, j'invite par complaisance... car franchement le-

* De Clercy, Octave.

jambes me rentrent dans le corps! Nous avons fait hier, dimanche, une partie de chasse... Êtes-vous chasseur ?

DE CLERCY.

A l'occasion.

OCTAVE.

Nous avons tué onze lièvres, vingt-deux lapins et quinze faisans.

DE CLERCY.

Très-beau !

OCTAVE.

J'ai une action dans la forêt de Sénart... chacun a le droit d'amener un ami... Sans façon, voulez-vous être des nôtres dimanche prochain ?

DE CLERCY.

Mais je ne sais si... (A part.) Chambrelan a beau dire... ce n'est pas pour ma femme... elle ne chasse pas.

OCTAVE.

Entre jeunes gens, pas de cérémonie... acceptez!... si toutefois madame vous autorise à la quitter...

DE CLERCY.

Madame ! (A part.) Je vais biens avoir... (Haut.) Madame !... Mais vous faites erreur.

OCTAVE.

Comment ?

DE CLERCY.

Je suis garçon, monsieur.

OCTAVE.

Ah ! pardon, je vous prenais pour... mais je n'insiste pas... mettons que je n'ai rien dit ; j'ai été indiscret.

DE CLERCY, à part.

Il me désinvite !

OCTAVE, à part.

Je me suis trompé... C'est le gros qui est le mari...

j'aime mieux ça... (Haut.) J'ai bien l'honneur... (Il sort vivement.)

DE CLERCY, seul.

Ça me parait clair... éclipse totale du mari par la jolie femme ! Ah ! la jolie femme ! la jolie femme ! Ça commence à m'agacer !

SCENE X

JEANNE, DE CLERCY, puis HECTOR, puis CHAMBRELAN.

JEANNE, paraissant au fond à gauche.
Mais que devenez-vous, mon ami ?

DE CLERCY.
Enfin vous voilà ! ce n'est pas malheureux !

JEANNE.
Qu'avez-vous donc ? vous paraissez contrarié...

DE CLERCY.
Si vous croyez qu'il est agréable pour un mari, de voir sa femme poursuivie par une meute de petits jeunes gens.

JEANNE.
Mais vous devriez être fier de mon succès... est-ce ma faute, si l'on me trouve agréable ? Vous m'avez dit vous même que j'étais jolie.

DE CLERCY.
Ah ! jolie ! voilà !... mais ce n'est pas une raison pour danser avec tout le monde.

JEANNE.
Si on m'invite, puis-je refuser ?

DE CLERCY.
Et moi !... le mari ! si je réclame une simple valse on me donne le n° 49.

JEANNE.

Ça, c'est peut-être votre faute, il fallait vous y prendre plus tôt.

DE CLERCY.

Alors, c'est une course au clocher.

JEANNE.

Un salon est un terrain neutre, où les maris n'ont pas plus de prérogatives que les autres.

DE CLERCY.

Elle n'est pas de vous cette phrase là... elle est de votre pere!... Je reconnais sa marque. . elle est tout à fait commode pour laisser les maris dans les petits coins. (Il s'assied sur le canapé.)

JEANNE.

Mais qu'avez-vous? Je ne vous comprends pas. Pouvez-vous me reprocher d'avoir été coquette ou légère? (Elle s'assied a côté de lui.)

DE CLERCY.

Oh! non! je ne dis pas ça!

JEANNE.

Eh bien?...

DE CLERCY.

Jeanne, il faut que nous causions... que nous causions sérieusement... car on fait ici à votre mari une position, que ni vous, ni moi ne saurions accepter; certes je n'ai pas la prétention...

HECTOR, entrant et l'interrompant.

Pardon, madame... c'est la polka *.

DE CLERCY, à par, se levant ainsi que Jeanne.

Que le diable l'emporte! Je ne peux plus même causer avec ma femme!...

* Hector, Jeanne, de Clercy.

HECTOR, à Jeanne.

Voulez-vous me faire l'honneur de me présenter à monsieur votre mari?

JEANNE, le présentant.

Mon ami... M. Hector Grandin...*

DE CLERCY.

Elle sait leurs petits noms... déjà!

HECTOR, à de Clercy, très-aimable et en offrant le bras à Jeanne.

Je crois, monsieur, que nous avons été camarades de collége.

DE CLERCY, avec humeur.

Je ne me souviens pas... je n'ai jamais été dans ce collége là...

HECTOR, étonné.

Hein?

DE CLERCY.

Pardon... on m'attend au whist (Il entre vivement à droite.)

HECTOR, d'un air rodomont, à part.

Il est bien heureux d'avoir une jolie femme!

CHAMBRELAN, paraissant à la porte du fond, très-affairé.

On polke! vite! vite!

HECTOR.

Voilà! (Il sort avec Jeanne par le fond.)

SCENE XI

CHAMBRELAN, puis ERNEST.

CHAMBRELAN, seul, il s'assied à gauche et prend son carnet.

Mettons de l'ordre dans ma comptabilité... ah! sapre-

---

* Jeanne, Hector, de Clercy.

lotte!... j'ai accordé le n° 22 à trois personnes!... je ne vois qu'un moyen, c'est de tirer au sort dans un chapeau. (Il continue à pointer son carnet.)

ERNEST, entrant par le côté gauche.

J'ai dormi par là... je me suis réveillé sous une montagne de pelisses*. (Reconnaissant Chambrelan.) Hein!... vous! son père!... Ah! mon Dieu!

CHAMBRELAN, se levant très-étonné**.

Qu'est-ce qu'il a, ce jeune homme?

ERNEST

Je ne dors pas! je ne rêve pas! c'est bien vous?

CHAMBRELAN, surpris.

Oui, monsieur, c'est moi.

ERNEST.

Ah! que je suis heureux de vous retrouver!... il y a si longtemps que je vous cherche!

CHAMBRELAN.

Vous venez un peu tard... je ne peux vous accorder que le n° 50... Non, le 49, celui du mari.

ERNEST.

J'ai parcouru toutes les villes d'Italie, Rome, Naples, Florence, Venise...

CHAMBRELAN.

Pourquoi faire?

ERNEST.

Pour vous retrouver... vous et votre adorable fille.

CHAMBRELAN.

Ah!

ERNEST.

Vous ne me remettez pas?

* Chambrelan, Ernest.
** Ernest, Chambrelan.

CHAMBRELAN.

Non.

ERNEST.

Dans la grotte d'azur... c'est moi...

CHAMBRELAN.

Ah! les allumettes! parfaitement!

ERNEST.

Ah ! monsieur! voir votre fille, c'est l'aimer.

CHAMBRELAN, heureux.

C'est vrai !

ERNEST, avec feu.

Jamais je n'ai rencontré tant de grâce, de charme, d'esprit, réunis à une beauté si parfaite !

CHAMBRELAN.

C'est vrai !

ERNEST.

Alors, sous son regard si bienveillant, si doux, si...

CHAMBRELAN.

Magnétique...

ERNEST.

Oui, magnétique. . j'ai été pénétré d'un sentiment profond, inaltérable ; enfin, je l'aime, monsieur, je l'aime !

CHAMBRELAN,

C'est fatal ! je ne peux pas vous en vouloir.

ERNEST.

. Je cours chercher mon père, je le précipite à vos genoux.

CHAMBRELAN.

Pourquoi faire ?

ERNEST.

Pour vous demander la main de votre fille.

CHAMBRELAN.

Non... ça ne se peut pas... je le regrette.

ERNEST.

Pourquoi?

CHAMBRELAN.

Parce que ma fille est mariée.

ERNEST.

Mariée! elle!... ah ! (Il défaille dans les bras de Chambrelan.)

CHAMBRELAN, le consolant.

Voyons, jeune homme... du courage, remettez-vous !

ERNEST, se redressant et avec véhémence.

Mariée!... monsieur, le nom de son mari... je le tuerai !

CHAMBRELAN, à part.

Le tuer!... ah! il va trop loin !

SCÈNE XII

LES MÊMES, JEANNE.

Jeanne paraît au fond, ramenée par son danseur qui la salue et la quitte.

ERNEST, l'apercevant *.

Elle!... ah! mademoiselle! mademoiselle !

JEANNE, a part.

Le jeune homme que nous avons rencontré à Naples !

ERNEST.

Vous êtes mariée!... Vous n'avez donc pas compris mes regards qui vous suppliaient d'attendre...

JEANNE, interdite.

Mais, monsieur...

ERNEST **.

Ou plutôt vous n'avez pas su résister à la contrainte imposée par un père barbare !

* Jeanne, Ernest, Chambrelan.
** Ernest, Jeanne, Chambrelan.

CHAMBRELAN.

Moi ? barbare !

ERNEST.

Mais soyez tranquille... je saurai vous rendre à vous-même... le nom. . le nom de votre mari !

CHAMBRELAN, vivement.

Ne le dis pas !

DE CLERCY, à la cantonade.

Merci, mille fois trop bon !

CHAMBRELAN, à part.

De Clercy ! (A Ernest.) * On vient, monsieur, pas de scandale... retirez-vous !

SCÈNE XIII

LES MÊMES, DE CLERCY.**

DE CLERCY, entrant à part.

En voilà un qui veut m'inviter à dîner par là !... (Apercevant Ernest.) Tiens ! te voilà... je vais te présenter à ma femme ***.

CHAMBRELAN, vivement.

Non !,..

ERNEST, à part.

Sa femme !

DE CLERCY, présentant Ernest.

Ma chère amie... je te présente notre cousin, Ernest Montgiscar ****.

* Ernest, Chambrelan, Jeanne.
** Ernest, Chambrelan, de Clercy, Jeanne.
*** Ernest, de Clercy, Chambrelan, Jeanne.
**** De Clercy, Ernest, Chambrelan, Jeanne.

CHAMBRELAN, à part, effrayé.

Ah! le malheureux!

DE CLERCY.

Un garnement que j'aime de tout mon cœur.

ERNEST, saluant Jeanne.

Madame!

JEANNE, de même.

Monsieur!

ERNEST, à part avec joie.

Sa femme! je pourrai la voir tous les jours.

CHAMBRELAN.

Vous dites?

DE CLERCY, continuant la présentation.

Monsieur Chambrelan, mon beau-père.

ERNEST, saluant.

Monsieur!

CHAMBRELAN, de même.

Monsieur!... (A part.) Il ne tue personne!... c'est un poseur!

ERNEST, à de Clercy d'un air contraint.

Reçois mes félicitations, mon cher, je suis très-heureux...

DE CLERCY.

J'aurai bientôt à t'adresser les miennes... ton père m'a parlé d'un mariage...

ERNEST, vivement.

Jamais!

CHAMBRELAN, à part.

Il ne manquerait plus que ça...

DE CLERCY.

Jamais! (Riant.) Est-ce que tu veux te faire chartreux?

ERNEST, avec émotion.

Non... mais j'aime une personne... que je ne puis

épouser... et jamais mon cœur n'appartiendra à une autre.

CHAMBRELAN, à part.

A la bonne heure !

JEANNE, à part.

Pauvre jeune homme ! ce n'est pas ma faute !

SCÈNE XIV

LES MÊMES. MONGISCAR, DE GOBERVILLE, MADAME DE GOBERVILLE, OCTAVE, MOULINOT, HECTOR, HERMANCE, DANSEURS et DANSEUSES.

Les invités entrent en valsant — Octave avec Madame de Goberville et Montgiscar avec une dame mûre. — La valse s'arrête, les dames sont reconduites à leur place.

MONTGISCAR, à part tout en finissant sa valse.

J'ai invité une tante... à droite... puisque mon fils dort *.

OCTAVE, à Montgiscar.

Bravo! bravo! (Changeant de ton.) Ah! ça, messieurs, qu'est-ce qui conduira le cotillon ?

MONTGISCAR.

Ce n'est pas moi.

MADAME DE GOBERVILLE.

Oh ! le cotillon... c'est bien usé... Hier au bal de la baronne du Tillac on l'a remplacé par une idée charmante.

CHAMBRELAN.

Quoi donc ?

MADAME DE GOBERVILLE.

On a joué aux enchères.

'Octave, Mme de Goberville, Montgiscar, Chambrelan.

MONTGISCAR.

Qu'est-ce que c'est que ça?

MADAME DE GOBERVILLE.

Chaque dame a fourni un lot... que les messieurs ont poussé au profit des pauvres.

TOUS.

C'est charmant! c'est charmant!

MONTGISCAR.

Eh bien! faisons comme chez la baronne.

TOUS.

Oui! oui!

OCTAVE.

Vite! une table. (Il va chercher une petite table.)

MONGISCAR, à un domestique.

Et un marteau. (On lui donne un marteau à casser du sucre.) Comme aux commissaires-priseurs. (A Madame de Goberville.) Vous allez commencer.

MADAME DE GOBERVILLE.

Oh! non... pas moi. (A part.) Le lever de rideau... merci! (Elle redescend à droite.)

MONTGISCAR, à Jeanne.

Alors ma nièce... votre lot?

JEANNE, hésitant.

Mais je ne sais quoi mettre... je vous jure.

CHAMBRELAN, à sa fille.

Ton bouquet!

DE CLERCY vexé.

Par exemple !

CHAMBRELAN.

C'est un lingot ! (Octave a placé devant Jeanne une table, Montgiscar se tient debout près de cette table comme les crieurs de l'hôtel des ventes, les autres personnages sont groupés en demi-cercle) *.

* Ernest, Moulinot, un Invité, Hector, Goberville, un Invité, Montgiscar, Jeanne, Chambrelan, de Clercy, Octave, Mme de Goberville, Invités, les autres Invités au fond.

JEANNE à la table prenant le marteau.

Messieurs, mon bouquet ! (Montgiscar le prend.'

TOUS.

Bravo ! bravo !

MONTGISCAR à la manière des crieurs.

Nous mettons en vente un bouquet de lilas blanc, porté par Madame... ça n'a pas de prix.

DE CLECY à part.

Le bouquet de ma femme !... Je ne le laisserai adjuger à personne !

ERNEST bas à Moulinot pendant que Montgiscar montre le bouquet.

Père Moulinot, rendez-moi un service.

MOULINOT bas.

A vos ordres, M. Ernest.

ERNEST bas.

Poussez ce bouquet jusqu'à ce qu'on vous l'adjuge.

MOULINOT étonné

Hein ?

ERNEST bas.

C'est pour mon compte... gardez-moi le secret.

MONTGISCAR, revenant à la table.

Combien disons-nous ? Commençons comme vous voudrez.

MOULINOT.

Il y a marchand à six francs.

TOUS riant.

Oh !

DE GOBERVILLE.

Douze !

DE CLRCY.

Cent francs !

OCTAVE.

Cent vingt ! (Madame Goberville le pince) Aie !

MONTGISCAR,

Cent vingt ! pas d'erreur, c'est de mon côté.

CHAMBRELAN qui est remonté et s'est caché dans la foule.

Un !

MONGISCAR,

On a dit un ... Cent vingt et un !

MOULINOT,

Deux cents !

UN INVITÉ.

Cinquante !

DE CLECY.

Trois cents !

MONTGISCAR.

Trois cents ! Voyons, messieurs !

HECTOR.

Cinquante !

MONTGISCAR.

Trois cent cinquante !

CHAMBRELAN a droite, se cachant.

Un !

MONTGISCAR.

On a dit un, trois cent cinqnante et un !

MOULINOT intimidé.

Diable !

ERNEST bas.

Allons donc... Cinq cents !

MOULINOT.

Cinq cents !

CHAMBRELAN (qui est revenu à sa place d'un air radieux.)
Quel succès !

MONTGISCAR à part, regardant Moulinot.

Il ne pourra jamais payer... Pourvu que ça ne lui reste
pas... (haut) Cinq cents... personne ne dit mot !

JEANNE souriant.

Bien vu, bien entendu .. Je vais adjuger.

MONTGISCAR.

Une fois... deux fois... sans regret...

DE CLERCY avec force.

Mille francs !

MONTGISCAR.

Mille francs, messieurs !

CHAMBRELAN a de Clercy.

Etes-vous fou ?

DE CLERCY bas et regardant Moulinot.

Je ne me laisserai pas battre par ce monsieur !

CHAMBRELAN bas à de Clercy.

Vous, le mari ! Un mari ne pousse pas !

MONTGISCAR.

Mille francs !... allons, messieurs, ça vaut mieux que
ça...

OCTAVE timidement.

Si on le détaillait (Madame le Goberville le pince) Aie !

MONTGISCAR.

Mille francs, messieurs.

CHAMBRELAN même jeu que plus haut.

Un !

MONTGISCAR.

On a dit un ! mille un ! On demande à voir ? Qui est ce
qui demande à voir ? (Il remonte).

ERNEST bas à Moulinot,

Quinze cents !

MOULINOT stupéfait, bas à Ernest.

Voyons... vous me compromettez !

ERNEST bas.

Non... allez donc !

MONTGISCAR revenant à la table.

Mille un francs ! messieurs, mille un !

MOULINOT avec effort.

Quinze cents !

TOUS.

Ah !

DE CLERCY a part.

J'y renonce... mais j'aurai une conversation avec ce gros banquier !

MONTGISCAR.

Quinze cents !... personne ne dit mot ?

JEANNE.

C'est bien vu... bien entendu... une fois, deux fois... je vais adjuger... non... rien ? (Frappant avec le marteau.) Adjugé !

HECTOR.

Passez à monsieur. (On passe le bouquet à Moulinot.)

TOUS.

Bravo ! bravo !

MOULINOT à part, regardant le bouquet.

Je n'en donnerais pas trente sous.

MONTGISCAR à part.

Avec dix-huit cents francs d'appointements... alors il me vole ! (Jeanne quitte la table, on la félicite.)

CHAMBRELAN bas à Jeanne.

Marche dans ton triomphe ! ma fille, marche dans ton triomphe !

DE CLERCY près de Moulinot et à voix basse.

Nous nous reverrons, monsieur.

MOULINOT étonné.

Hein ! quoi ? (De Clercy s'éloigne de lui).

MONGISCAR.

Voyons, mesdames, à qui le tour ?

HERMANCE.

Oh ! non !... ce n'est pas amusant ! (Elle remonte avec les autres dames.)

CHAMBRELAN (à Jeanne.)

Elles ont peur !... Elles fuient la lutte !

JUSTIN annonçant au fond.

Le souper est servi,

MONGISCAR.

La main aux dames. (Tout le monde remonte, Montgiscar s'approche de Moulinot.) Ah ! vous achetez des bouquets de quinze cents francs, monsieur !... Vos appointements ne sont pas à la hauteur de vos passions... Vous pouvez souper comme tout le monde !... Mais nous causerons demain !

(Il sort à la suite de ses invités. Moulinot le regarde d'un air stupéfait. Le rideau baisse.

* Montgiscar, Moulinot.

FIN DU DEUXIÈME ACTE

ACTE TROISIÈME

Un salon chez de Clercy.

Au premier plan à droite, une fenêtre ouvrant sur un jardin ; auprès de la fenêtre, un petit meuble sur lequelle est un verre d'eau, à gauche, une cheminée ; près de cette cheminée, un canapé A droite une table avec ce qu'il faut pour écrire. Porte au fond. Portes dans les pans-coupés.

SCÈNE PREMIÈRE

DE CLERCY, seul, arrivant par le fond et posant son chapeau en entrant.

J'aurais aussi bien fait de ne pas aller chez ce Moulinot... que le diable l'emporte!... J'arrive chez lui, pour lui demander des explications sur sa folle enchère d'hier soir: Au cinquième, au dessus de l'entresol, me répond le concierge... un banquier, ça m'étonne... je monte, et je me trouve, dans une mansarde, en face d'un vieux bonhomme qui faisait sécher des gilets de flanelle devant le feu... et qui toussait... qui toussait !... il m'a pourtant avoué entre deux quintes, que le bouquet n'était pas pour lui... que c'était une commission... mais il n'a jamais voulu me

dire pour le compte de qui il opérait .. j'ai fait mine de me
fâcher, et il s'est remis à tousser de plus belle... impossible d'avoir une affaire avec un pareil rhume! Mais qui
donc a poussé le bouquet de ma femme? Oh! je veux le
savoir... et je le saurai!

SCÈNE II

DE CLERCY, JEANNE, CHAMBRELAN, puis un domestique.

JEANNE, entrant.

Bonjour, mon ami.

CHAMBRELAN.

Bonjour, mon gendre.

JEANNE.

Comme tu es sorti de bonne heure ce matin...

DE CLERCY.

Oui... j'avais un renseignement à prendre... et toi, te
ressens-tu des fatigues du bal?

JEANNE.

Du tout... Je suis prête à recommencer.

CHAMBRELAN.

Voilà les femmes! infatigables! Quel début! quel
début!... on peut appeler ça une jolie première!

DE CLERCY.

Quoi?

CHAMBRELAN.

La scène du bouquet surtout a beaucoup impressionné.,.

DE CLERCY.

Mais vraiment, beau-père, à vous entendre, on croirait
que ma femme est une actrice qui monte sur les planches.

CHAMBRELAN.

Le monde n'est-il pas un théâtre?

* Jeanne, de Clercy, Chambrelan.

JEANNE.

J'ai bien peur maintenant d'avoir toutes ces dames contre moi.

CHAMBRELAN.

Tant mieux, morbieu ! Ce monsieur Moulinot doit être un homme considérable. (à de Clercy) Il faudra lui faire remettre votre carte.

DE CLERCY.

Je la lui ai portée ce matin... savez-vous ce que c'est que ce Moulinot ?

CHAMBRELAN.

Un gros banquier.

DE CLERCY.

C'est un modeste employé à 1800 francs d'appointements...

JEANNE.

Allons donc !

CHAMBRELAN.

Alors c'est qu'il opérait pour quelque mystérieux amateur.

DE CLERCY.

C'est probable.

CHAMBRELAN.

Je voudrais bien le connaître.

DE CLERCY.

Moi aussi.

CHAMBRELAN.

Pour lui envoyer ma carte.

DE CLERCY.

Moi ! pas pour ça !...

(Un domestique entre portant des lettres sur un plateau.)

DE CLERCY.

Des lettres !... (Il les prend. — Le domestique sort. — à Jeanne lui tendant une des lettres.) Une pour toi. (à Chambrelan même jeu.) Une pour vous .. et une pour moi... (Chacun ouvre sa lettre.)

JEANNE.

Tiens ! c'est une loge pour les Italiens.

CHAMBRELAN.

Moi aussi.

DE CLERCY.

Moi aussi !

CHAMBRELAN.

Trois loges pour le même jour ! qui est-ce qui nous envoie ça ?

DE CLERCY, à part.

Il est évident que le galant au bouquet est un de ces trois là.

JEANNE, lisant une carte.

Monsieur de Goberville...

DE CLERCY, même jeu.

Ernest Montgiscar... mon cousin.

JEANNE.

Ah !...

CHAMBRELAN, lisant une carte.

Octave Blandar... mon sculpteur.

DE CLERCY.

Comment, votre sculpteur !... vous avez un sculpteur ?

CHAMBRELAN

Oui, hier, il m'a demandé la faveur de faire mon buste... il trouve que j'ai une tête d'empereur romain... Galba... et il doit venir aujourd'hui ..

DE CLERCY.

Ici ? vous allez introduire un étranger dans notre maison !...

CHAMBRELAN.

Où est le mal ?

DE CLERCY, avec colère.

Ah ! vous ne comprenez rien ! *

* De Clercy, Jeanne, Chambrelan.

CHAMBRELAN.

Comment! je ne comprends rien! mais vous le prenez avec moi sur un ton...

JEANNE, intervenant

Voyons, mon père...

CHAMBRELAN, à de Clercy.

Je ne reconnais à personne le droit de surveiller mes relations!... j'aime les artistes, moi! et si j'ai une tête d'empereur Romain, ça ne regarde que moi!

DE CLERCY.

Vous! (A part.) Une tête de patissier... honoraire!

CHAMBRELAN.

Vous êtes depuis hier d'une humeur massacrante. On dirait que vous jalousez les triomphes de votre femme.

DE CLERCY.

Non, mais je les voudrais plus calmes.

CHAMBRELAN.

Des triomphes calmes à présent!

JEANNE.

Voyons, ne vous disputez pas... et d'abord, irons-nous aux Italiens?

CHAMBRELAN.

Certainement...

DE CLERCY.

Si tu le désires. (A part) J'espère bien que là, je découvrirai quelque chose.

CHAMBRELAN, à sa fille.

Quelle coiffure mettrons-nous?... des roses ou des prunes?

DE CLERCY.

C'est bien... Ma femme décidera.

CHAMBRELAN.

C'est très-important... Les lorgnettes vont encore nous dévorer, comme à l'Opéra.

DE CLERGY, à part.

Mon Dieu ! que j'ai un beau-père agaçant !...

SCÈNE III

LES MÊMES, MONTGISCAR.

MONTGISCAR, entrant très agité *.

C'est moi.. vous voyez un homme tout retourné.

DE CLERCY.

En effet... qu'avez-vous donc ?

MONTGISCAR.

Ah ! si vous saviez la découverte que je viens de faire..
Ernest...

DE CLERCY.

Mon cousin, eh bien ?

MONTGISCAR.

Mon ami, il aime ta femme !

DE CLERCY.

Lui ! allons donc ! c'est impossible ?

CHAMBRELAN.

Pourquoi donc, impossible ?

DE CLERCY.

Un camarade... un ami !.. (Jeanne va s'assoir à gauche.)

MONTGISCAR.

Il en est amoureux comme un fou ! comme un possédé...
et moi, ça ne me va pas !

DE CLERCY **.

A moi non plus, parbleu !

---

* De Clercy, Jeanne, Montgiscar, Chambrelan
** Jeanne, Chambrelan, de Clercy, Montgiscar.

MONTGISCAR.

Voilà pourquoi il a refusé la main de la petite Burnett, Baring et Compagnie.

JEANNE, à part.

Pauvre garçon !

MONTGISCAR.

Et il m'a déclaré tout net, qu'il ne se marierait jamais... jamais !... jamais !...

DE CLERCY.

C'est une folie... un enfantillage...

MONTGISCAR *.

Et le bouquet !... le bouquet... c'est lui qui l'a poussé, c'est moi qui l'ai payé... 4,500 francs de perdus !.., et maintenant il le contemple, il lui parle, il lui envoie des baisers... comme à une femme.

CHAMBRELAN, à part, indiquant Jeanne.

Encore une existence broyée sous les roues de son char !

DE CLERCY.

Ceci ne peut être sérieux, il faut user de votre autorité, le raisonner...

MONTGISCAR.

J'ai déjà commencé.. Je lui ai dit : Voyons, en supposant que ta cousine consente à se laisser fléchir...

DE CLERCY.

Hein ?

JEANNE.

Par exemple !

MONTGISCAR.

C'est une supposition... il me semble qu'elle n'a rien d'invraisemblable, quand ou considère les avantages extérieurs de mon fils Ernest...

* Jeanne, Chambrelan, Montgiscar, de Clercy.

DE CLERCY.

C'est aimable pour moi...

MONTGISCAR.

J'ai été plus loin... Je l'ai poussé dans ses derniers re-
tranchements... j'ai ajouté : ta cousine te cède... je
l'admets ! très-bien !

DE CLERCY, se récriant.

Comment très-bien !

MONTGISCAR, continuant.

Et après ? songe aux conséquences · Je ne parle pas du
mari, qui ne le saura pas... mais où cela te conduira-t-il ?
à une de ces liaisons bâtardes, à un de ces ménages à trois,
qui enchaînent à tout jamais l'avenir d'un jeune homme...
Ernest, pense au monde qui te regarde, pense à ton père...
à ton malheureux père ..

DE CLERCY.

Et à ton cousin.

MONTGISCAR.

Non... je n'ai pas parlé du cousin...

DE CLERCY.

Vous avez eu tort... Certainement, je suis bon garçon...
mais je suis homme à lui mettre trois pouces de fer dans
la poitrine.

MONTGISCAR, vivement.

Ah ! Jules ! tu ne ferais pas cela... un duel en famille...
avec mon enfant...

DE CLERCY.

Que votre enfant reste chez lui !

MONTGISCAR.

Écoutez... aux grands maux, les grands remèdes... il
faut couper le mal dans sa racine... vous allez m'aider.
(A Jeanne) Vous surtout.

JEANNE, qui s'est levée *.

Moi ! Que faut-il faire ?

* Chambrelan, Jeanne, Montgiscar, de Clercy.

MONTGISCAR.

Il faut lui défendre votre porte... il ne faut plus le voir...

CHAMBRELAN.

A la bonne heure !... parceque s'il la voit... c'est fatal !...

MONTGISCAR.

Il vous a envoyé une loge pour les Italiens... Je le sais... Eh bien ! je vous demande, comme un service, de ne pas y aller.

JEANNE.

Ah ! ça ! bien volontiers !

DE CLERCY.

J'accorde.

CHAMBRELAN, à part.

Comme c'est agréable !

MONTGISCAR, à Jeanne.

Et si, malgré toutes vos précautions, le hasard vous le faisait rencontrer, soyez implacable, soyez impitoyable !... Dites-lui qu'il n'a rien à espérer, que vous ne manquerez jamais à vos devoirs

DE CLERCY.

Très-bien !

MONTGISCAR, continuant.

Ajoutez même que vous aimez votre mari. . allez jusque-là !

DE CLERCY.

Comment jusque-là !

MONTGISCAR.

Ça lui fera de la peine, je le sais bien, mais tant pis ! c'est pour le sauver ! me le promettez-vous ?

JEANNE.

Mon Dieu ! je ferai tout ce qui dépendra de moi.

MONTGISCAR.

Merci... je vous laisse... Je retourne près de lui... je crains qu'il ne fasse quelque sottise... (A de Clercy) Et toi, Jules, surveille ta femme. Je te confie son honneur... Adieu !

DE CLERCY.

Je vous accompagne, mon oncle. (A part.) Je vais faire défendre ma porte au cousin. (Montgiscar et de Clercy sortent par le fond.)

SCÈNE IV

CHAMBRELAN, JEANNE, puis DE CLERCY.

JEANNE.

Eh bien ! nous voilà revenus des Italiens.

CHAMBRELAN.

C'est insupportable. Ce M. Montgiscar est étonnant avec son fils !... s'il croit que nous allons renoncer au monde, nous claquemurer !

JEANNE.

Ah! il ne nous est pas défendu de sortir... d'abord nous avons une petite course à faire aujourd'hui.

CHAMBRELAN.

Chez la couturière ?

JEANNE.

Mais non !... chez M. de Goberville... à quatre heures.

CHAMBRELAN.

C'est juste... pour cette place... (Tirant sa montre.) Nous n'avons que le temps.

JEANNE, sonnant.

Je suis prête dans une minute. (Une femme de chambre paraît à droite.) Mon chapeau... mon mantelet, je sors. (La femme de chambre disparaît.)

CHAMBRELAN.

Il est convenu que nous ne parlons pas de cette dé-
marche à ton mari.

JEANNE.

Non... je veux qu'il ne se doute de rien... et lui prouver
que les femmes sont quelquefois bonnes à quelque chose.
(La femme de chambre est rentrée et lui a mis son chapeau et son
mantelet, Jeanne va à la glace)

DE CLERCY, rentrant, à part*.

Le cousin est consigné. (Haut) Tiens! vous sortez?

CHAMBRELAN.

Oui.

DE CLERCY.

Ah!... et où allez-vous?

CHAMBRELAN.

On ne peut pas le dire.

JEANNE, à de Clercy.

Vous le saurez plus tard... c'est une surprise. (L'em-
brassant.) Adieu, monsieur...

CHAMBRELAN, bas à de Clercy.

Cette femme là est un ange! (Il offre son bras à Jeanne, ils
disparaissent par le fond.)

SCÈNE V

DE CLERCY, puis un Domestique, puis OCTAVE.

DE CLERCY, seul.

Je suis sûr qu'ils vont acheter mystérieusement un
baba... le beau-père les adore, moi, ça m'étouffe. . alors
nous en mangeons souvent. Mais comprend-on Ernest qui
se met à aimer ma femme?... D'abord, entre cousins, ça

---

* Jeanne, de Clercy, Chambrelan.

ne se fait pas... Eh ! eh ! les cousins ! heureusement je suis prévenu... je le verrai... et nous traiterons la question à fond...

UN DOMESTIQUE, entrant.

M. Octave Blandar demande si madame est visible

DE CLERCY, à part.

Encore un ! le sculpteur de mon beau-père ! (Haut.) dites que madame est chez elle et faites entrer. (Le domestique sort) Dame ! quand on a épousé une jolie femme, il faut s'attendre à recevoir des visites.

OCTAVE, entrant*.

Excusez mon indiscrétion, madame... (Apercevant de Clercy.) Tiens, c'est vous !

DE CLERCY.

Madame de Clercy est sortie... mais je la représente, je suis son mari.

OCTAVE.

Son mari... Hier vous m'avez dit que vous étiez garçon.

DE CLERCY.

Hier, je voulais faire une expérience... Je désirais savoir si toutes les gracieusetés dont vous avez eu la bonté de me combler, s'adressaient bien à moi... J'ai acquis la preuve du contraire... recevez tous mes remercîments.

OCTAVE.

Mais vous vous êtes mépris, Monsieur... je me serai mal expliqué...

DE CLERCY.

Oh ! non, très-clairement... vous avez eu l'obligeance de nous envoyer ce matin une loge pour les Italiens.

OCTAVE.

En effet... je serais très-heureux... si vous pouviez...

* De Clercy, Octave.

DE CLERCY.

Oui, mais nous ne pourrons pas... nous avons tous les trois la migraine.

OCTAVE.

Ah! tous les..

DE CLERCY.

Oui... dans les ménages bien unis, c'est comme cela... on n'a pas la migraine les uns sans les autres... Veuillez donc reprendre votre coupon... que vous pourrez placer sans doute plus fructueusement. (Il le lui rend, le saluant) Monsieur, j'ai bien l'honneur. .

OCTAVE.

Pardon... j'avais aussi pris rendez-vous pour une séance avec monsieur.. monsieur... un gros monsieur.

DE CLERCY.

Galba!... c'est mon beau-père, le gros monsieur.

OCTAVE.

Il m'a accordé l'autorisation de faire son buste.

DE CLERCY.

Ah! ah! une œuvre d'art!... voyons, franchement, vous le trouvez donc joli, mon beau-père?

OCTAVE.

Il a des côtés plastiques.

DE CLERCY.

Vraiment!... Lesquels?

OCTAVE, embarrassé.

Mais, dame... le front... le nez...

DE CLERCY.

Et les oreilles? avez-vous remarqué les oreilles?

OCTAVE, à part.

Il se moque de moi. (On entend le roulement d'une voiture.) Une voiture!... c'est sa femme qui rentre... gagnons du temps. (Haut.) Vous le savez, monsieur, les artistes ont des fantaisies, ce n'est pas toujours le beau idéal qui les touche ; ainsi voyez, au moyen âge... les gargouilles du moyen âge...

SCÈNE VI

LES MÊMES, MADAME DE GOBERVILLE.

MADAME DE GOBERVILLE *, entrant comme une trombe.

Ah !

OCTAVE, à part.

Héloïse!...

DE CLERCY, à part.

Madame de Goberville!... Ah bah ?...

MADAME DE GOBERVILLE, à Octave

J'étais bien sûr de vous trouver ici... je vous ai suivi en fiacre... je me doutais de quelque chose... Que faites-vous dans cette maison ?

OCTAVE.

Moi, je...

MADAME DE GOBERVILLE.

Vous n'osez pas le dire...

OCTAVE.

Mais si...

MABAME DE GOBERVILLE.

Alors, dites-le...

OCTAVE.

Je viens voir Monsieur Chambrelan qui m'a prié de faire son buste.

MADAME DE GOBERVILLE.

Ah! son buste! vous avez fait aussi celui de mon mari... On sait ce que cela veut dire...

OCTAVE.

Mais il me semble que je suis bien libre.

* De Clercy, Mme Goberville, Octave

MADAME DE GOBERVILLE.

Non monsieur.

OCTAVE.

Si madame !

MADAME DE GOBERVILLE.

Non !

OCTAVE.

Si !...

DE CLERCY, à part.

Ils oublient que je suis là !... (Toussant.) Hum ! hum !

MADAME DE GOBERVILLE, l'apercevant.

Ah ! Monsieur de Clercy !... Comment va madame ?

DE CLERCY.

Très-bien... je vous remercie...

MADAME DE GOBERVILLE.

J'ai tenu à venir moi-même prendre de ses nouvelles.

DE CLERCY.

Trop bonne...

MADAME DE GOBERVILLE.

Vous voyez souvent monsieur Octave ?

DE CLERCY.

C'est la première fois qu'il vient ici.

MADAME DE GOBERVILLE, se calmant.

Ah !...

DE CLERCY.

Il a eu la bonté de nous envoyer une loge pour les Italiens.(Il va s'asseoir sur le canapé.)

MADAME DE GOBERVILLE, bondissant.

Une loge ! (A Octave, s'oubliant.) Vous m'avez dit ce matin que vous n'iriez pas !

OCTAVE.

J'ai probablement changé d'avis...

MADAME DE GOBERVILLE.

Vous espériez m'empêcher d'y aller... vous redoutiez ma présence !

OCTAVE.

Mais madame !

MADAME DE GOBERVILLE.

Je vous gênais.

OCTAVE.

Permettez !

MADAME DE GOBERVILLE.

Taisez-vous !

DE CLERCY, à part.

Ah ! ça, est-ce qu'ils ne pourraient pas aller se disputer ailleurs ? (Il tousse.) Hum !... hum !...

MADAME DE GOBERVILLE, à de Clercy.

Vous vous étonnez de me voir parler ainsi à ce jeune homme ?

DE CLERCY, se levant.

Mais non.

MADAME DE GOBERVILLE.

Il nous a été confié par sa famille qui habite la province, Monsieur de Goberville est son correspondant, nous l'aimons beaucoup.

DE CLERCY.

Je m'en doutais.

MADAME DE GOBERVILLE.

Nous sommes chargés de veiller sur lui... il est un peu léger, un peu mauvaise tête... mais le cœur est bon.

DE CLERCY.

C'est le principal.

MADAME DE GOBERVILLE.

Nous nous retirons... mes compliments à madame de Clercy... charmante femme !.. charmante femme !

DE CLERCY, saluant

Madame !...

MADAME DE GOBERVILLE.

Monsieur...

OCTAVE, à de Clercy.

Veuillez présenter mes hommages...

MADAME DE GOBERVILLE, l'interrompant.

C'est bien... votre bras.

OCTAVE

A vos ordres. (A part.) Je reviendrai. (Il sort vivement en donnant le bras à Mme de Goberville.)

SCÈNE VII

DE CLERCY, puis JEANNE.

DE CLERCY, seul.

Eh bien! j'ai là un joli petit intérieur... c'est à faire murer sa porte... pauvre Jeanne, ce n'est pas sa faute... Je n'ai rien à lui reprocher.. que sa beauté... mais je serais bien fâché qu'elle ne l'eût pas. (Voyant Jeanne qui entre par le fond.) C'est elle *! (A Jeanne) Eh bien ?... et la surprise ?.

JEANNE, d'un air contraint.

Elle est faite, mon ami...

DE CLERCY.

Alors démasquons le baba !

JEANNE.

Oh ! ce n'est pas de cela qu'il s'agissait... je suis allée chez monsieur de Goberville...

DE CLERCY

Hein ?..

* Jeanne, de Clercy

JEANNE.

Avec mon père et... tu as ta place.

DE CLERCY.

Comment ?

JEANNE.

Dans ce moment on expédie ta nomination... papa l'attend pour te l'apporter.

DE CLERCY, la regardant.

Mais de quel ton tu me dis cela... tu as l'air contrariée. .

JEANNE.

Oh ! du tout. (Vivement.) Mais je ne me chargerai plus de ces démarches-là !

DE CLERCY.

Pourquoi ?... voyons, tu as quelque chose...

SCÈNE VIII

LES MÊMES, MONTGISCAR.

MONTGISCAR, bouleversé *.

C'est encore moi !.. mes amis, tout est changé.

DE CLERCY ET JEANNE.

Quoi donc ?

MONTGISCAR.

Je vous avais prié de ne pas paraître aux Italiens... il faut y aller.

DE CLERCY.

Pourquoi ce changement !

MONTGISCAR.

Pour Ernest... nous avons été trop durs avec lui ! si vous aviez été témoin de sa douleur quand je lui ai dit qu'on n'acceptait pas sa loge... J'ai coloré votre refus en

* Jeanne, Montgiscar, de Clercy

lui faisant entendre que Jeanne était souffrante... alors, il
va venir prendre de ses nouvelles...

JEANNE, vivement.

Non ! je ne veux pas le recevoir !

DE CLERCY.

Il n'entrera pas... je l'ai consigné à la porte.

MONTGISCAR

J'ai levé la consigne... en passant.

DE CLERCY.

Ah ! bien !... très-bien !

MONTGISCAR.

Il est si malheureux !... il a refusé de déjeuner, et pourtant il y avait des huîtres... il a déclaré qu'il ne dinerait
pas... j'ai voulu lui faire écrire une lettre à mon agent de
change, pour le distraire ; il lui a parlé tout le temps de la
grotte d'azur.

DE CLERCY.

Qu'est-ce que c'est que ça ?

MONTGISCAR.

Ça ne te regarde pas... C'est entre ta femme et moi.

JEANNE, à de Clercy.

Plus tard... je te dirai...

MONTGISCAR.

Et il pleurait... lui, si gai !... il répétait à chaque instant... elle ne m'aime pas .. elle ne m'aime pas ! J'avais
beau lui dire : mais ne te désole pas, avec les femmes, il
y a toujours de l'espoir.

DE CLERCY.

Je vous remercie.

MONTGISCAR.

Dame ! on ne sait ni qui vit, ni qui meurt, tu te portes
bien aujourd'hui... mais demain...

JEANNE.

Par exemple !

DE CLERGY.

C'est ça, enterrez-moi tout de suite.

MONTGISCAR.

Ça ne tue personne ce que je dis là.

DE CLERCY.

Tenez, sans vous en douter, vous poussez l'amour paternel jusqu'à la férocité... vous êtes un monstre de tendresse.

MONTGISCAR.

Si tu l'avais vu comme moi, la tête dans ses mains, le regard fixe... c'était effrayant !... j'en tremble encore... et s'il devait lui arriver un malheur... (Pleurant.) Je n'ai que lui, moi... Qu'est-ce que je deviendrais... tout seul au monde ?.. (Sanglotant.) Mon pauvre enfant! mon pauvre enfant! (Il se jette dans les bras de de Clercy.)

DE CLERCY, le consolant.

Voyons, mon oncle, remettez-vous... à son âge... on oublie.

MONTGISCAR.

Oh non ! pas lui !.. (A Jeanne, comme un homme qui fait une déclaration.) Ce n'est pas un amour vulgaire, un amour banal que le sien !... (Se passionnant.) Il vous aime profondément, de toutes les forces, de toutes les ardeurs de son âme... Il vous a vue, madame, une minute a suffi !... (Il est prêt à tomber à genoux.)

DE CLERCY, l'interrompant *.

Dites-donc ! dites-donc ! je suis là, moi !...

MONTGISCAR.

Je le sais bien, malheureusement.

DE CLERCY.

Comment ?

* Jeanne, de Clercy, Montgiscar.

MONTGISCAR.

Mais c'est ta faute aussi !... c'est toi qui a fait tout le mal.

DE CLERCY.

Moi ?..

MONTGISCAR.

Tu as voulu absolument épouser une jolie femme, par amour-propre... par orgueil.

DE CLERCY, à part.

La tête n'y est plus.

MONTGISCAR.

Qui sait, sans toi, c'est peut-être Ernest qui aurait épousé ta femme ; elle serait heureuse.

DE CLERCY.

Mais il me semble qu'avec moi !...

MONTGISCAR *.

Enfin le mal est fait !... il faut le réparer maintenant. (A Jeanne.) Il va venir, ne soyez pas trop sévère. Faites-lui l'aumône d'un regard.

DE CLERCY.

Ah ! permettez !...

MONTGISCAR.

Un regard, qu'est-ce que ça te fait ?

DE CLERCY.

Vous êtes superbe !

MONTGISCAR.

Comment ! quand un seul regard peut sauver ton cousin, tu refuses ?...

DE CLERCY.

Oui...

MONTGISCAR **

Toi, que j'ai élevé, toi, que j'ai marié !

* Jeanne, Montgiscar, de Clercy.
** Jeanne, de Clercy, Montgiscar.

DE CLERCY.

Vous m'avez marié... pas pour ça!

MONTGISCAR.

Tiens! veux-tu que je te dise.. tu manques de sens moral.

DE CLERCY.

Ah! allez au diable!

UN DOMESTIQUE, annonçant.

M. Ernest Montgiscar.

MONTGISCAR *.

Lui... (A Jeanne.) Vous ne savez rien... un peu de bien-veillance... de compassion. (A de Clercy.) Et toi, du calme .. je te le demande au nom de la famille!

DE CLERCY.

Soyez tranquille. (A part.) J'aurai avec lui une explica-tion sans témoins.

SCÈNE IX

LES MÊMES, ERNEST.

ERNEST, entrant **.

Madame! (A de Clercy.) Bonjour, cher ami.

MONTGISCAR, bas à de Clercy.

Hein ?... comme il est pâle.

DE CLERCY, bas.

Je ne trouve pas.

ERNEST, a Jeanne.

J'ai appris par mon pere que vous étiez souffrante... et j'ai tenu à venir m'informer moi-même...

---

* De Clercy, Montgiscar, Jeanne.
** Montgiscar, de Clercy, Ernest, Jeanne.

JEANNE.

Ce n'est rien, un peu de fatigue seulement, le bal d'hier. Je vous demande la permission de me retirer...

ERNEST, décontenancé.

Ah !... certainement. (Jeanne salue et sort par la droite.)

MONTGISCAR. à part.

Qu'elle est cruelle !

ERNEST, se remettant.

Ma cousine paraît délicate... elle a besoin de grands ménagements. (A de Clercy.) Tu est responsable de sa santé.

DE CLERCY.

Ce cher Ernest... mais, toi-même, comment vas-tu ? Ton père nous disait à l'instant que tu étais malade... bien malade.

ERNEST, regardant son père.

Ah !

MONTGISCAR.

Je n'ai parlé que d'une simple indisposition.

ERNEST.

Oh ! qu'importe ! Qu'un garçon vive ou meure, ça ne compte pas... (Souriant.) C'est une non-valeur dans la société.

MONTGISCAR, bas à de Clercy.

Sa gaieté me fait mal.

SCENE X

Les Mêmes, CHAMBRELAN, puis un Domestique.

CHAMBRELAN, entrant par le fond *.

Vivat ! L'affaire est dans le sac !

* Montgiscar, de Clercy, Chambrelan, Ernest.

DE CLERCY.

Vous m'apportez ma nomination.

CHAMBRELAN *.

M. de Goberville avait dit à Jeanne : « Venez demain à quatre heures... » J'ai tenu à l'accompagner, parce que c'est plus convenable.

DE CLERCY, lui serrant la main.

Merci, beau-père.

CHAMBRELAN.

Seulement, comme je n'avais pas de lettre d'audience, je suis resté dans l'antichambre.

DE CLERCY et ERNEST.

Ah !

CHAMBRELAN.

Mais Jeanne n'a eu qu'à dire son nom, elle est entrée tout de suite... avant cinq personnes qui attendaient... dont un monsieur décoré... qui faisait un nez.

DE CLERCY.

Après?

ERNEST **.

Après ?

CHAMBRELAN.

Elle a été reçue admirablement. Elle m'a tout raconté, ce Monsieur de Goberville est un homme d'une courtoisie parfaite... il l'a fait asseoir près du feu... dans son propre fauteuil, s'il vous plaît! Il lui a mis un tabouret sous les pieds... un homme de cette importance là.

ERNEST.

Il est bien poli... ce n'est pourtant pas dans ses habitudes.

MONTGISCAR, bas à Ernest.

Tais-toi donc!... qu'est-ce que ça te fait ?

* De Clercy, Chambrelan, Montgiscar, Ernest.
** De Clercy, Chambrelan, Ernest, Montgiscar

DE CLERCY, à Chambrelan.

Continuez.

ERNEST.

Continuez.

CHAMBRELAN.

Ensuite il s'est informé de ses nouvelles... (A Clercy.) des vôtres... des miennes . il a dit qu'il espérait la voir ce soir aux Italiens... et il a prié qu'on lui gardât un petit coin dans la loge qu'il nous a envoyée.

ERNEST.

Comment ! il s'est permis d'adresser une loge.

DE CLERCY.

Oui, la même idée que toi.

ERNEST.

Mais moi, je suis...

DE CLERCY.

Son cousin. (A Chambrelan.) Enfin, cette place...

CHAMBRELAN.

Il l'a accordée... avec une grâce charmante : en lui disant qu'on ne pourrait rien refuser a un pareil ambassadeur... ce qui est un peu vrai... et comme Jeanne allait le remercier... (Se redressant avec orgueil.) Il a embrassé ma fille !

DE CLERCY.

Hein ?

ERNEST.

Par exemple !

CHAMBERLAN.

Sur le front ! un homme de cette importance là... et il a ajouté en la reconduisant : Jolie comme un ange.

DE CLERCY.

Morbleu !

ERNEST, de même.

Vieux drôle !

MONTGISCAR, bas à Ernest.

Tais-toi donc.

CHAMBRELAN, radieux.

Mon gendre vous êtes nommé. (Il lui tend un pli.)

DE CLERCY, le prenant.

Merci.., (Le déchirant en deux.) Tenez, voici le cas que je fais de sa nomination.

CHAMBRELAN,

Comment !

DE CLERCY.

Et je vais la lui retourner avec une lettre qu'il ne fera pas circuler dans son bureau. (Il sort furieux par le fond.)

CHAMBRELAN, étonné.

Qu'est-ce qu'il a ?... Eh bien ! voilà un original !

ERNEST, furieux,

Il a bien fait !... et si j'étais à sa place j'irai trouver ce monsieur !...

MONTGISCAR, bas à Ernest.*

Mais tais toi donc ?... tu n'es pas le mari !

UN DOMESTIQUE, entrant.

M. Octave Blandar, demande si M. Chambrelan peut le recevoir.

CHAMBRELAN.

C'est pour mon buste... (Au domestique.) Faites entrer chez moi. (Le domestique sort.) C'est mon sculpteur... un garçon charmant... il nous a aussi envoyé une loge pour les Italiens.

ERNEST.

Encore !

MONTGISCAR, à part.

·Toute la feuille de location y a passé ! (On entend le roulement d'une voiture.)

---

* Chambrelan, Montgiscar, Ernest.

CHAMBRELAN.

Tiens ! une voiture !... une visite... Nous commençons à recevoir beaucoup de monde.

LE DOMESTIQUE, revenant.

Madame de Goberville demande si M. Octave Blandar est ici.

CHAMBRELAN.

Certainement, faites entrer chez moi. (Le domestique sort, à Montgiscar). Elle vient sans doute pour causer de son buste... faites-moi le plaisir de m'accompagner, vous me donnerez vos conseils sur la pose que je dois prendre... vous êtes un peu artiste.

MONTGISCAR.

Oh! j'ai fréquenté le musée des Antiques... je recolle.

(On entend au dehors un grand bruit de porcelaine cassée.)

CHAMBRELAN.

Ah! mon Dieu! qu'est-ce qu'on casse chez moi... venez vite! (Chambrelan et Montgiscar sortent vivement par la gauche.)

SCÈNE XI

ERNEST, puis JEANNE.

ERNEST, regardant autour de lui.

Seul.. si ce bruit pouvait la faire venir. (Il remonte.)

JEANNE, entrouvrant la porte de droite.

On a brisé quelque chose. (S'avançant et apercevant Ernest*.) Ah! ciel!

ERNEST.

Madame !... un seul mot de grâce.

JEANNE.

Non, monsieur.

* Jeanne Ernest.

ERNEST.

Je vous en prie, daignez m'écouter. (Il fait un pas vers elle.

JEANNE.

Plus loin... ou je me retire.

ERNEST, s'éloignant.

Oui, d'ici... tenez, d'ici !... Je n'approcherai pas, mais
ne refusez pas d'entendre un homme qui vous demande
avec respect d'avoir pitié de lui.

JEANNE*.

Mais qu'est-ce que vous voulez?

ERNEST.

Accordez moi la faveur de vous aimer discrétement...
en silence.

JEANNE.

Mais c'est impossible... Je suis mariée... Monsieur
Ernest, je vous en prie. . Oubliez moi.

ERNEST, allant à elle.

Vous oublier ! vous!...

JEANNE.

Ah ! vous me faites peur ' (Elle rentre vivement et ferme la
porte.)

SCÈNE XII

ERNEST, puis MONTGISCAR.

ERNEST, courant à la porte.

Madame! madame!... Elle refuse de m'entendre... que
faire?... si je lui écrivais?... oui, essayons. (Il se met à
la table et écrit vivement.) Quelques lignes seulement... peut
être se laissera-t-elle fléchir... c'est mon dernier espoir...
oui, le dernier !... (Pliant le billet et se levant.) Comment lui
faire parvenir ! (Revenant à la porte.) Hein !... le frôlement

* Ernest, Jeanne.

4.

d'une robe... elle est là! Ah! sous la porte... (Il passe le billet sous la porte.) On le prend....

MONTGISCAR, à la cantonade.

Oui, du mastic d'Athènes...

ERNEST, près de la porte du fond.

Quelqu'un!...

MONTGISCAR, entrouvrant la porte de gauche et parlant au dehors.

En face le guichet du Louvre.

ERNEST.

Mon père!.. (Il sort vivement par le fond.)

SCÈNE XIII

MONTGISCAR, puis JEANNE, puis DE CLERCY.

MONTGISCAR.

Je ne sais pas ce que madame de Goberville peut avoir à reprocher à monsieur Octave... mais elle vient de lui flanquer trois potiches à la tête... heureusement qu'avec du mastic d'Athènes...

JEANNE, entrant vivement*.

Ah! monsieur Montgiscar... si vous saviez ce qui se passe... le malheureux... est-il parti?

MONTGISCAR.

Qui ça?...

JEANNE.

Votre fils!

MONTGISCAR.

Mon fils!

JEANNE, lui tendant un billet.

Lisez.

* Montgiscar, Jeanne.

MONTGISCAR*

« Ah ! mon Dieu ! (Lisant.) « Madame, je ne prends plus
« conseil que de mon désespoir. — Cette tentative sera la
« dernière .. Je suis dans le jardin, si vous consentez à
« m'entendre faites le moi savoir en ouvrant la fenêtre...
« qu'elle reste fermée comme votre cœur et je me fais
« sauter la cervelle !. » — Ah ! le malheureux ! (Il va ouvrir
la fenêtre.)

JEANNE.

Que faites vous !. . si mon mari ..

MONTGISCAR.

Eh ! votre mari !... il y a force majeure ! (De Clercy entre
par le fond **.)

JEANNE et MONTGISCAR, à part.

Lui !

DE CLERCY, les observant.

Eh bien ! qu'avez-vous donc tous les deux ? ce trouble...

MONTGISCAR.

Rien, va t'en !

JEANNE.

Oui, mon ami.

DE CLERCY.

Moi ? pourquoi ?

MONTGISCAR.

Va t'en !... si tu savais... cette lettre... (Il gesticule avec
la lettre.)

DE CLERCY, la prenant.

Cette lettre !...

MONTGISCAR et JEANNE.

Ah !

* Jeanne, Montgiscar.
** De Clercy, Montgiscar, Jeanne

DE CLERCY, après l'avoir lue.

Mais c'est insensé... il est fou !

MONTGISCAR.

Oui... il va venir... va t'en !

DE CLERCY.

Rentrez!... c'est moi qui le recevrai.

MONTGISCAR.

Par exemple!

DE CLERCY.

Oh! ne craignez rien... Je suis calme... je lui ferai entendre raison... D'ailleurs Jeanne ne peut assister à cette explication.

MONTGISCAR.

Oui, mais de la douceur, je t'en prie, de la douceur.

DE CLERCY.

Soyez tranquille...

MONTGISCAR.

Tâche de t'emparer tout de suite de son pistolet... c'est la première chose.

DE CLERCY.

Oui... allez !

MONTGISCAR.

Nous serons-là... si tu as besoin de nous... de la douceur... de la douceur et le pistolet. (Montgiscar et Jeanne sortent par le fond à droite.)

SCÈNE XIV

DE CLERCY, puis ERNEST.

DE CLERCY

Eh bien ! il ne manquait plus que ça, c'est le bouquet !... en voilà un qui veut se brûler la cervelle sous mes fenêtres... oh ! les jolies femmes !... et cet imbécile... un ami... un camarade... un gamin! je l'entends.. (Il remonte et se tient près de la porte du fond.)

ERNEST, entrant vivement sans voir de Clercy.

Ah!... merci, madame!...

DE CLERCY, le prenant à bras le corps *.

A nous deux !

ERNEST.

Toi ?

DE CLERCY.

Pas d'enfantillage ! tes armes ! il me faut tes armes?...

ERNEST, se débattant.

Non... Laisse-moi !

DE CLERCY.

Je les veux ! (Il lui arrache un revolver de sa poche.)

ERNEST.

Rends moi ce revolver !

DE CLERCY, l'écartant de lui.

Malheureux ! tu n'as donc pas pensé à ton père... à tes amis... à ta famille... au scandale. . et tu voulais... (Regardant le revolver et à part.) Tiens'... il n'est pas chargé.

ERNEST.

Oui, je suis fou! criminel... raison de plus pour en finir.

DE CLERCY, avec calme.

Au fait... tu as peut-être raison... je ne peux pas t'offrir ma femme... d'un autre côté tu ne peux pas y renoncer.

ERNEST.

Oh!

DE CLERCY.

Non... je ne te le demande pas (lui tendant le révolver.) Il n'y a donc que ce moyen d'en sortir.

ERNEST.

Donne.

* Ernest, de Clercy.

DE CLERCY examinant l'arme.

Attends !... je crois que tu as oublié les cartouches.

ERNEST decontenancé.

Ah ! vraiment !... le trouble.

DE CLERCY.

C'est bien naturel... dans ces moments là on ne pense pas à tout.., on veut se tuer... on oublie les cartouches... C'est bien naturel.

ERNEST, tendant la main.

J'en ai chez moi.

DE CLERCY.

Ne te dérange donc pas... j'en ai aussi là... dans mon tiroir. (Il s'assied devant la table et ouvre le tiroir.) Je t'en mets quatre... en veux-tu six ?... Je t'en mets six.

ERNEST à part.

Sapristi !

DE CLERCY lui tendant le révolver après l'avoir chargé.

Tiens !... va !... je ne regarderai pas. . je suis trop sensible.

ERNEST regardant le révolver sans le prendre.

Hum ! (il va s'asseoir sur un fauteuil à gauche.)

DE CLERCY se levant,

Mais alors tu es un farceur ! c'était un truc... dis le donc.

ÉRNEST

Ah ! peux-tu croire.

DE CLERCY.

Il n'est pas neuf... Il a déjà servi au théâtre... *Etre aimé ou mourir* !

ERNEST se levant.

Je te jure... que je ne connais pas la pièce.

DE CLERCY.

Sais-tu que ce n'est pas honnête ce que tu as fait là... chercher à séduire la femme d'un ami... presque d'un frère . Je pourrais t'en demander compte... mais je me trouve assez vengé.

ERNEST.

Comment ?

DE CLERCY.

Sans doute, après avoir écrit... ton billet de faire part... reparaître dans le monde gros et gras... ces dames ne t'apelleront plus que : le monsieur qui ne se tue pas.

ERNEST.

C'est vrai... Je vais être couvert de ridicule.

DE CLERCY.

C'est bien ainsi que je l'entends.

ERNEST.

Comment me tirer de là... voyons... je t'en prie donne moi un conseil.

DE CLERCY.

Tue toi !

ERNEST.

Je vois bien que tu m'en veux,

DE CLERDY.

Il n'y a peut être pas de quoi ?

ERNEST.

Eh bien ! j'ai eu tort... je le reconnais... j'ai eu un moment d'égarement, de folie... mais toi, tu ne t'es pas gêné avec moi... tu m'as soufflé la petite...

DE CLERCY.

Quelle différence ! tu me parles d'une monnaie qui était dans la circulation.

ERNEST.

Ah ! très-joli !

DE CLERCY.

Oui...Tu me flattes pour me désarmer.

ERNEST.

Voyons, tu ne peux pas me laisser dans cette position

grotesque... pour l'honneur de la famille, arrangeons quelque chose, qui sauvegarde mon amour propre.

DE CLERCY.

J'ai peut-être un moyen.

ERNEST.

Ah ! parle !

DE CLERCY.

Oui... mais à deux conditions.

ERNEST.

Lesquelles ?

DE CLERCY.

La première, (avoue que je suis un bon enfant...) La
première, c'est que tu seras marié avant trois mois.

ERNEST.

Ah ! tu es cruel.

DE CLERCY.

Avec une jolie femme !.. ça t'occupera... et c'est une
garantie pour l'avenir .. la seconde... tu diras à ma femme
textuellement ces paroles : Aimez votre mari, madame,
c'est le plus noble et le plus généreux des hommes.

ERNEST.

Ah ! non !... je peux pas dire ça...

DE CLERCY.

Alors... tue toi !...

ERNEST.

Allons, soit !... (De Clercy lui tend le revolver.) Je le dirai.

DE CLERCY.

Ah ! très-bien... maintenant faisons notre mise en
scène.

ERNEST.

Comment ?

DE CLERCY.

Tu vas voir. Ébouriffe-toi... du désordre dans les cheveux, défais ta cravate, déboutonne ton gilet. Tu ne pour-

rais pas être un peu pâle .. ça ne fait rien... tu y es?...
pousse un cri... je tire... (Il tire un coup de revolver.)

ERNEST, tombant sur le canapé.

Ah!

SCÈNE XV

LES MÊMES, MONTGISCAR, JEANNE, puis CHAMBRELAN.

MONTGISCAR et JEANNE entrant, avec effroi *.

Ah!

DE CLERCY.

Il s'est manqué! il s'est manqué.. j'ai détourné le
coup.

CHAMBRELAN, venant de la gauche.

Que se passe-t-il?

MONTGISCAR, courant à Ernest **.

Malheureux!

JEANNE.

Pauvre jeune homme.

ERNEST.

Je vous l'avais promis, madame.

JEANNE, à Ernest, avec émotion.

Monsieur Ernest, vous avez voulu mourir pour moi. Je
sens là, que je ne l'oublierai jamais!

ERNEST.

Ah! madame.

DE CLERCY, a part

Ah! mais non! je l'ai trop réhabilité! je n'entends
pas ça...

* Ernest, de Clercy, Montgiscar, Jeanne.
** Chambrelan, Ernest, Montgiscar, Jeanne, de Clercy.

7

MONTGISCAR.

Il pâlit... un verre d'eau.

JEANNE, avec empressement.

Voilà ! voilà !... (Elle court a droite et y prépare un verre d'eau *.)

CHAMBRELAN, à Montgiscar.

Mais expliquez-moi...

MONTGISCAR.

Un évènement effroyable. Mon fils a failli se tuer pour votre fille.

CHAMBRELAN.

Ça ne m'étonne pas.

MONTGISCAR, mettant un flacon sous le nez d'Ernest.

Tiens ! respire !... respire !...

JEANNE, redescendant avec le verre d'eau.

Vite, buvez !...

DE CLERCY, l'arrêtant au passage, et prenant le verre d'eau

Pardon !...

JEANNE, etonnée.

Mais, mon ami...

DE CLERCY, à demi-voix.

C'est moi qui ai tiré en l'air... une petite comédie arrangée entre nous... (Il boit le verre d'eau.)

JEANNE, désapointée.

Ah ! je ne veux plus aimer personne

DE CLERCY, à part.

Eh ! bien !... il n'était que temps ..

MONTGISCAR, palpant Ernest.

Tu es sûr de ne pas être blessé.

* Chambrelan, Ernest, Montgiscar, de Clercy, Jeanne.

ERNEST, se levant.

Non... ça va mieux... rentrons, mon père...*

MONTGISCAR.

Quel caractère ! il est en bronze !

DE CLERCY, bas à Ernest.

Et nos conditions.

ERNEST, bas.

Je les oubliais...

DE CLERCY.

Comme les cartouches.

ERNEST, à Montgiscar.

Mon père, je vous donne trois mois pour me chercher une femme...

DE CLERY, bas à Ernest.

Maintenant aimez votre mari, madame... chaud !...

ERNEST, à part.

Sapristi ! ** (Haut, et prenant son parti, à Jeanne.) Aimez votre mari, madame, c'est le plus noble et le plus généreux des hommes ! (Il remonte.)

JEANNE, courant à son mari et se jetant dans ses bras ***.

Ah ! c'est bien vrai !

DE CLERCY.

Je ne lui ai pas fait dire. (Il l'embrasse.) Chère petite Jeanne ! (A part.) Eh bien !... on dira ce qu'on voudra, il y a des moments où les jolies femmes ont du bon !..

* Chambrelan, Montgiscar, Ernest, de Clercy, Jeanne.
** Chambrelan, Montgiscar, de Clercy, Ernest, Jeanne
*** Chambrelan, Montgiscar, Ernest, de Clercy, Jeanne.

FIN

Poissy. — Typ. S Lejay et Cie.

Lightning Source UK Ltd.
Milton Keynes UK
UKOW07f2156051215

264186UK00008B/141/P

RISE

A LANTERN CITY ILLUSTRATED NOVEL

WRITTEN BY
MATTHEW JAMES DALEY

CREATED BY
TREVOR CRAFTS AND BRUCE BOXLEITNER

BLUECANVAS

Rise: A Lantern City Illustrated Novel
By Matthew James Daley

Cover design By Trevor Crafts and Alex Sanchez
All illustrations by Section Studios
Book Design by Trevor Crafts

Published by Bluecanvas
316 W. 2nd St. Third Floor – Los Angeles, CA 90012
www.bluecanvas.com

Macrocosm Entertainment
Los Angeles, CA
www.macrocosm.tv

Library of Congress Cataloging-in-Publication Data

Daley, Matthew James

Rise: A Lantern City Illustrated Novel Written By Matthew James Daley
Created by Trevor Crafts and Bruce Boxleitner

ISBN 978-0-9859022-2-3

First Edition: July 2013

Partners:
Section Studios, Inc. | www.sectionstudios.com

Printed in Korea in collaboration with

R
I
M
ASSOCIATION

RIM Association

To my wife Arlene. Whom I have loved since we met. In a library.

— *Matthew James Daley*

To my wife Ellen, who is my everything, and my wonderful parents who always pushed me to greatness.

— *Trevor Crafts*

To my fellow voyagers Trevor and Matt, partners on this incredible journey that begins with this story.

— *Bruce Boxleitner*

Prologue

Killian wasn't bothered by the whistling sound of his mother's breathing as she struggled to fill her lungs, and it disturbed him that he couldn't force himself to feel something for the dying woman. Servants came and went, bringing foods and beverages and wondrous concoctions of medicine, all whispering prayers to the goddess Uryston before they left, fearing that Martha Grey, the woman they fussed and busied over, would soon be dead.

All of the faces had started to look the same to Killian; even Desmond Welhorn, his father's advisor—a man he saw more often than his father—looked like a stranger. There wasn't a thing Killian could do for his suffering mother. She wasn't supposed to be sick. No one in the Ruling Class, especially the wife of the Great Ruler, should succumb to a commoner's disease. Yet here she was, imprisoned in her own bed, looking more like a skeleton with thin, leathery skin stretched across her bones than the healthy woman Killian had called Mother. Not only was she unrecognizable; he could not bear to look at her. And all she wanted was her son's attention.

"Here . . . here . . . please," said Martha, her voice like a distant murmur.

Desmond rushed to the bedside and stopped just short of stepping on Killian. Killian sat with his back to the bed frame, sharpening his pencil with a small blade. He just wanted to go to his room and draw; he hadn't been allowed to his room since she'd first shown symptoms, and it was the only place he wanted to be. He hated all the servants pretending to know what was best, even after every credible doctor in Lantern City had examined her. There was little hope for her and Killian did not want to watch her die. He certainly didn't want to be close to her, nor could he be a loving son when he no longer recognized her.

"She wants you," said Desmond. Desmond, round in belly and meek in voice, spoke to everyone except the Great Ruler, James Jay Grey, with contempt. He refused to look at Killian when he spoke to him, as if Killian was some abomination. Killian hated his father's advisor.

"What?" said Killian, pretending not to hear.

"Your mother . . . is calling for you," said Desmond.

Desmond snapped his fingers at two male servants, who leaped to attention at the advisor's signaling. "Open the curtains," said Desmond. The servants turned and pulled on the ropes to draw the curtains open. Killian shaded his eyes, expecting to be blinded by the suns. To his astonishment, it was nighttime. He had lost all track of time during the past few days, his internal clock disabled.

"Please," said Martha. "Kil—"

Desmond threw up his hands. "You mustn't speak. I sent that Coolridge boy to a trusted apothecary in the north district. If you can hold on long enough, we might have the cure for you. Do not—"

"Killian," said Martha.

Killian stood. He went to the side of the bed opposite from Desmond. He stared at his mother's hands. She was no more than thirty, and yet her hands looked like they belonged to a withered old woman. The hands, no matter how grotesque, were better than her face.

"Sit," said Desmond.

"I've been sitting," said Killian.

"He's behaved. Surprisingly," Desmond said to Martha.

"Go," said Martha.

Desmond turned to walk away.

"No . . . Killian," said Martha. "Don't see me like this. Go."

Killian made the mistake of looking at his mother. The skin underneath her eyes was dark purple. Her eyes were yellowing. As she breathed, her blackened tongue fell out of her mouth.

Desmond walked around to Killian. He pulled him by the shoulder and walked him to the door; a servant opened it. Killian walked through the door and Desmond grabbed him by the shoulder. Killian didn't turn around. Desmond's beard scraped Killian's neck as he leaned in to whisper to the boy.

"Why don't you run along and try to find your daddy. I'm sure our Great Ruler has a solution for his dying wife," Desmond said.

Killian pulled away from Desmond's grip. He ran, with no destination in mind—the only thing that mattered was getting as far from

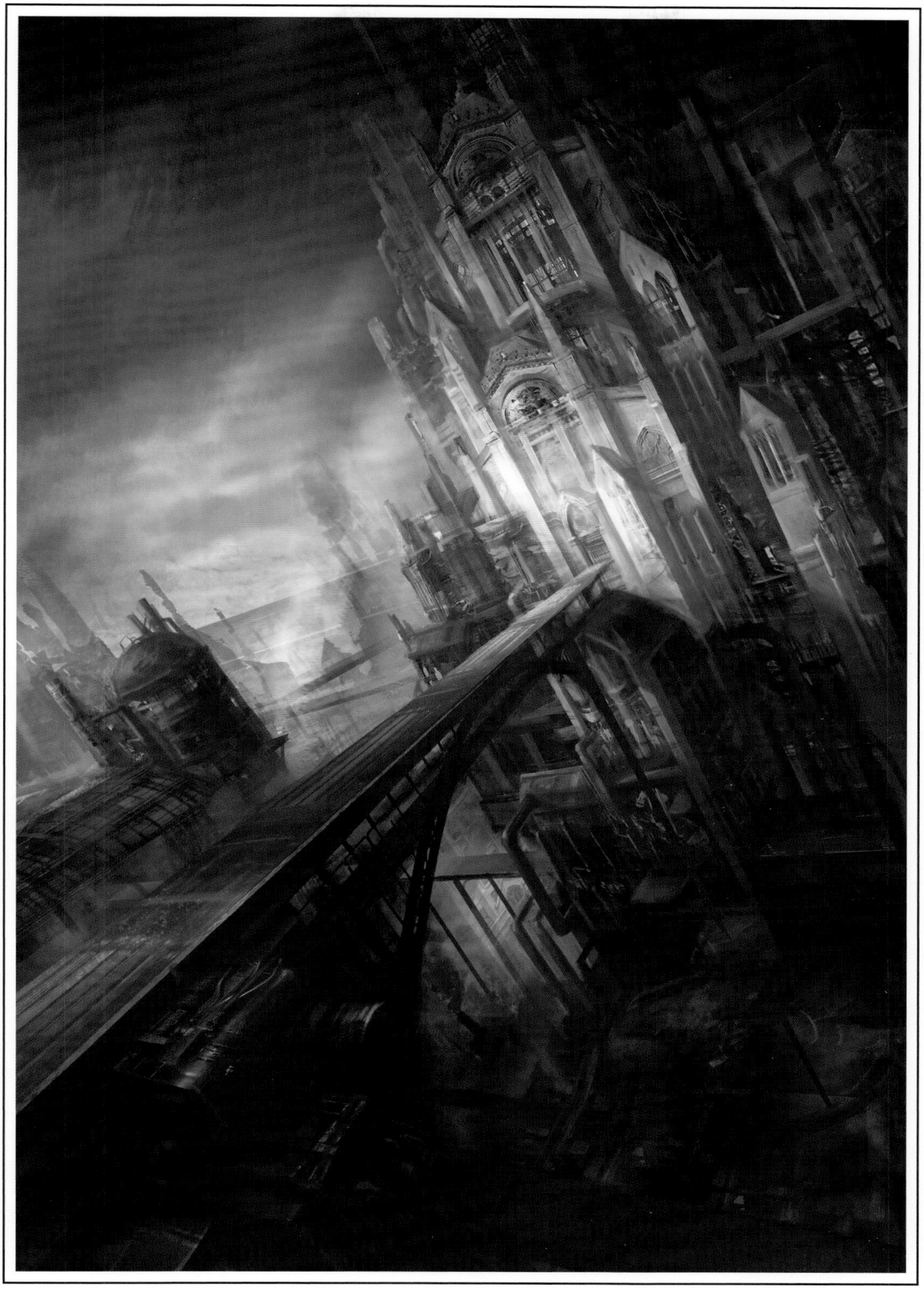

his mother's room as possible. He passed many servants, all of whom looked like they were going to stop him and direct him back to his mother. He kept his head down and moved forward, giving none of them a chance to find out where he was going.

Once he realized he hadn't brought his pencil or blade, he decided to go to his favorite place in Grey Tower: the space he would inherit at age eighteen. Sure, he had a room now, with all of the amenities he needed, including servants, but it was not as glorious as his space-to-be.

The Grey Tower was comprised of a series of impressively built towers, all reaching well over 600 feet, the central spire rising over 1,500 feet. It dominated Lantern City like a god. The top floor of the central tower was reserved for Killian, who would one day become the Great Ruler of Lantern City. Killian, at age eight, was not concerned about ruling anything—but he was excited to have his own space separate from everyone else. Ten years could not pass quickly enough for him.

Many of the buildings were connected by walkways and some were reserved exclusively for the Grey family. Killian ran from the West Tower to the Central Tower, watching the city below. He had no fear of heights and thought nothing of what a four-hundred-foot drop would do to him. Once he reached the Central Tower, he took the private lift to the top floor. All he wanted to do was sit on the balcony and watch the city below. There were always things to see and hear, and he looked down on the world below like it was an organic toy, moving at his whim and fancy. During the day, he enjoyed looking out beyond the wall, allowing his imagination to fill in the space with great mountains, forests, and cities. Though he was young and never allowed to leave Grey Tower, he knew that he was privy to something no common citizen was privy to: a view of the wasted world beyond the wall.

Killian stopped in front of the main entrance to his apartment. He could sense someone else was inside. The handle clicked loudly and the door opened with a great whoosh. The space was not furnished, save for a bed in one of the small bedrooms, and its vastness pleased Killian. He loved walking across the pristine floors, as if he were making a grand entrance every time. The windows stretched from floor to ceiling, more than forty feet high, letting the world shine into the room.

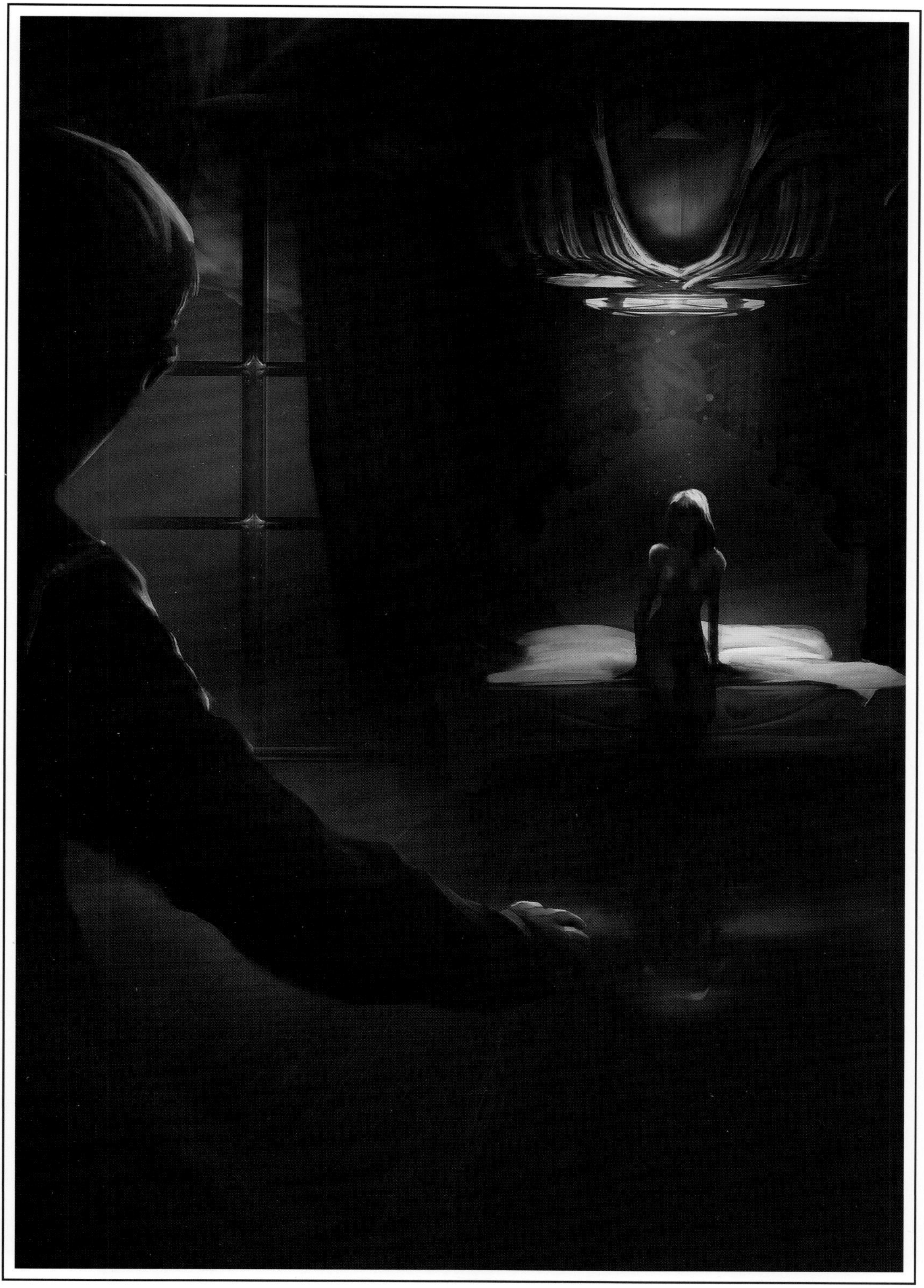

The curtains were now open, and Killian could see a figure silhouetted against the faint glimmer of moonlight shining through the window. At first he thought it was an apparition, then a shadow, until he was close enough to see that it was a young woman. She was naked, unashamed and beautiful. Killian knew he wasn't meant to see her, yet he couldn't prevent himself from walking to the window. He stopped next to her and stood where he always did.

"I don't know you," said Killian.

"You don't look like your father," her voice like quicksilver. She covered her left breast with her right hand and smiled. "Or your mother."

"Who are you?" said Killian.

The woman leaned in, whispering as if she knew every secret in the world. "I'm next."

Killian didn't understand—but then he heard his father's voice coming from the bedroom, and he turned and raced through the main door to the lift. He didn't want to see his father, though he knew the woman would tell James his son had been there.

He took the lift to the basement level, then found the door that led to the sub-basements. Killian had never been so deep into the building's bowels, but he'd heard of secret tunnels and passageways that led all the way out of the city. He'd wanted desperately to explore them, but this had never been an option before—a servant was assigned to him permanently, and if he or she allowed Killian free reign, the servant would be killed. But now the world was too distracted with his mother's illness to bother with where he was going, and he planned on finding a passage that would set him free.

He was lost almost instantly, unable to determine the direction in which he was headed. Everything looked the same. He wished he'd brought his pencil so he could mark a trail. Killian cursed himself and sat down. He wasn't ready to quit. He just needed a minute to think. He remembered his mother's face and his imagination twisted it into something more macabre than it was. Killian stood and walked again. He reached the end of one corridor and turned left, then right at the end of another one. At last he found a door and opened it—but it led only to more passageways, these more complicated than the previous ones. His feet ached. He sat again, his nervousness that he wouldn't find his way back giving way to resignation; he'd thought of death so much since his mother's illness that he was no longer bothered by his own mortality. He would die of starvation, and he would be nothing more than bone dust when someone eventually found him. He would—

"Just a little further down," came a voice. Killian looked back in the direction he'd come from. "The other way." Killian turned and looked down the corridor. He didn't see anyone. If he was hearing things, he was glad for it—this was a friendly voice. He got up and walked toward the voice. The hallways intersected, and Killian walked down the one with an open door. The door led to a staircase, the staircase to another hallway. Just as Killian convinced himself that the voice was only in his head, he heard, "Yes, yes," and he followed the voice further. He found another open door and walked through it.

He was greeted by an old man's smiling face. "I'm Hugh Spender," said the man, his thinning white hair in shambles on his head and a patchy white beard covering his face. He was dressed in what looked like an old military uniform, the red jacket faded from years of wear.

"You were leading me here. How?" Killian said.

"I may be eighty-nine, but I am spry. I attribute it all to stretching. Stretching keeps you limber and fools your body into thinking that it's not aging. Very good to do," Hugh said. He bobbed about the modest space, decorated only with a table and bed, looking for something. "It may not seem like much, especially to someone of your lineage, but I don't mind calling it home. That I have no other choice has no bearing on my saying so."

"You don't know who I am," said Killian.

"The whole world knows who you are. And you're wearing the uniform," said Hugh. Killian looked down; he'd forgotten that he was wearing the Great Ruler's colors, blue and grey. "Don't worry. I won't report that you've been here. In fact, I was expecting you."

"That can't be true," said Killian.

"Did you know that there are only two people in the world who know about this place?" said Hugh.

"Who?" said Killian.

"Me . . . and you," said Hugh.

"My father knows," said Killian.

"There's a lot your father doesn't know. And his closest advisor—Mr. Welhorn, I believe?—he doesn't know either. Just the two of us. They know it probably exists, but they've never found it. Or bothered to find it. I'm impressed you did. Then again, from what I've heard about you, I'm not surprised you were the one to find it," said Hugh.

"I've heard a lot about what was down here, but this isn't what I was hoping for," said Killian in bewilderment.

"That's because I haven't shown you anything yet," said Hugh.

"It's nothing," said Killian.

"I realize that one day you will rule this city, and you're under the impression that this city is all there is in this world—but one of the things you've got to realize, more than your father and grandfather and everyone who surrounded them, is that nothing is as it seems," said Hugh.

"So what am I supposed to realize?" said Killian.

"This is the most important place in Lantern City," said Hugh. "Move the bed for me."

"I don't—"

"I don't care that you've never lifted a finger to do any work in your entire life. Move the goddamn bed!" said Hugh, losing patience.

Killian pulled the bed away from the wall, revealing a trapdoor in the floor. Hugh kneeled down, removed a key from around his neck, and unlocked the door. He pulled the door up, exposing a staircase.

"Future rulers first," said Hugh, stepping aside. Guided by the hanging lights, Killian descended the stairs and continued along a narrow tunnel. At the end of the corridor he found another locked door. Hugh stepped around him, holding a second key. "One can never be too safe." Hugh unlocked the door and opened it for Killian.

Inside that room was a different world. Killian stepped onto a track a quarter mile around with eight stories of library shelves, descending one by one into the earth, filled with books and cases.

"Your great-grandfather built this. I would say he and I were friends. He hired me to collect and look after this stuff. Technically, the job doesn't exist anymore, but I don't have anything else to do. You would have liked him," said Hugh.

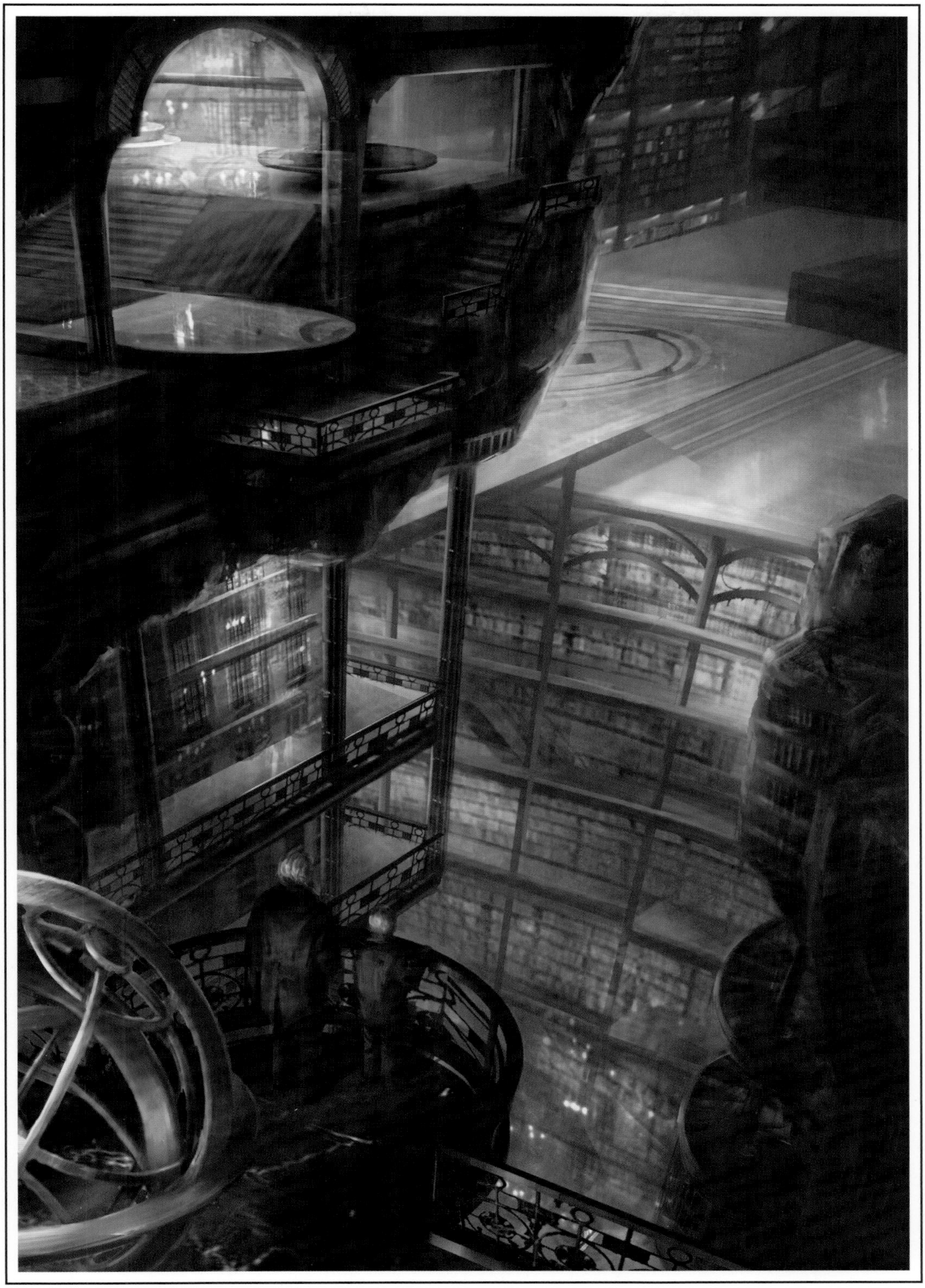

"He was a tyrant," Killian said, his voice flat.

"That's a nice rumor, started by the same people who have changed what's contained in here," said Hugh.

"What's that?" said Killian.

"The truth," said Hugh. "This is the history of our world. All of which was changed by your grandfather. The world did not begin with Lantern City."

"You're calling my grandfather a liar?" said Killian.

"Him, and your father, and everyone else in the Ruling Class. The thing is, everyone is so far removed from what happened that now the lies are the truth," said Hugh.

"I like reading—sort of—but I can't read everything in here," said Killian.

"The reason you don't like reading is because the books made available to you are rubbish. I know, because I've read all of them. But there is one book that you must read immediately," said Hugh.

"Maybe I'll read it some other time, but right now I have to find a way out of the city. I know one of the tunnels gets me there," said Killian.

"This book is your way out. Trust me. Come, come," said Hugh.

Hugh walked around the track, his feet clanking on the metal, until he reached a small enclave. It was his office, consisting of a desk, chair, lamp, and small bookshelf.

"Sit, sit," said Hugh.

Killian sat in the chair. It was uncomfortable, but still better than sitting on his mother's floor. Hugh slid the bookshelf to one side, revealing a smaller bookshelf concealed behind it. There was only one book on its shelves; Hugh removed it and carefully placed it in Killian's hands. The cover was faded red leather with a buckled strap preventing it from flapping open. The letters "IFG" were carved into the cover.

"Your great-grandfather wanted you to have this," said Hugh.

"He didn't know I would exist," said Killian.

"Very true, but soon after writing that book that you're holding, he told me that the right person would come for it one day. And that reader would be the only person who can make things right . . . undo all the wrongs," said Hugh. "No pressure."

"Thanks," said Killian. He unbuckled the strap and opened the book. The smell was something foreign to Killian, like cinders mixed with iron ink.

"I'll get you some food. Anything you don't like?" said Hugh. Killian shook his head, and Hugh dashed off. Killian felt the weight of the book in his hands, intimidated for a moment, then placed it in his lap and opened to the first page. The inscription haunted him:

"Dear Reader, you will know what to do when you're finished."

The Journals of Isaac Foster Grey

On this very day I begin, I am nearly ninety-years old, though as fit as a man a third my age. I know, however, that time is running short, and I can only share what is most important.

Reducing a life to a few handwritten pages is insulting to any man—especially, I would argue, to a man of my accomplishments. Take from these tales what you will; remember that this is a half-painted portrait. It is my hope, in writing this and, hopefully, in completing it, that it will be held in the hands of one of my distant relatives, perhaps a grandchild or fair cousin many generations removed. Through the reading of this, such relative, living in the age of the Grey Empire (a power that bears my name but not my soul), will attempt to overthrow the ignorance that reigns. Understand fully that the people who populate Lantern City, regardless of how far removed from me they are, will rise with true leadership and bring the Empire down. Although I will be long dead and returned to the earth before this is read, this book must only find itself in trusting hands; otherwise, it will be lost like so many treasures before it.

My curiosities and ambitions had little to do with venturing out beyond my world. The places in which my family and I resided were always quite wonderful, especially for a boy of eight. Perhaps if my mother and father had refused me unlimited access to those city and villages, I would have broken the bonds that held me and journeyed to places beyond my imagining. Instead, my interest, outside of exploring the city of Timpast with my older brother Joshua and venturing through the great and dangerous Blackbin Forest, was reading. This love was inspired by my mother, who read to me by candlelight every night, long after I knew how to read by myself. And it was on one of my Timpast adventures with Joshua that I discovered the book that set the course for the rest of my life.

One of Joshua's favorite pursuits in Timpast was bothering a grizzled old man named Kelman, who operated a little outpost off Storish Street in a small district known as Claremond, a part of the city that was like a time capsule from a bygone era. Storish Street was one of the final reminders of what Timpast had been like prior to the takeover by the Steppe Army. It had been a peaceful passing of power, insofar as any negotiations between a general with forty thousand troops behind him and a governor with no ability to provide for his city can be.

The takeover occurred long before I was born, when Steppe was the charismatic, youthful savior for all of Hetra and my father was one of his commanding officers. Old maps of Timpast display a small metropolis of scattershot design, but Steppe, in the twenty-five years since, had transformed Timpast into a robust stronghold, the shining city of Hetra. The military presence had an effect on all facets of Timpast life: the buildings grew taller, the streets safer, and a sense of order existed in nearly every place. But Storish Street was uneven and rough, suitable only for feet, and the buildings were occupied by drifters and ruffians, while the shops provided vices of every variety.

Steppe had never really imposed upon Claremond, because its existence was a reminder of what the city would become if Steppe decided to transport his influence elsewhere. Joshua loved Claremond and I was less fond of it, mostly because our mother and father insisted that they would kill us if we ever went there (and I did not think they were exaggerating). They certainly did not frequent Claremond themselves, and I was riddled with anxiety every time we went there, concerned that someone acquainted with my father would spot us and pass word along to him. The only thing that eased my nerves was that Joshua was most pleased with Storish Street, which was conveniently close to Gross Street, which led directly to the more modern Timpast—if anything happened, we could make a quick getaway.

This Kelman gentleman ran an outpost that was never in fashion, for he only provided goods for sea bandits and buckmen. Joshua loved to look through the old man's weaponry, maps, and trinkets, all promising a grander world beyond Hetra. Kelman was bothered by both of us because we never bought anything. This was true for all of Kelman's customers; the difference between us and the rest of them was we had money. But while our mother always gave us pocket change for food, Joshua kept it for himself.

Kelman stared us down as we walked amongst his wares. "Yous'n come'nere every week and steal with yous'n eyes what yer' pockets can afford," he said.

Joshua typically responded with questions about Kelman's youth or how he came to possess so many useless things. I remained near the front of the store, ready to flee at the sight of a familiar face. On that particular day, Joshua was more rambunctious than normal, having earlier been the unfortunate recipient of a verbal lashing by my father. He seemed like he might do something cruel and regrettable, so I took leave of my post near the entrance to peruse some of the books piled high next to a collection of Black Whale hooks. Many of the books were written in languages I did not recognize, though many contained fascinating sketches.

Kelman ignored Joshua for a change and walked over to stand behind me. I felt pressured to purchase something, and before I could select a book in those piles, Kelman said, "probably'n you'll find in 'dem piles over der' what it is you can read." He pointed to a small collection underneath a box of withered maps. I realized then that he liked me better than Joshua because I didn't try to incite a reaction from him.

These books were all small, bound in black leather, and branded with exquisite gold lettering. Most of them were histories of one sort or another, nothing that held my attention—that is, until I spotted the book whose cover had been tarnished, the engraved titled scratched out by a blade. It was there for me to find, and I knew this as soon as my fingers held it. The title page was torn, but all that was missing was the author's name; the book's title, Eniam: A True Account, was left fading into the page.

"I'sn never seen that'n one yet," said Kelman.

Joshua joined us, glanced at the book, and realized he could not sway Kelman's attention, so he said, "Let's get out of here."

His words startled me, for I knew I could not leave Kelman's outpost without the book, yet I had no money with which to pay the old man. I looked at Joshua, wishing we could communicate without speaking, and he backed away with a grin, knowing I needed to ask him for money. Retaining power and control over me was of great importance to Joshua, and I railed against it as best I could. I knew that I would have to beg for whatever small change Kelman would charge for the book.

For once in a long moon, Kelman had merchandise someone wanted. But to my surprise, instead of delighting in my inability to pay for it, he tapped the book three times with his crooked knuckle and said, "You'n should keep it," and walked away. My intention was to thank him, but I was too overjoyed to muster any words.

Joshua was too disappointed by my excitement to continue on with our misadventures in Timpast and sulked home. I said nothing, reserving my energy for the book in my hand.

I did not sleep that night and invariably thought of nothing but Eniam for the weeks that followed. It was not the first time I had forgone sleep in favor of reading, though no book had ever enveloped me like the story of Eniam.

Her tale is the story of our existence, tracing the lineage of man through the gods in a single brilliant young woman. She was touched by both Uryston and Wareis, who had granted her two inhuman abilities: immortality, and the ability to tell men's futures. Through touching her, the gods left Eniam in a mangled, horrific state, a figure no human could bear to observe. Eniam did not use her ability to tell futures willingly, for what she told those souls brave enough to hear her prophecies, both the good and the bad, would haunt the listener forever. But the most remarkable thing about Eniam was the fact that her tale had continued to unfold long after her story was committed to paper. She is still, possibly, alive and walking among men, embodying the highest qualities we can achieve, with all of the unexplainable powers of the gods.

When I completed Eniam's tome early that morning, I declared to myself that my purpose was to find her. To any rational person, this would have been a terrible and dangerous idea—but I was eight years old, more concerned with experiencing something fantastical than worrying about the consequences of such an encounter. Finding Eniam would be no simple task, for it should be noted that the anonymous author of the book made it quite clear that Eniam had relegated herself to exile in Blackbin. This, however, did not dissuade me in the least.

My plan was to sneak away to Blackbin, but such plans are easier spoken than acted upon, especially when you are incapable of masking your intentions. As a preemptive strike against such action, my mother, who sensed I was planning something reckless, sent me away with my father. Under normal circumstances, I would have reveled in such opportunities, for my father's work fascinated me. I had begged so often for him to take me with him, and each time received a firm "Never" in response—as it was, my father being forced to escort me was almost as good as searching for Eniam.

My father, lieutenant general of Steppe's Army, prided himself on his ability to take any man and make him a soldier. "Within each boy is a man, and within each man, a soldier." He recognized great potential in me, much more so than in Joshua, and my father was incapable of hiding this sentiment. He expected Joshua to study law or make his mark in engineering and spoke of this path as a noble one, though any talk of my soldiering and eventually leading great armies was an obvious sign of favoritism, something that Joshua never allowed me to forget. For the first eight years of my life, this was exciting for me to forecast—but once I read Eniam's tale, I wondered if it was true. Was I, in fact, destined to be a general, or was there something else in store for me? This question haunted me, stirring that great desire within me to find Eniam.

To my father, meaningful training involved gradually shaping the recruits' spirits and bodies, through rigorous routines and exercises, into confident and capable soldiers; their faces would be recognizable to those they left behind, but their figures and minds would be new. Soldiers trained under Philip Grey were instantly identifiable, with a determinism and professionalism that other troops lacked. My father expected this attribute to be his lasting legacy.

There was no way for him to predict how wrong he would be. If he would have known then, as he and I walked behind the line of troops, that this would be his final training, would he have done anything differently? Knowing my father's commitment to Steppe, I'm afraid that

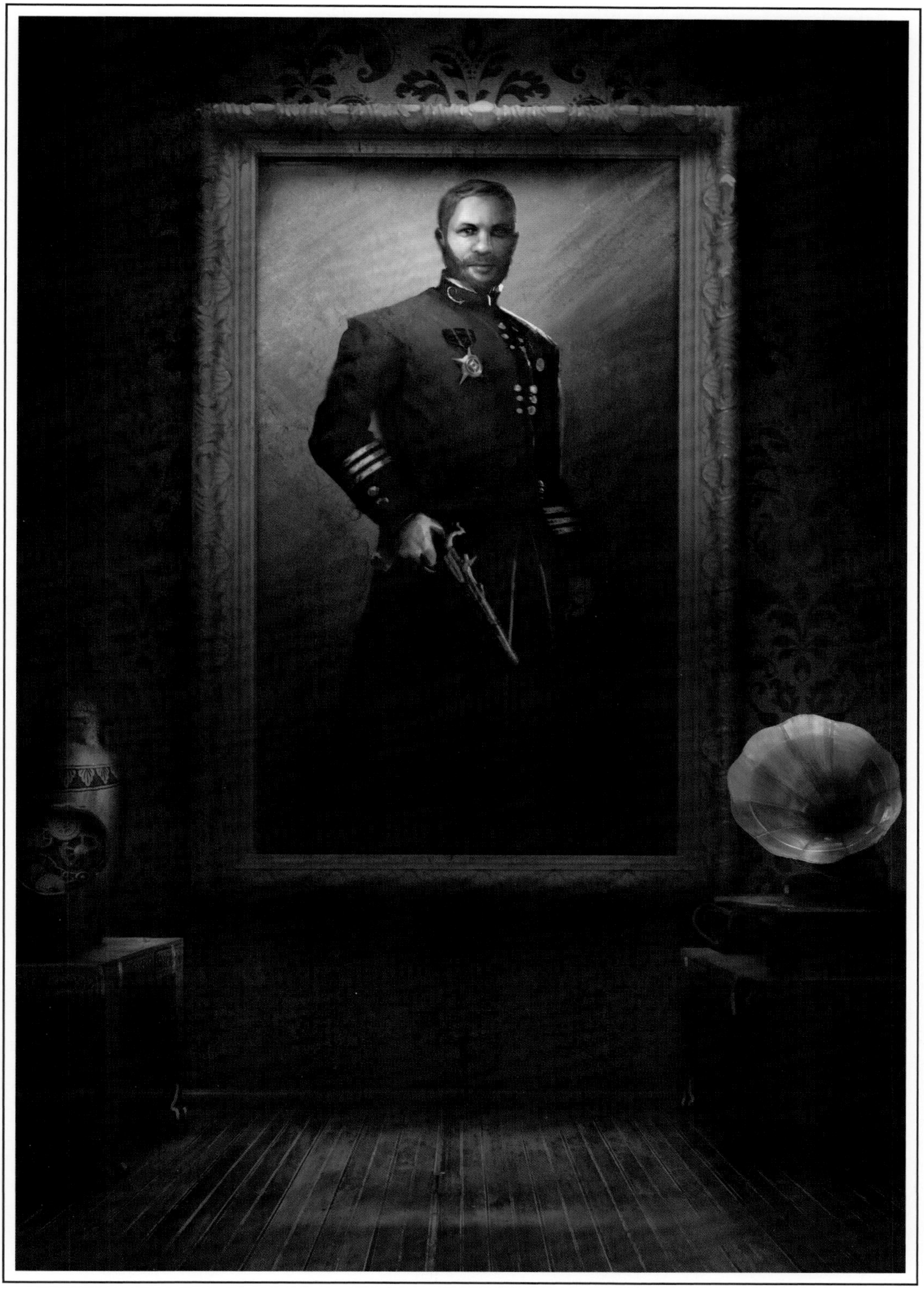

he wouldn't have, though I like to believe that he would have gathered our family and fled.

He tugged on my earlobe and grinned, slowing his stride to a casual pace. I did the same, understanding that we were going to speak privately. The thirty-five young recruits pressed on ahead.

"Does something seem wrong to you?" my father said, looking at me with the seriousness he would my mother.

"I don't know what usually happens. You never let me come with you before," I said.

"Not with this. I have a firm grip on what's happening here. Save the weather or an attack from a White Wolf, I have things under control," he said. "It's just that, with your unusual behavior lately, I wondered if you felt something . . . different."

"Maybe," I said, not wanting to reveal that I had the book about Eniam or what was contained in it.

"This is something that I really can't help you with, but your great-grandmother Avona, my grandmother, had a strange ability to predict what was going to happen. Not everything, mind you, just certain things. I thought you might be having a spell like Avona used to," said my father.

This was the first I'd ever heard of Avona's capabilities, even though my father had always spoken highly of her.

"It's not that," I said.

"There won't be much time for us to talk once we reach camp, but if you want to tell me what's bothering you, don't hesitate. Things are changing very quickly, faster than I can keep up with," he said.

I looked up at my father and witnessed doubt in his expression for the first time. Philip Grey, the stalwart of confidence and certainty, was pressed by something dark in his heart.

"What do you mean?" I said.

"I'm prepared to tell you everything I know, although I haven't said a thing to anyone else, including your mother. I'm trusting I have your confidence to keep this between us," he said.

No child can refuse being privy to information held for adults. I nodded eagerly.

"So I suspected. Before I say another word, understand that I have not fully comprehended all that I now know. And it bothers me to no end that I must admit this, but I am afraid. That is something I haven't experienced since I was your age," he said.

"I won't tell anyone," I said, not intending to be funny, but my father laughed.

"That's an even bigger secret than what I'm about to tell you," he said. He held out his right hand and my hand disappeared in his; he gripped my hand and shook it, then released it as he began to speak. "I've served General Steppe since I was thirteen. Essentially, we rose together and built the Steppe Army to the behemoth it is today. My entire life's work is stitched into this army's fabric, and I am now fearful of the direction in which Steppe is taking things. He and I built this army to protect Hetra, and now he wants to use it to rule the world. I cannot say for sure what is going to happen, but if Steppe's intentions reflect his actions to be, then we will need to leave. It won't be easy and it could prove impossible. I cannot say for sure—but I will not use my power and influence toward an evil means," he said.

A stocky young man tripped and fell and didn't get to his feet quickly enough.

"Excuse me. I have to address this," my father said. He walked away, and that was the last thing he said in regard to General Warren J. Steppe's plans for his army. In all fairness, he did not have time to continue our conversation.

What later struck me about this conversation—other than that it was the first and only time my father had ever opened up to me—was the thought that he might have been the one with Avona's ability, not me. If in fact he was, he would have certainly concealed this from everyone. I had assumed at the time that Steppe had confided in my father and shared his intentions to take over Hetra. This would not be a rare occurrence, since the two men had been close for most of their lives; if Steppe trusted anyone in the world, it would be my father. But as time progressed and Steppe's character became clearer to me, I started to wonder if Steppe had ever uttered such claims to my father; it is quite possible that my father had merely sensed the inevitable altering of course and could not foresee himself as part of it. Although my father was a man of war by training and profession, his nature was closer to that of a scholar. His life was a contradiction, as is true, I believe, for most men.

The training facilities were at Camp Locias, on the easternmost point of Blackbin, nestled on the western bank of the Gorndon River. It was a wonderment, everything a young boy could wish from a place: the eastern edges of Blackbin provided ample yellowberry bushes and trails that led to the Radmon Mountains, the shallow banks of the Gorndon River were perfect for swimming and fishing, and Locias itself had tunnels and shooting ranges aplenty. My father permitted me free reign and I roamed from the first sunrise till the second sunset. It was perfect. When I wasn't off by myself, I would watch my father train the men. It was my good fortune to experience this, to see the full character of my father—something my siblings, regrettably, were never able to do.

At night I would reread Eniam's tale over and over again, learning both the intricacies of the story and the importance of self-restraint. The more I read, the greater was my urge to venture into the Blackbin Forest and search for her. I wanted the answer to life's darkest secret, and I would have to risk my life to get it.

One night I fell asleep while reading, and I awoke a few hours later to discover the book missing. I sat up frantically, only to notice it next to my father, who was sitting on his bed, shining his boots. I walked to him and reclaimed the book. He did not turn to me but spoke: "Is it good?"

"Fine."

"You've read it the past nine nights and you've not brought another book with you. There are some excellent histories in the colonel's tent," he said.

"I'll just read this."

"I hope you understand, Isaac, that there are things in this world that can be proven and other things that cannot. The acts and intentions of the gods, if they do or ever did exist, is one such thing. Many men have wonderful imaginations and exploit those who do not," he said.

"Yes, I know."

"It is my hope that you are reading this as a fiction," he said.

"But . . ." I hesitated, knowing that I could not win an argument

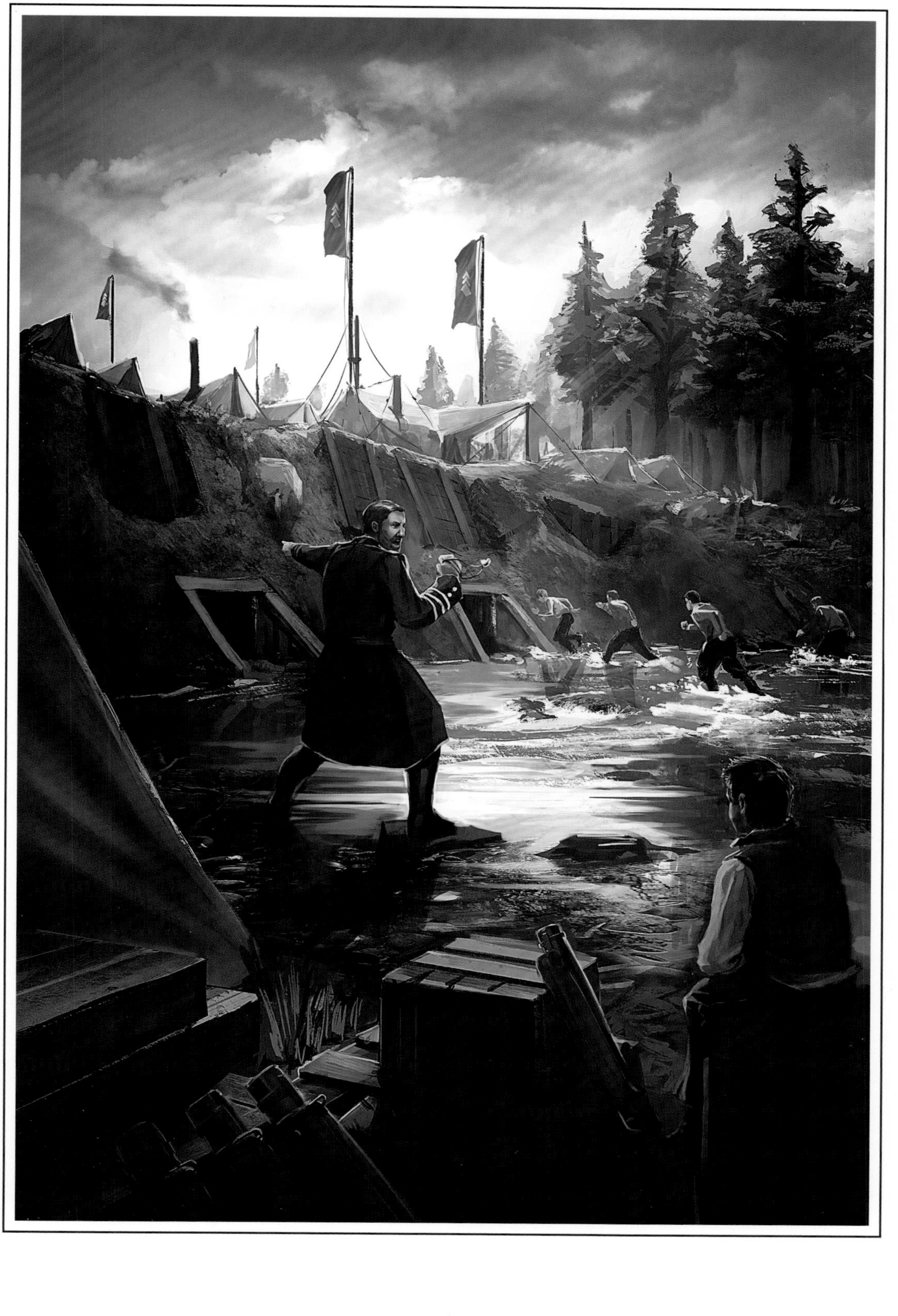

with my father. And yet I was too overwhelmed with passion for the book to hold my tongue. "It could be real."

"And I could fly like a Hamil Jay if I so imagined it," he said.

"Why don't you believe it's real?"

My father took the candle from the bedside table and held it between us.

"There are men who believe that whole worlds are held in a single flame. That god upon god dances in its contained glow, and that if you blow it out, your spirit is forever cursed. Does that sound like something believable?" he said.

"It's foolish."

"As foolish as a woman holding a man's future in her touch," he said. "We grow smarter every day, answering questions with science that our ancestors thought to be the work of the gods."

"But you said Avona had—"

"Having a sense of things is very different from the ability to watch a life unfold in an instant," he said.

"I like the book."

"I don't dispute that. But two things you must keep in mind: first, devote yourself to other works. There are many volumes of brilliant histories and philosophy waiting to be devoured," he said.

"Okay. What's the other thing?"

"Don't get any ideas," he said, extinguishing the light. I returned to my bed, upset but unwilling to argue with him.

The training was cut short a mere three days later, when a rider approached the camp. He carried specific instructions for my father to return immediately to Timpast; the orders came from General Steppe directly. My father wanted to know the details of the unusual request, but the rider knew little other than that a replacement for my father would arrive shortly. The soldiers-in-training looked relieved, so my father sent them on a fifteen-mile hike through Blackbin, fully dressed and armed. I expected a begrudging attitude from my father; instead, he quietly packed his things and helped me do the same.

We went by horse, which cut our travel time down by a third, although we did not return on the same route we had taken to Locias. We stopped off at the small village of Cafrush, just south of Timpast.

The great city loomed over Cafrush. My father dismounted the horse and helped me down, then led the horses to a water trough. The villagers stopped their lives for a few moments as my father passed— his uniform and stature were both impressive and imposing.

A young child, no more than three, ran from his mother's side and jumped into a mud puddle near us. Muddy water splashed all over my father's boots and pants. The boy laughed innocently and the village stopped in silence. They nervously awaited my father's reaction, as did I; he treated his uniform like a precious family heirloom.

My father hunched over and signaled for the boy to come to him. The boy walked sheepishly toward my father, then stopped a few feet away. He waved the boy closer, and the boy took the last few steps with great hesitation. My father said, "Stand there," and pointed to a spot near the puddle. "I will show you how it's done." The villagers held their breath as my father took four great strides and leapt into the air, pummeling the muddy water with his boots. The water traveled in all directions, covering the boy from head to toe. My father laughed uproariously, and the villagers quickly joined him, their relief tinged with hysteria. The boy looked none too pleased, but my father wiped his face and told him to join us. Even I didn't know where we were going, though I figured it would be worth the young boy's time. And I was absolutely right.

It turns out that one of the men my father had fought alongside lived in Cafrush, and this man's wife made the most famous yellowberry tarts in all of Hetra. I sat and ate four yellowberry tarts as my father and his friend, Connor Billing, recounted their days together in colorful brushstrokes. I had never seen my father happier and my stomach had never been so satisfied. Even the young boy, still caked in mud, forgot about his embarrassment after two yellowberry tarts. It was a moment I wish I could have remained in forever. But as the day drew to a close, my father and I returned to Timpast.

My mother was surprised by our premature return, and my father was incapable of hiding the weight of the situation. He called the family to the table. My sisters, Mariam and Lillian, only five and four, sat on my father's lap. Joshua stood at the end of the table with his arms crossed, still insulted that he'd been left behind. My mother, in her nervousness, began to search the kitchen for food.

"Lady, sit," said my father and my mother fought back tears at the sound of his voice. His tone was not intimidating, yet his words were laced with a seriousness that pulled her back to the situation. She sat next to me and ran her finger along the back of my hairline.

Philip Grey looked at all of us as he spoke. "We are leaving here in three days' time. I can't say exactly where we'll end up, but we're going south. We may leave Hetra altogether—I'll know how safe we'll be in this country after I speak with General Steppe tomorrow. It might be that we could stay, though I think it's best for all of us to start anew elsewhere. Not everyone will understand—maybe even you don't. We can speak about it in further detail once we are settled elsewhere. Pack only what you need and say nothing to anyone. Am I understood?"

"Why?" said Joshua.

"As I said, we will speak on it later," said my father.

"No. Now," said Joshua.

"Your tone, Joshua, is—"

Joshua interrupted my father. "You can't expect us to leave without you explaining anything!"

"Never speak to me that way!" my father said, eyes flashing. "I have told you what to do, so do it."

My sisters were frightened and clung to my mother. My father called to them and they obeyed; he wrapped them in his arms.

We were sent to bed, and I tried conversing with Joshua. He turned his back to me and refused to speak. I knew that he would thaw eventually and I focused my attention on a more pressing matter: determining how I would sneak away to Blackbin in the next three days to search for Eniam.

I didn't necessarily expect to find her, but I had to make one valiant attempt or I would live with the regret forever. If we were to leave Hetra, which was a great possibility, I would be too far from Blackbin for Eniam to read my future. Fortunately for me, my mother was so distracted with the preparations and stress of having to pick up our lives and leave that she didn't deny my request the next morning when I asked to go outside. She didn't inquire why I would want to, only asking that Joshua accompany me, but Joshua feigned illness so as to not have to join me or help my mother.

This was perfectly according to my plan. My father had left hours earlier, and he wasn't due back till late in the night. Things were tense enough and I wouldn't make it worse by returning at an inappropriate time; this still allowed me at least twelve hours to seek out the great Eniam.

I did not expect to cover all of Blackbin in a day, nor did I assume that Eniam remained in one place like a statue. This, however, did not deter me in the least, for I had youthful naiveté on my side, foolish enough to believe that I could hold the world in my palms. If my suspicions were correct, many people had sought Eniam in the past and failed—and the reason they failed is that they were not me. This was not a display of hubris on my part, but rather a life led with minimal failure. I was eight years old and expected to accomplish everything I set out to do. And I considered myself an expert on Eniam, since I had reread the book more times than I could recall. The book said very little about her location, just that her last known whereabouts were the Blackbin Forest.

I took with me some stale bread and my slingshot, something my father had helped me to carve and fashion, though I'd never used it for its intended purpose: to hunt galrabbits. My father promised that one silver stone, aimed accurately and fired with enough speed, could crush a galrabbit's skull; a shot to the body would impair it, but not slow it down enough for a hunter to catch. Hitting a galrabbit in the head was of no waste to the creature, for its brains were inedible and its black tongue apparently poisonous. The problem for a hunter was that the galrabbit's head was disproportionally small, making it a challenging target to hit. The slingshot was a tool I'd never had the opportunity to use, though I wouldn't dare leave home without it.

The city was brimming with soldiers, something quite unusual, and I knew that what my father had supposed was coming to fruition. I could barely move without bumping into a soldier, which was less bothersome to me than their new uniforms. Gone were the full blue uniforms, replaced by dark red coats and black pants. They looked not like soldiers, but conquerors. I pushed through as best I could, no doubt losing some time, but I was at the mercy of the city. It was too late

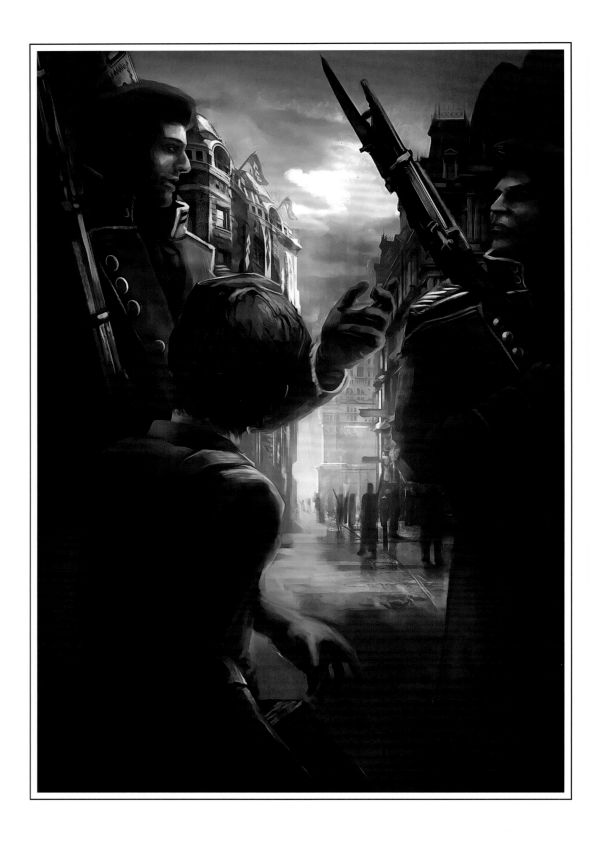

to backtrack southward and take the trails to the east of Timpast; the best entrance to Blackbin was just north of the city.

My first plan of business was to snake around the Pelman Gorge and head straight for the family of Brown Oak trees, the tallest trees near the city. From the top of a Brown Oak, I could determine the next best destination. This plan seemed so foolproof that I didn't pay much attention to where I was walking. My mind was so occupied with Eniam that I didn't notice the two soldiers standing by a tree, just to the west—not at first, at least—but the benefit of me not seeing them was that they didn't notice me either. It was a perfect accident. The only reason I eventually spotted them was that they were wearing those new red coats, which, against the cluster of White Hand trees, looked like splotches of blood. I slid underneath a group of bushes and watched them for a few minutes. Blackbin wasn't territory patrolled by the Steppe Army, and in all of my experiences in Blackbin, I had never encountered soldiers. They stood as if on guard, and I needed to see what they were protecting. Yes, this would steal time from my primary pursuit, but I wouldn't be satisfied if I didn't investigate.

The bushes were perfect camouflage, and I followed their trail till I was just north of the soldiers. They were not looking in the direction of the bushes, and if I wanted to gain access to what they were guard-ing, I needed them to leave their post. I strategized quickly, pulling my slingshot from the back of my pants. I grabbed a handful of loose rocks, loaded them, then shot them to the opposite side of the clearing. The rocks landed at sporadic intervals, sounding much like footsteps.

This seized the soldiers' attention, yet they did not move from the White Hand trees. I repeated my action four more times until one of the soldiers said, "We have to see what that is."

The other was quite hesitant, understandably, because they were raised on horror stories of White Wolves and Korbears. "I don't think so," he said.

The first soldier stepped away from the White Hand trees and said, "It's why we trained." As soon as the reluctant soldier followed after the first, I made my way toward the cluster of White Hand trees.

There was nothing to see initially, though I heard voices other than the guards in the near distance. I maneuvered to a pile of logs, placed by man and not nature, near the top of the clearing. Once behind the logs, I slithered on the ground to the far side. From here I could see to the bottom of a small hill, its growth trampled and killed by horses. Two more soldiers stood on either side of three prisoners, humbled and unclothed. The prisoners looked like they'd been bathed in mud. The two soldiers held a new style of rifle by their sides; from what I could see, there were three revolving barrels, and a bayonet fastened to a second chamber and cylinder atop the first. I could not process how the gun would work, and I did not need to: a voice boomed out.

"These are just the first in our new developments. The weapons of the future, Philip," said General Steppe, speaking to my father. The General stepped into my view, a man of great physicality and stature, standing taller than most men. His hair, so blonde it was nearly white, was perfectly combed back, no gust of wind disturbing it. Strangely, he wore a massive black overcoat, concealing his uniform. "That you are not persuaded by these advances troubles me." My heart started to race, and not because I would be in a world of trouble for traveling through Blackbin by myself; it beat out of my breast for fear of what Steppe would do to my father. My mind told me to stand up, announce my presence, change the course of what was about to happen—yet my body refused to obey the orders. Nothing I demanded of myself resulted in me budging from my hiding place.

Philip Grey walked into my line of vision, dressed in the former Steppe Army blue. He stood next to the General, but looked at the prisoners as he spoke.

"I'm not unimpressed by these advances—my concerns lie with why you would spend so many precious resources developing weapons we do not need," said my father.

"Armies require the best weaponry," said Steppe.

"In times of war, perhaps, or in the very least, when war looms. We have been at peace for more than thirty years. Raiders do not storm our shores, nor is the population of Hetra restless. We have been at peace for more than half our lives, so why—"

"Prepare? Is that what you're wondering? Besides once being a good soldier, you were also a student of history. When a city or a nation becomes complacent, it opens itself to invaders. Thinking we

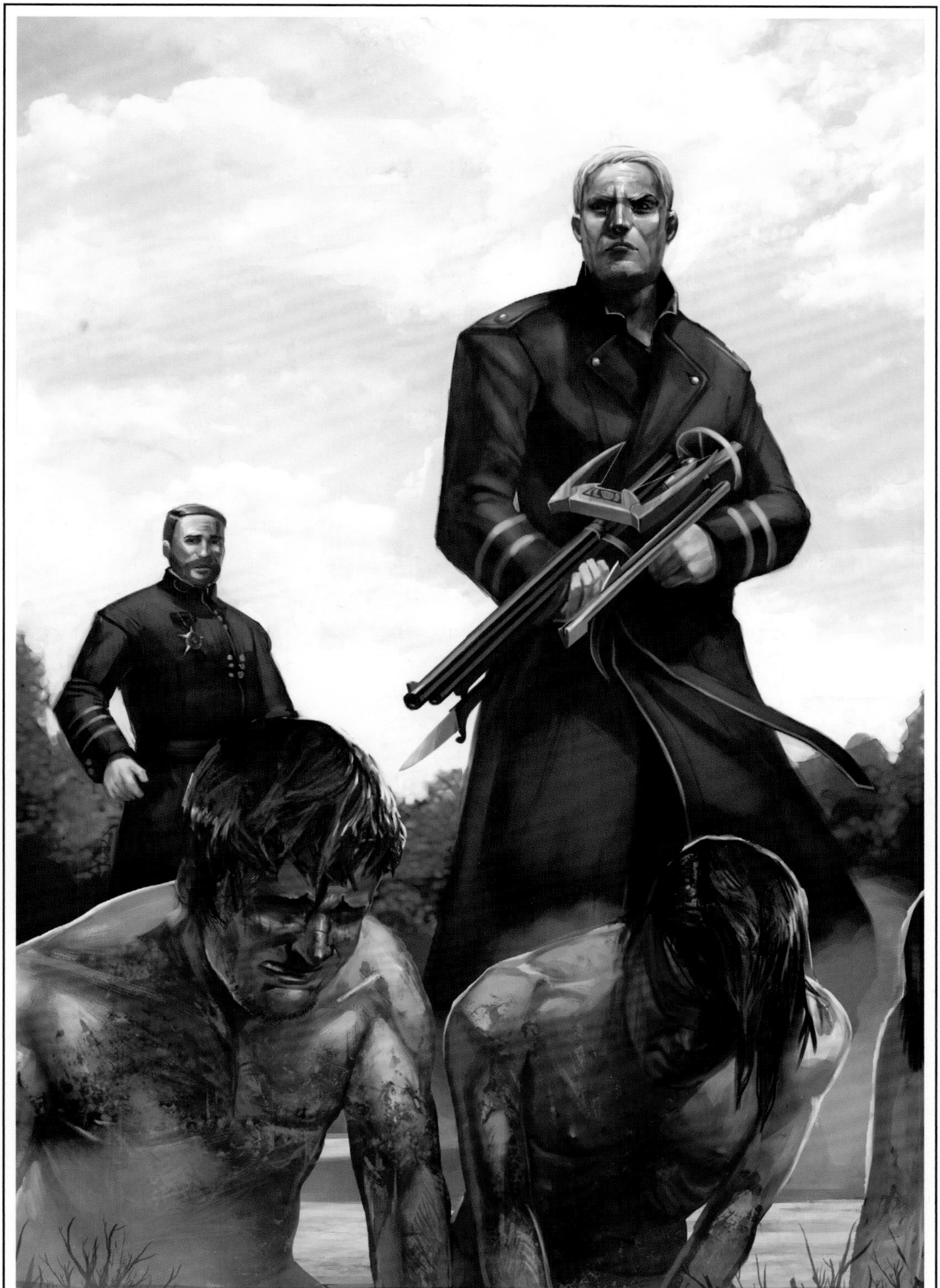

don't need new weapons and tactics makes you a vulnerable fool," said Steppe. He walked in front of my father, and my father's steadfast gaze focused on the prisoners.

"You're confusing soldiering and mongering. I will not destroy this nation for your benefit. You cannot name one man from the history texts who became an absolute ruler and didn't ultimately suffer at the hands of his people. If this is how you wish to shape your fate, you will accept my resignation," said my father.

"I wish I would have recognized this weakness in you long ago," said Steppe.

"If it is weakness that causes my stomach to wrench at the sight of these three helpless men, then yes, you may consider me a coward," said my father.

Steppe summoned one of the soldiers, and I saw a young man run to the General. Steppe took the soldier's gun and held it in front of my father.

"This is a remarkable piece of machinery. I encourage you to try it. Using it just once might sway you to see things my way," said Steppe. He held the gun out for my father's taking, but my father only looked at Steppe, a look of resigned sadness on his face.

Steppe turned and faced the prisoners. "I certainly won't waste the opportunity to use it." Steppe aimed the gun at the prisoner closest to me as I watched, stunned. He fired three quick shots into the man's chest; the man flew backwards. With quick precision, Steppe grabbed the small handle on the side of the bayonet and pulled it toward himself. The first chamber and cylinder were replaced by the second chamber and cylinder, and the general fired three more shots, this time into the second prisoner. This prisoner's legs kicked out from under him and he lay dead next to the first. "Six shots with fast reloading make for interesting results. Of course, you cannot always rely on reloading—which is easily remedied with this." Steppe pulled back on the bayonet's handle and this time turned it to the right, creating a weapon more akin to a crossbow than a rifle. "This is yet another advantage we have." Steppe pulled a different trigger and the bayonet shot straight through the third prisoner's neck; the man fell to his knees, then face first to the ground.

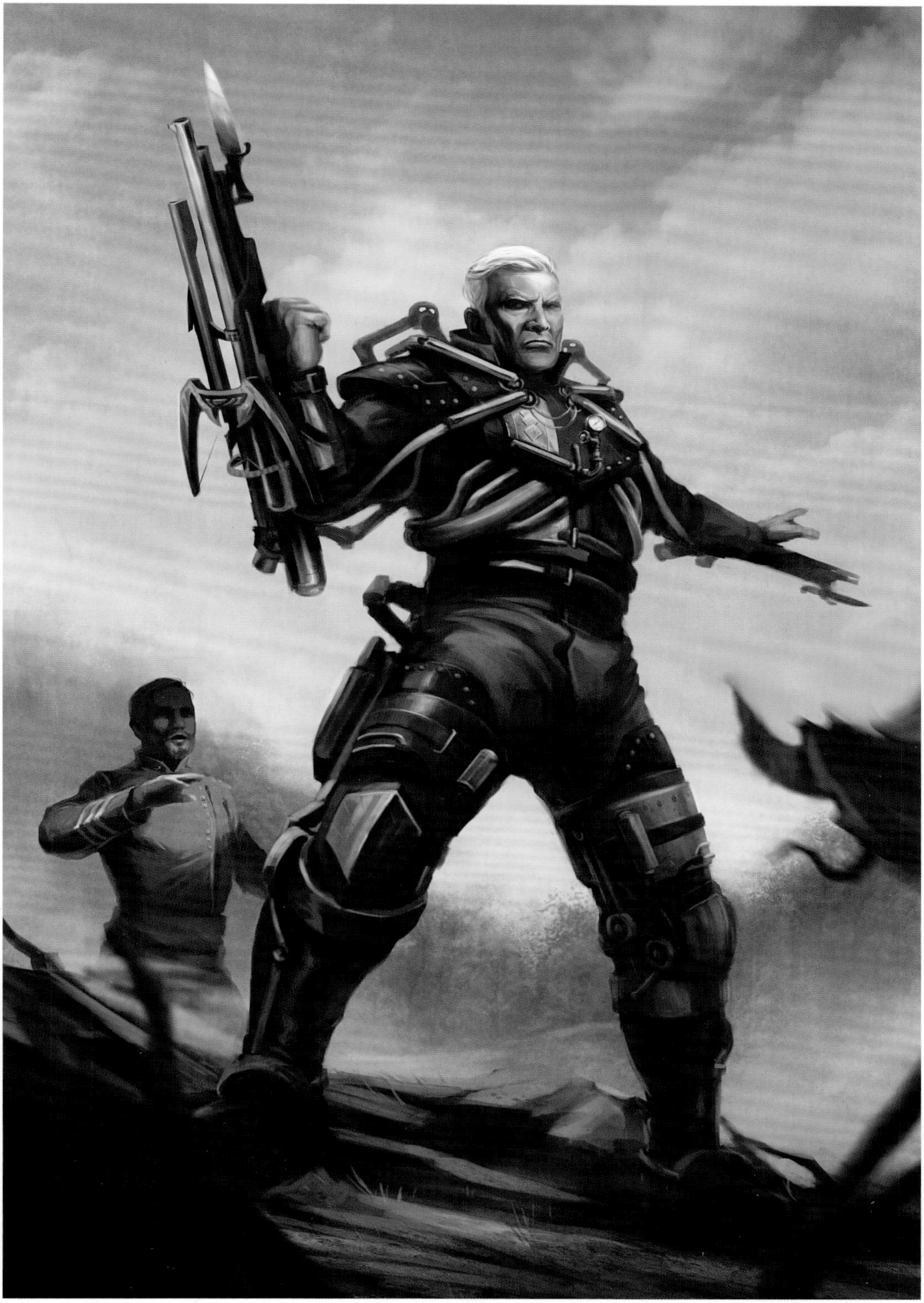

My father lowered his head. Steppe held the gun under his nose. "You will feel differently once you try."

Philip Grey walked toward the bodies, shaking his head. "You're wrong. If you see this as our future, then you see only our demise," my father said.

"Perhaps this will convince you," said the General. In the most dramatic fashion, Steppe undraped himself from his shadowy cloak, unveiling a frightening amalgamation of man and machine. Across his chest coiled a webbing of pipes, poles, brackets, and fasteners; from this skeletal shield extended two craning arms that attached themselves to Steppe's shoulders and forearms. Fastened to each of these arms was a three-barreled rotating rifle; continuing downward from the main chest frame, completing the fantastical effect, were leg braces that locked at the knees and held two pistols on the outside of each leg. Steppe turned so my father could see the back of the apparatus, which clung tightly to his back—the arm, chest, and leg sections conjoined in a large brass-colored plate decorated with a network of various-sized gears. The General looked like a man who had walked into our world from the future.

"You look as unnatural as a fish would walking in the woods," said my father.

"Say what you will, but your reaction merely masks what you know to be true," said Steppe.

"Please, explain to me what I believe the truth to be," said my father.

"That you are not enough of a man to do what we should have done years ago: show this pitiful nation what it should be," said Steppe.

"What makes you think you know what's best for Hetra? Or that you have the requirements to rule it?" said my father.

"All I need is the force and will to rule. Everything else will fall into place. These men and women will recoil in fear. You may view this suit of armor as foolish, but I promise you your opinion will change once you see its capabilities. And an army outfitted with these does not need to settle on Hetra alone," said Steppe.

"You have no understanding of the world outside Hetra," said my father.

"This is why I need you," said Steppe. "We are strong now, but we could be so much more powerful."

"I say this as a friend: you have lost all sight. Walking a path of domination leads only to a tragic end," said my father. "Whether you accept my resignation or not, I am leaving today and taking my family. You will never know what becomes of us—and if you attempt to find us, I will kill you."

Steppe smiled. He pointed his left arm toward the one soldier.

"Maybe you'll believe me if you witness our potential," said Steppe.

"Don't kill them," said my father.

The smile faded from Steppe's face and he stared at my father with dangerous intent. "No?" he said.

Steppe ignited the guns. Bullets ripped through the soldier. I covered my ears with my hands, blocking them from the deafening sound. The second soldier ran and was thrown down by the rapid succession of bullets that chewed through his back. The gears on the back of the gun suit whirled loudly to reload the chambers. When the deafening barrage ceased, Steppe turned back to my father, smiling.

"You only leave when I say you leave, so remain by my side and train our next army," said Steppe.

"I train soldiers to protect, not to kill," said my father.

"That's very interesting, how you distinguish between protecting and killing," said Steppe.

"You cannot see anything clearly anymore," said my father. He removed his jacket and dropped it at Steppe's feet.

"Why are you satisfied with having nothing?" said Steppe.

"I'm afraid you do not know me very well. I have everything a man could want," said my father.

"A simple man. Realize before it's too late that you are not free. Your family will belong to me. Your sons will serve me. Your beautiful wife will lie beneath me and clean the blood from my boots. Your daughters will mount me like the whores of Varron Street. And they, along with everyone else, will know you as a traitor. Your sons especially will be ashamed of how you betrayed your country and ruler. When the world bows to me, they will think of you and what I did to you anytime they consider rebelling. There will be no praying to Uryston or

Wareis—there will be me and me alone. Join me now and be worshiped as a saint forever, or refuse and be damned as a devil," said Steppe.

"I've made my choice," said my father. Tears streamed down my cheeks and I wanted to shout to him, to make him aware of my presence, to let him know that I would always know the truth. My father turned his back on Steppe and began to walk away. I expected the General to shoot my father. Instead, Steppe knelt down and appeared to fix his boot.

"Wait," said Steppe, halting my father with his words. In one swift motion, Steppe lunged forward and stabbed my father in the lower back, twisted the knife, and dragged it upward six inches. My father fell, trying to grasp the knife. Steppe planted his boot on the butt of the knife and pushed it deeper into my father's back. I should have run, to warn my mother and siblings of what would happen to us, but instead I grabbed a jagged silver stone near my foot and loaded it into my slingshot. I sprang upward and positioned my left foot on one of the fallen branches, poised to shoot the General in the back of the head.

He sensed my presence and turned, facing me down, a small boy with a silver stone and slingshot standing up against the most powerful man in Hetra. He aimed both of his arms at me, reveling in the opportunity with a smile that burned to my core. I let go of the strap, and the silver stone became a blur that cut through the air, smashing into his mouth with an eruption of blood. The General reeled and tripped backwards over my father's body, firing gunshots toward the sky. I dipped back down and foolishly sought a second silver stone when I should have run—but by the time I found a suitable second shot, readied it in my weapon, and perched myself for an able shot, Steppe was approaching the fallen trees with veracity. He unloaded the rifles, sending shards of tree in every direction. Just before I covered my face and ducked behind the trees, I glimpsed his face: both lips were split open and his front teeth were missing, his once-handsome visage mangled. My feet carried me faster than they ever had before, thumping the ground with each step and leap. Bullets rained everywhere, all narrowly avoiding me. I moved as if I had no control over my body, and I felt for a moment that I could take off and soar like a bird.

And then I made the mistake of glancing to my left and seeing—or

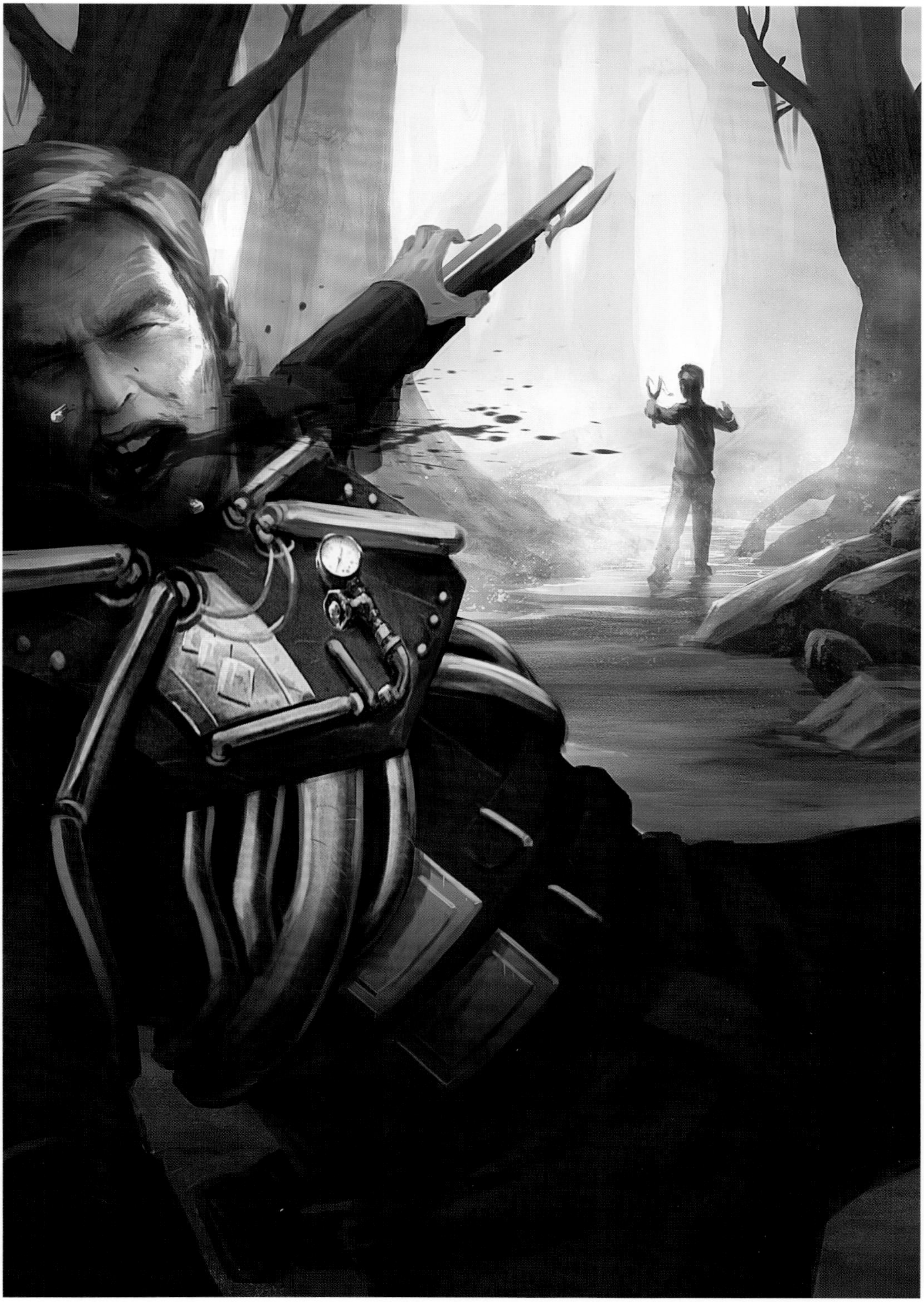

believing that I saw—a figure that could be none other than Eniam, hunched over near a family of White Hand trees; she acknowledged me and pointed in the direction I should run. I followed the line of her finger and caught my right foot on a protruding root. My fall was broken by a rock. I tried to see Eniam again, but she was gone. My ankle was twisted so badly I could not move, and the side of my head was split open. Blood mixed with the ground beneath me. I expected this to be the last thing I saw before Steppe killed me. His shadow loomed over me.

"Turn over," he said. I refused, so he grabbed me by the back of the head and twisted me around and dropped me. He hissed through dangling lip and gapped grin, blood and saliva dripping onto my shirt. "The men who paint my portraits will fix this." He tapped his mouth with his right pointer finger. "History won't be so kind to you."

"You could have let him go."

"You're smart for a boy your age, and quite resourceful, but there's a lot you haven't figured out," said Steppe.

"Like what?"

"Like knowing when your father is being a fool. He should have understood his decision to walk away would not sway me from my course of action. He chose to ignore certain things, things that were right under his nose, for years. He pretended my decision to flex my power was surprising. He chose ignorance. That makes him a fool," said Steppe.

"Somebody will stop you."

"Only if I permit it. It certainly won't be your father—or you." Steppe removed the pistol from his right leg holster and aimed it at my head. "When we meet in the next world, tell me what your final thoughts were." The hammer drawing back sounded as loudly as a cannon shot. He fired a shot above my head, quaking the earth below me, then withdrew his weapon. "You were meant to suffer, not die."

The promise the General made, about my purpose being one of suffering, came to fruition. I was bound like a sow and dragged through

Blackbin to an internment camp for dissenters, defectors, and anyone else deemed unworthy of a normal existence.

My family arrived two days later, bound in the same fashion as me, and our restraints were loosened after an arbitrary amount of time passed. Having the freedom to walk about was no relief at all; the camp, affectionately named Purg, was a putrid place that forced men and women and children to behave like beasts. Food and water were essentially nonexistent. The purpose of Purg was to slowly and painfully kill its residents. We were kept alive rather than executed because Steppe believed in the suffering of all dissenters—especially those in the Grey family.

Over time, a hierarchy had developed inside Purg; to get anything you needed, you had to fill a role. My siblings and I were too young to understand completely how this worked because we were not yet cogs in its system—though my mother was, and I did not comprehend how she kept us alive. Once per week, for our first three years, she would disappear at night and return a few hours later with a bag of runt potatoes that the five of us would share for the week. My mother did not think any of us knew that she abandoned our fold in the nighttime and I never said a word, especially after realizing she willfully allowed brutish men to use her body for a mere pittance.

I hold no ill regard toward Lady Grey, for she had no other means to sustain us. And those potatoes, always eaten raw, barely kept us alive, transforming our once-robust bodies into emaciated doppelgangers. Mariam and Lillian fought through illness after illness, and Joshua stopped sprouting up as he was projected to do; only I continued to grow healthily, by what means I will never understand. Though two years younger than Joshua, I outpaced him, and by the time I was eleven and he thirteen, I was a full head taller than him. When alone with my mother, which rarely occurred, she would whisper to me, "There's something special with you." I always assumed she said this because I was responsible for us being in Purg, though I now realize we would have ended up there regardless of whether I had been there when Steppe killed my father.

The other detail I must mention about these horrific four years is the time Steppe visited Joshua and me. It was six months into our tenure, and Purg was certainly breaking our bodies and spirits; more often than not, we wished for death rather than survive another day of suffering.

He came in the black of night and separated us from our mother and sisters, taking us to a small outpost a few miles north of Purg. It was there that he sat us in a tent and fed us galrabbit stew, bread with yellowberry jam, and milk. We ate till we were sick, fearing that we'd never enjoy another meal. He watched us devour the food, relishing the power he held over us. After two soldiers cleared our plates, Steppe lit four candles atop his desk and stared at us. The flickering light painted his face orange and yellow and red. A scar burrowed into his face from the base of his nose to the top of his chin, like a chasm in the earth; the four teeth I took had been replaced with copper ones. His handsome looks were still present, though distorted unsettlingly when arranged into certain expressions.

"How are you finding your accommodations?" he said, not expecting or waiting for an answer. "I wonder—not very often, mind you—what your father would think to see his family in squalor. Would he have chosen differently? Or was this his plan all along—to betray like a coward and force his family into imprisonment? Do you still hold him in high regard, or has he fallen a few pecks in your order? No matter," he said, settling back. "It's not what we're here to discuss. I need not bother asking how your meals were. Neither of you breathed while eating. Has it really been that long since you've been nourished? Is it that the love you share for each other or the legacy of your father you insist upon does not feed you? Might you need something more? I only ask because it seems quite unusual to choose this life—and whether you are aware of it or not, you did choose this. And that is why I am prepared to make the two of you an offer. Just this once.

"My army is expanding—rapidly and robustly. Even though a private must be fifteen to serve, I am willing to ignore the requirements and allow the two of you to join. At first, you will not train with the others. There are many roles for you. You'll be messengers, mostly, but you can also clean the living quarters and learn to cook. All valuable skills that most soldiers begrudgingly accept. During this time, you will have sufficient food and shelter and clothing. And when you reach the age of fifteen, which will not happen if you remain in the camp, you will be made officers of my army. Those positions are highly coveted, and men have killed for them in the past—your father included. The catch is that you will leave your mother and sisters, and they will remain in Purg until they die. There will be nothing you can do for them, because this option is your only hope of escape. Refuse me, and you will suffer the same fate as them. What a waste of life it would be to die in that place at your ages. Undoubtedly, you will miss them and be filled with sorrow when they die—not that you would know about the specifics of their deaths. What you should do is think of them as being dead already. As if they died with your father. Commit to my offer and you are guaranteed greatness. Refuse me, and—"

"We'll never serve you." The sound of my voice appeared to startle Steppe, as if he'd forgotten he was addressing others. I cannot say for sure that Joshua shared my conviction—he was much weaker than me and susceptible to the General's promises. I had, of course, told him how Steppe killed our father; that he wasn't present at the murder abstracted the event to him. Yes, our father was dead and he mourned him, but it seemed that my brother's reaction was no different than if he had died in combat.

I doubt to this day that Steppe expected a different response from me. He sat back in his chair and smiled.

"Everyone serves me," he said and summoned his two personal guards to see that we be returned to Purg immediately. At that moment, I did not care if he was right or not.

Once I reached the age of twelve and the camp had established itself, a new rule was enacted: the eldest male of each clan could leave daily for potential positions of labor. The salary was food, albeit a meager allotment, yet small portions were enough to prolong dying. Joshua was sent every day and every day returned with nothing. He was too frail for work, and he had no discernable skills. Most days, when Mother would wake him to leave, he would turn his back to her and sleep, knowing his day would be wasted with long hikes to a worksite, expending energy only to watch others awarded with work.

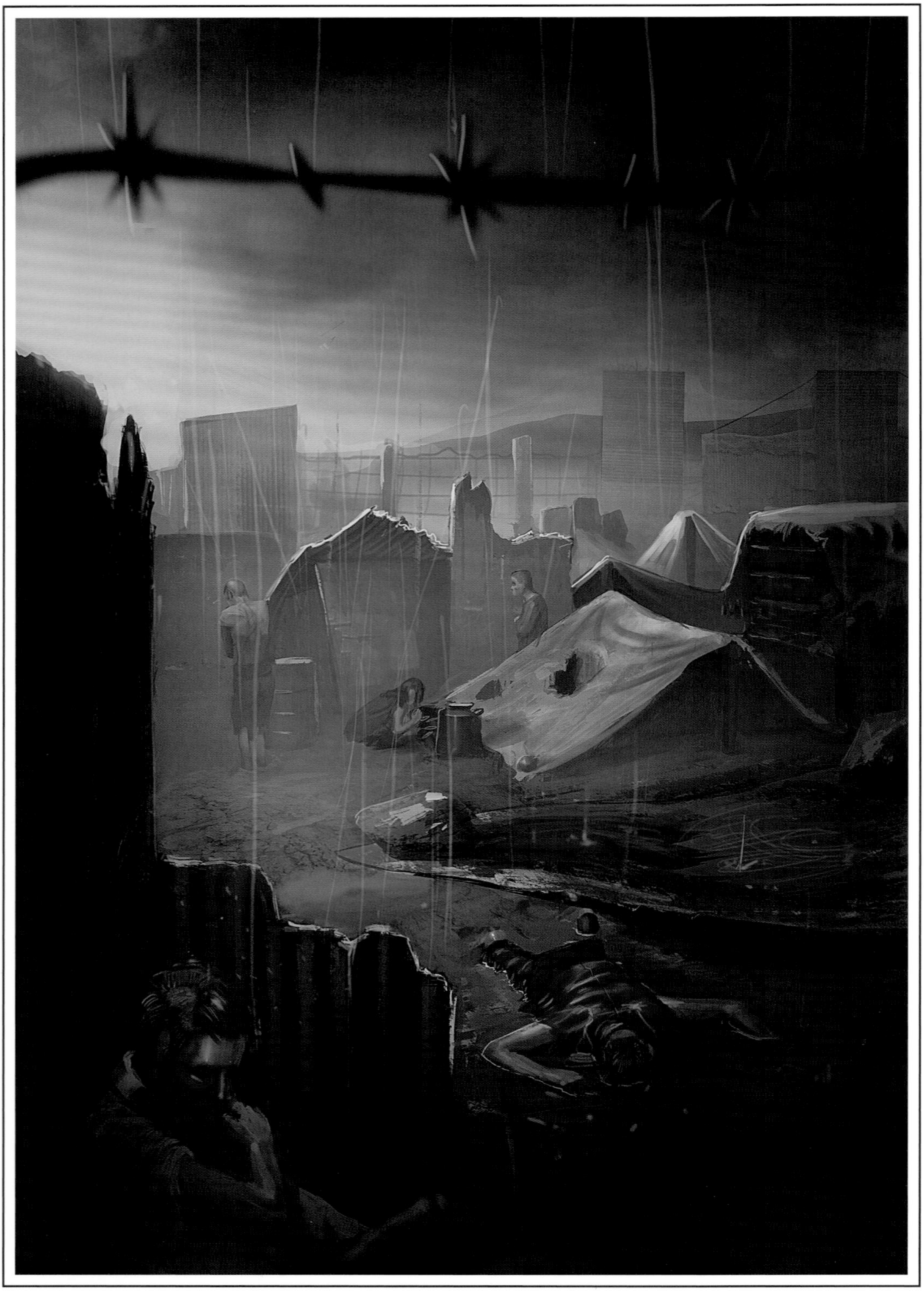

The man in charge of the program, John Gill, refused my offers to replace Joshua. "There are rules for a reason," he would say, never explaining the rules and ignoring the rest of my pleas.

It seemed almost impossible that we were still alive after four years of life in Purg. After a few months, Joshua refused to leave with Gill altogether, which Gill reported to Lopdan, the prisoner who operated the camp. It became quite apparent to me that we would not live much longer when my mother returned from her weekly night of work bruised and unpaid—her efforts would not be compensated from that point forward. My mother was so distraught that I took it upon myself to deal with Joshua. He had accepted death and his selfish nature was unwavering; he would let us all die instead of trying to work.

With great confidence I sought out a meeting with Lopdan, a wiry, middle-aged man who had once distilled the best liquor in all of Timpast. He was as pleasant as a caged Vaxon Snake, but all dealings were handled by him. After waiting for hours, I was let into his tent. It was comprised of pants and shirts sewn together haphazardly, though it was preferable to nothing at all. He was one of the few people in Purg that had shelter. Lopdan had piles of potatoes, cooking pots, and liquor bottles everywhere. He sat upon a stool that only had three legs, and sitting down looked to be more a balancing act than a relief for his feet. He spoke in low, quick bursts.

"I know your mother," he said, not attempting subtlety in the least. "She's been here. She's been there. Does good work, but you know there's rules for things. Even in places like this. I got business, they got business. So if you want me to let your mother go out and keep working her business with some of the guys here, I can't. I can't. I just got rules I got to follow."

"That's not why I'm here."

"Good-good-good. I hope she didn't send you to beg for food neither because this ain't charity, just like your mother's work wasn't. Always got paid," he said.

"Not always."

"Yeah well there's rules and that's what we gotta' follow. Here. Even here. Get out of here, kid," he said.

"I'm not done."

"Well you didn't come with nothing to say, at least I can't tell you did," he said.

"Stop talking."

Lopdan laughed to himself and looked around as if he were surrounded by others who were about to join him in his joyful noise. I stared at him without blinking, breathing slowly, composing myself as best as I could, knowing that overreacting would not benefit me.

"Alright-alright-alright. Say your peace and get the—"

"I want to work for you. I can do whatever you need."

"Anything I need?" he said.

"Yes. I'm good with calculations, I can read and write, or if you need, I can steal."

"A thief?" he said.

"I can."

"What'cha think I need a thief for?" he said, intrigued with the direction of the conversation.

"You tell me."

Lopdan laughed again.

"You're alright, kid. But tell me this if you're so goddamn smart: why do you need to be a thief for me, when you can be a thief for yourself and get what you want?" he said, pleased with his clever inquiry.

"Because I need protection."

He nodded aggressively. "You're a thinker. Not many like you around here. But you're what—ten, eleven?"

"Twelve."

"Guess not eating makes kids look younger, or I just don't know how old a kid's supposed to be. No matter, no matter. I like that you set out to help your family. That I respect. Like your mother did too. Real good too. A lot of people die off in here and you guys figured out a way to keep alive. Something to be said about that. So you want to work for me?" he said.

"I want food for my family."

"You ever think about why we keep ourselves alive here? Really think? Maybe I might be crazy to even ask that, but we acting real savage in here to stay alive, and for what? For what? They ain't letting us out. They ain't. Because ain't nobody stopping the General. He's more powerful than anybody that ever lived. If somebody were to run in here right now and say, 'General Steppe just moved the suns,' I'd believe it. Since nobody's stopping him, we all dying in here. Some faster than others. But I can't figure even for myself why I don't just let it happen. Why I do what I always done and run this place. It makes no sense. Even you coming to me makes no sense. You wanting to steal for me or work for me to get a little of this. But how far you going to take this? Because I don't need nobody to steal for me. But what I need is some-one to kill for me. You got that in you? You a killer, kid?" he said.

Lopdan knew the answer to his question, but I shook my head anyway.

"Exactly so. And I don't think that's a bad thing neither. People who start killing at your age end up dead real quick. Instead, you've got to get your brother to work," he said.

"He won't. Or he can't. Maybe both."

"It's the first. Everybody that gets sent out gets picked eventually. I hear from some of the guys that he goes out and when it comes time to picking workers, he finds a tree and props it up and sleeps. That's what your brother's doing. How's that for keeping the family alive? He's a little different from me and you—he's already given up living. He's too weak to even kill himself. But he don't think nothing more of this world than his own death," he said.

"That doesn't help me."

"It could, as long as you realize he's not helping you and your mother and your sisters. Ever," said Lopdan.

"There has to be something I can do."

"You could strangle me right here and run off with some potatoes, but that'll only keep you for a couple of months," he said. He winked, searched through a bin of potatoes, picked a few rotten ones, and handed them to me. I refused them. "You're a stubborn bastard, ain't you? Well, as I see it you're not leaving till I tell you something you want to hear, even if I ain't got nothing to tell you. So I'll let you in on a little private information. If it gets back to me that you told someone else, I'll kill your mother. Clear?" he said. I nodded my head. "Good. Mr. Gill, who you know was appointed by the General himself, has got a real fondness for galrabbit stew. Gets crazy for it. Problem for him is, being out here he gets the same lousy rations as the soldiers. Course he gets a little more, but is more lousy better than a little lousy? I don't know. What I've been told by a guy who ain't never lied to me before is that when that gate opens in the morning, Mr. Gill will let you out as long as you do two things: bring him back a galrabbit, and get back before they open the gate again to let the workers back. Then you're good. If you come back with no galrabbit you get used for target practice. On the spot. If you run away and don't come back then they send a little set of troops after you to kill you. They succeed, too. Them boys is trained good. Now to make all this happen, you just go get yourself a meeting with Mr. Gill and tell him your intentions. It's really easy as that."

"I don't know how to hunt."

"That's something you got to figure out. Now get the hell out of here and don't let me see you again unless you aim to kill someone for me."

I wandered around the camp for most of the day, trying to determine how I could teach myself how to hunt galrabbits. I knew the best method for killing them was a shot to the head, which was a suitable solution for a typical hunter, even one with access only to a slingshot. I had no weapon and little knowledge of galrabbits, other than that they fed on yellowberry bush leaves and were hunted by White Wolves. Instead of giving up, I was determined to fashion weapons from anything I could find. After patrolling the grounds near where we slept, I found a handful of strong branches and carted them off to a place I thought was private, next to the fence that kept us caged. I snapped the branches in half and used my teeth to peel back the first layer of bark; then I rubbed the jagged tips in between the fence posts to try to form sharp ends. My efforts failed. I tried next with my fingers to peel back more layers from the branches, desperate to create makeshift knives.

The work was so consuming that I did not realize a man stood just behind me, until he held a small, curved blade in front of me and said, "Try'n this." The handle was wrapped with sweat-stained leather. I looked up at the man, but his face was blocked by the second sun, hanging high above. The knife felt natural in my hands as I shaved the branch tips into deadly points. I held the branches up when I finished, proud of my work.

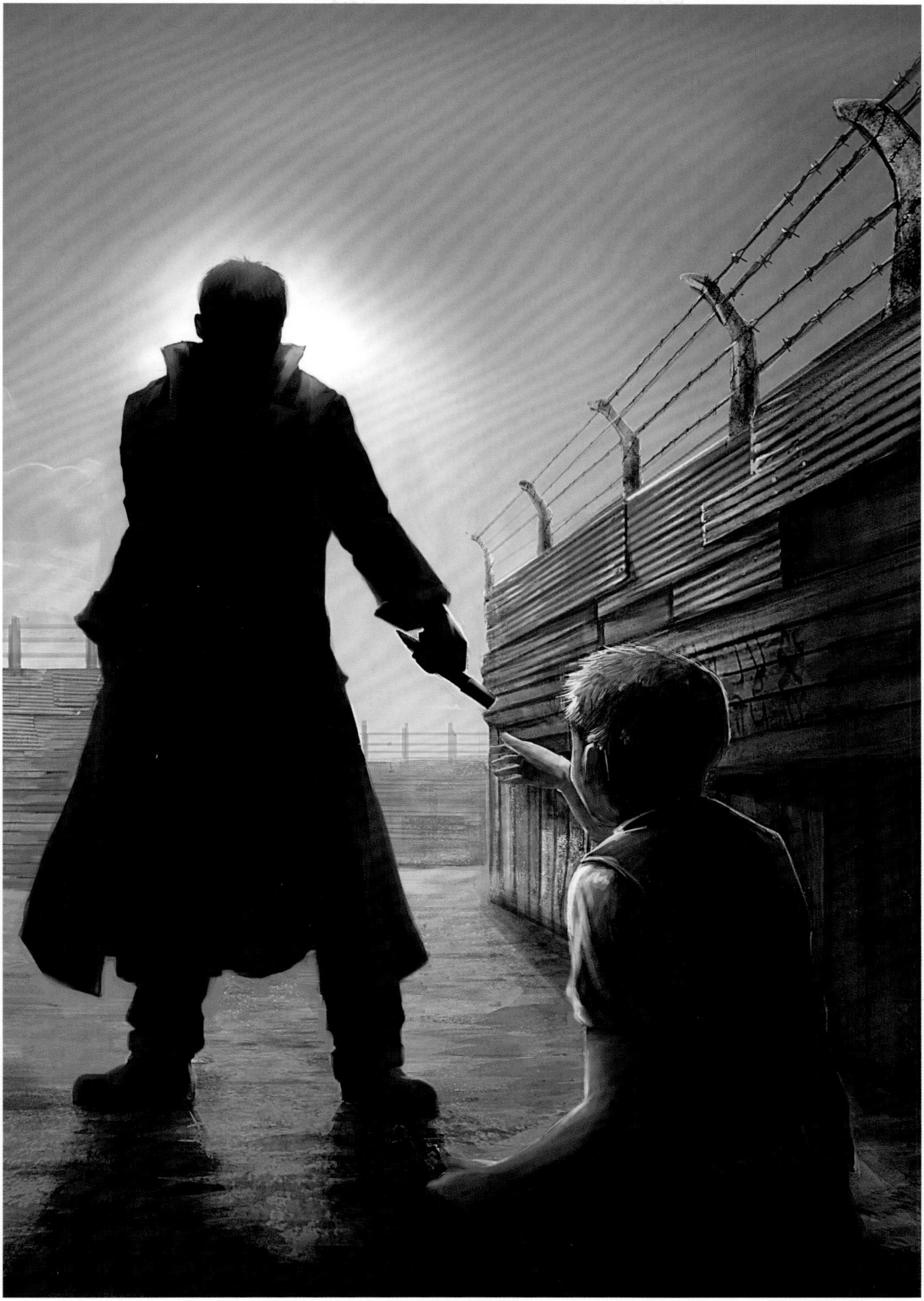

When I stood and finally saw the man's face, I recognized him instantly—it was Kelman, the man from Timpast who had given me the book about Eniam. I wondered why he was a prisoner and if he had known for a long time that I was there. I had never seen him there, but then I'd done my best to stick with my family. Perhaps he had just been waiting for the right moment to approach me.

"Thank you. Here." I tried to return his knife, but he surprised me by refusing it.

"You'n need it more than me. Just keep er' hidden. Someone knows you have it, they'll use it against you," he said. "And never'n on your life hunt with it. You try to stab down on something, it'll run off with it in its side, leaving you'n with no knife. Use those," he said, pointing to the branches, "for killing, and that," he pointed to the knife, "for skinning. You'n can't clean an animal with those branches." With that, he walked away and I never saw him again, almost as if he was part of a dream.

Jubilation raced through my veins, for not only did I have a formidable weapon with which to defend myself and my family, but I could now hunt—which was the only means for us to survive.

Upon returning to my family, I was surprised to find only Mariam and Lillian. They were huddled closely together, and my initial thought was that something terrible had happened to Mother and Joshua. My sisters were delighted to see me and I showed them the knife I'd acquired.

"What's that good for?" said Lillian.

"I'm going to hunt us some galrabbits. Mama can make her famous galrabbit stew."

"There's no rabbits in here," said Mariam.

"I know where to find them."

The girls wanted to play a game they'd recently invented called Over the Fence. It was a simple way to pass the time, and Mother and Joshua were never willing participants in the girls' games. Perhaps it was because I was closer to them in age, or because I realized they needed distractions in a place like Purg, but it was I who always played along with them. Keeping them preoccupied was difficult and necessary; there were few children in Purg and no places to play. Our circumstances were grim but they were fortunate to have each other's company. Together, they created games and other flourishes to keep busy, and once they settled on something, they lured me into playing. Over the Fence, their latest game, required each participant to behave like an animal found in Blackbin. They constantly fought over who would be a Korbear, since that player was guaranteed to win the game—or so they thought. Mariam chose first and, as predicted, chose to be a Korbear. Lillian was next and became a Black Tail Hawk. The girls expected me to be a White Wolf, so instead I chose galrabbit; they laughed so hard that they both fell over.

"Why even play?" said Mariam.

"Yeah, Isaac, you know we can both get you!" said Lillian.

They continued to laugh and taunt me. I enjoyed the sound of their laughter so much, even though it was at my expense, that I allowed it to continue. To this day it is one of the sounds I miss dearly: the laughter that used to fill our house in Timpast. At times it seemed that they would never find anything joyous to celebrate; if my own purposely foolish action was the cause, I accepted it gladly.

"The two of you don't know anything about galrabbit strategy."

"Yes we do," said Lillian.

"We do. It's scamper—hop—scamper and . . . die!" said Mariam. Her joke pleased her so much that her laughter turned into an uncontrollable cough.

"Let's see."

"Well, I guess you should go first, then," said Lillian, smiling at me, believing that no matter what decision I made as a galrabbit, she or Mariam would trample me with their first move. I winked at Lillian and she understood immediately that I was going to play in her favor; she was the youngest, and Mariam never allowed her to win at any game.

I circled around both girls, then clamped my right hand onto Mariam's back. She wriggled and turned, so I stepped behind her again and held my hand to her back. "My first move is to cling to the Korbear's back."

"Impossible!" said Mariam.

"How?"

"A galrabbit would never jump on a Korbear's back!" said Mariam.

"I didn't know you were an expert in the habits of galrabbits."

"I'm not, but they can't do that. They just can't," said Mariam.

"Maybe they could," said Lillian.

"No they can't!" said Mariam.

"The only galrabbits the two of you have ever seen have been inside a cooking pot. They do look quite docile, but they have nails that grow out from their paws and firm teeth that could hold onto any Korbear's hair. So I will position myself in the middle of your back."

"Then I go next," said Mariam.

"That's not fair!" said Lillian. "You picked first, so I should get to move before you."

"Let her go."

"Exactly," said Mariam. "My move is to grab the galrabbit off my back." Mariam tried to reach behind and grab my hand, yet my position eluded her. "I can't . . . quite . . . reach."

"Very interesting. Keep your hands where they are, Mariam. Lillian, go ahead."

"Okay. Okay. What I'm going to do is . . . take out the Korbear's left eye!" said Lillian. She placed her hand over Mariam's left eye, incapable of hiding her exuberance. She smiled at me.

"I believe it's my turn again. And I am going to leap into the hole in that tree."

"We never said there was a hole in a tree!" said Mariam.

"We never said there wasn't, either." I stood near the imaginary tree, pretending to hide.

"Stupid move, Isaac. I'll reach inside and grab you," said Mariam. She held onto my forearm with as much strength as she could muster.

"Then I'll take out your right eye!" said Lillian. She covered Mariam's other eye. Lillian was so giddy that nothing in the world could wipe the smile from her face.

"This leaves me in a bad position. What can I do when a blind Korbear has me in her grip?"

"Nothing!" said Mariam.

"That's not exactly true. You have me in your big paw, but I can still bite you." I bit down softly on Mariam's arm.

"That's nothing compared to this!" said Mariam. She bit down on my shoulder and I laughed.

"Good move. Your Korbear beats my galrabbit."

"And then I'll swipe this stupid Black Tail Hawk off my face," said Mariam.

"No you won't. It's my move next," said Lillian.

"No, it's—"

"Yes it is!" said Lillian. "And I think I'll fly up to the top of this tree."

"Another stupid move. Korbears can climb trees," said Mariam.

"I don't care what you can climb. You can't see!" said Lillian.

"Doesn't matter. I can still get you," said Mariam.

"How? How? Tell me—how you will hunt blind?"

"Yeah. Tell us," said Lillian. "Because if you think I'd sit and wait for you to get me, you're dumber than I thought."

"This doesn't mean you win," said Mariam.

"But there's no way you can get me, so yes it does," said Lillian.

"She's right."

"It's not fair," said Mariam.

Mother and Joshua returned just as our game concluded. Mariam wanted to propose the game's ending to Mother to get her feedback, but she could tell that Mother was distracted with something else.

"Where were you?" Mother asked me.

"Working on something."

"You must stop this wandering around. Understand?" she said. I nodded my head. "You have too much of your father's independence."

"It's a good quality."

"We can only survive if we stay together. At all times," she said. I wanted to argue with her, to explain how my disappearance was to help everyone, pointing out that in one afternoon I had accomplished more than Joshua had in four years, but it was not the time to mention things that were obvious to her. It was also an inappropriate time to mention the knife, which would make her nervous. "Things are going to be better tomorrow. Joshua and I spoke with Mr. Gill. He is understanding. Not anything like his reputation. And he's going to allow Joshua to go out with the workers in the morning. He's guaranteed a place. The General's building a bridge over the Gorndon River. Needs all the hands he can get. Joshua will work. He will work and get paid in enough food to feed us all. We will be okay."

Joshua stood in silence, then went to his usual spot to lay down. The girls sat with Mother and I busied myself with gathering the nearby branches. There weren't many to gather, so I sat down next to Joshua. He pretended to sleep, an impossible task with Mariam and Lillian's continued argument over who won the first round of Over the Fence. Mother asked them to be quiet and try to sleep, yet any time the two tried to sleep they invariably complained about hunger. After four years, they hadn't grown accustomed to hunger pangs—I cannot say for sure that I had either, though I realized speaking about it was certainly no remedy. To silence the girls, my mother lay between them and acted as a divide, hushing any rumblings of ensuing argument. Any time my mother positioned herself this way, she fell asleep with the girls. It was the nearest thing to serene anyone could experience in Purg.

An opportunity to speak with Joshua presented itself and I seized upon the moment. I nudged him until he swatted my hand away. "I'm sleeping," he said.

"Liar."

"Leave me. I am the General's slave. You're useless," he said.

"That's only because you were born first. I'm preparing for something."

"Games you play in your mind," he said.

"Once I start my new plan, I will get more food than you."

"That doesn't bother me. Because I know it's not true," he said. "We should have gone with the General years ago."

"Don't say that."

"We will be soldiers in his army soon enough," he said.

"I have a plan for us to escape."

"This isn't a fantasy, Isaac. You think if it was so easy to leave people wouldn't do it already?" he said.

"It's a big place. People might have escaped."

"There is only one way to get out of this place. And I'm doing it tomorrow," said Joshua.

"You have to work. We need the food."

"What happened to your wager that you could collect more food than I could earn?" he said.

"I'm not yet prepared, but I will be soon."

"Tomorrow I will handle things. For all of us," he said, in a tone I could not assess.

"Tomorrow you're going to work and bring back food."

"And if I don't?" He settled back into his sleeping position. His words rattled around my head, keeping me awake most of the night.

Mother insisted throughout the day that we all wait for Joshua upon his return from work. I protested that this would cause too much of a scene for him, a hero's welcome that was neither earned nor warranted. The further I argued, the more she insisted, drumming up great support from Mariam and Lillian. By the time we set out to the gate, just as the second sun was in its final lap, the two girls were expecting to see Joshua carried on the shoulders of the other workers and food dumped at our feet. I wasn't bothered by jealousy of all the attention Joshua received that day, but rather by the inclination that something had gone terribly wrong.

Nobody was permitted to stand too closely to the gate, especially while in a pack. Purg did not have many soldiers stationed there to keep its prisoners from rioting, and it really did not need them anyway; the perimeter fence, impossible to climb, was the ultimate deterrent from escape. There were always eight soldiers at the gate: fully armed, trained, and encouraged to fire upon anyone who moved toward uprising or rebellion. There were few incidents of prisoners being shot, and I doubted that any were truly trying to escape the grounds. Few people could have survived Blackbin, with or without a pursuing party of Steppe soldiers. My mother seemed to forget this momentarily and escorted us to the line of soldiers not more than fifteen feet from the gate.

"You know you got to go back, lady," said one of them, not much older than Joshua. My mother must have heard him and chose to ignore his words. I hooked my arm around my mother's and gently pulled her back. She would not budge, and the soldier recognized this. "Maybe it's your hearing that's a problem. I can do something for that if you like." The soldier raised his rifle, pressed it to my mother's shoulder, and shoved her back. There was a wildness in her eyes that I'd never seen before and I needed all my strength to restrain her. All of the soldiers were boys who were now trained to kill. Being assigned to Purg was a punishment, for there was no killing to be done—no official killing, anyway—and the soldiers were restless. They needed no excuse to fire their weapons, and they would face no repercussions for killing anyone there.

My mother fought against me until I spoke. "Do you want the girls to see you killed?" This was enough for a momentary respite from the violence building inside her. Purg had certainly pushed her to her limits. "They want you to attack them. And they will make examples of all of us. That cannot be the final word on the Grey family." Placing the situation in terms of legacy seemed to suppress the rage within her.

"Let go," she said and slid her arm out from under mine. She stared at the soldier who'd shoved her. "If only your mother could see you. What would she think?"

"Nothing at all. She's been dead since I was two. But I imagine she'd think I was wise to kill any crazy bitch who attacked me," he said.

He wanted to incite both me and my mother, but I made sure to appear subdued. We walked away, putting enough distance between ourselves and the soldiers to not be heard or hear any more rash talk. My mother seemed to have reached her breaking point, something I never expected to happen; if her strength betrayed her, only I could keep the family intact.

"Your father made men of those boys, not monsters," my mother said. "They behave like animals and that's how they expect us to act. There is little hope for anyone if this is what's to become of us."

"There are many good people out there. Like us."

"That is what Steppe is trying to eradicate," she said. "Sometimes I wonder if—"

"Remember the girls," I said quietly. "They have not been corrupted. Don't show them any signs that you have."

The gate, twenty-five feet in height, five feet higher than the fence it connected to, opened outward, pulled by four soldiers on the outside. The workers were led by Gill, who rode atop an auburn horse, dragging

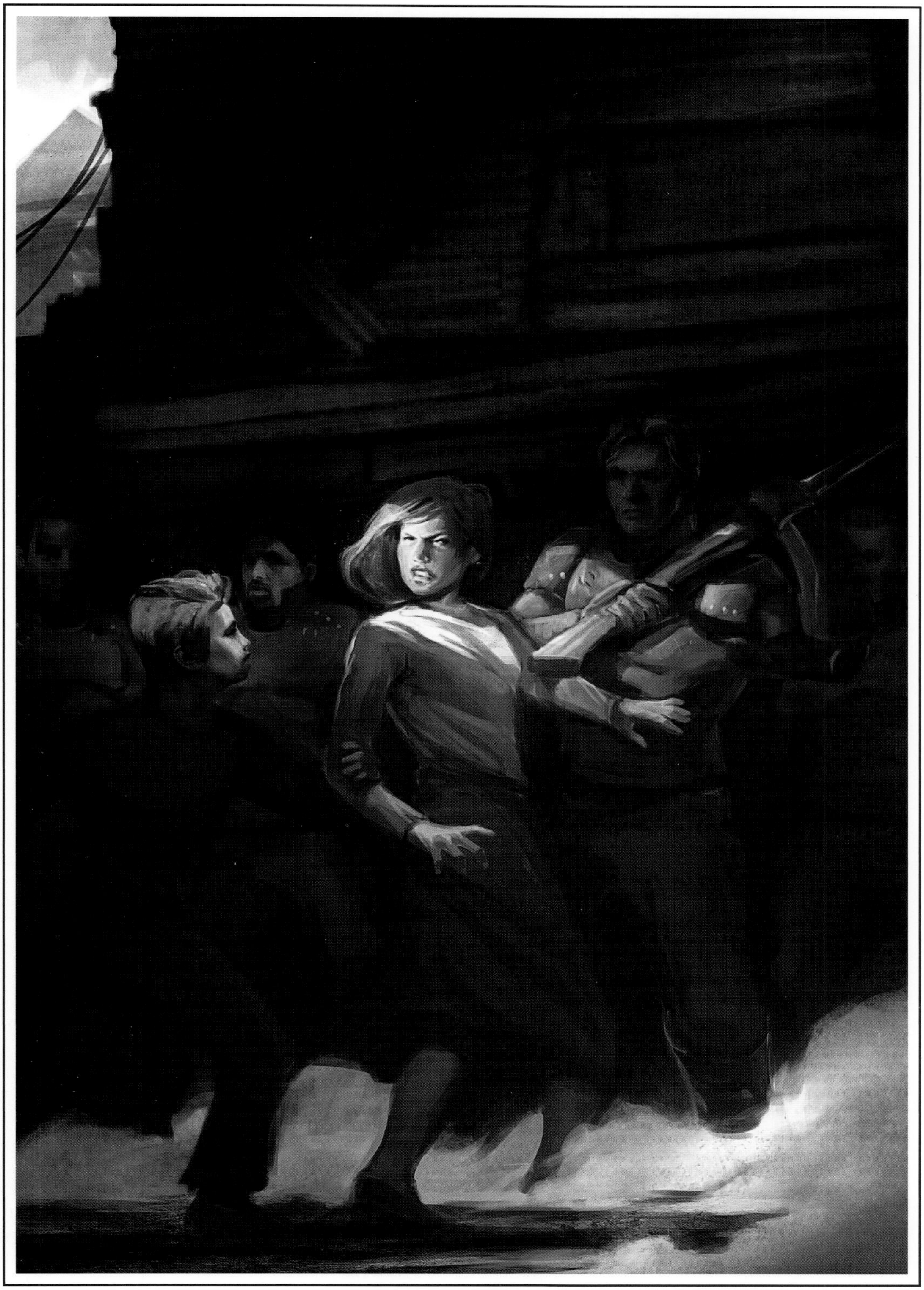

someone behind him.

Even before I could see who it was, I knew that it was Joshua. I didn't want Mariam and Lillian to see our brother like this, and the gods could not have moved my mother from the place in which she stood, so I created a diversion for my sisters. "Girls, there's something I wanted to show you."

"Yes, let's go," said Lillian.

"We must wait," said Mariam.

"Yes, they should," said mother. It was just as the words escaped my mother's lips that she realized that her eldest born was being dragged behind Gill. We did not know if he was alive or dead, and I was unprepared for an emotional outburst from my mother.

"It's not too far from here."

"Yes. Yes. Go on," said my mother.

"Come, girls—unless you're scared."

"What? Us, scared? Never," said Mariam.

"When have you ever seen us scared?" said Lillian.

"Today might be the first."

That I had nothing specific to show them was inconsequential at the moment. They were quite satisfied with anything new, so I took them on a quick tour of a section of camp they'd never been allowed to see before. Mother had kept them so sequestered in our spot that they had not realized some people lived in tents.

This was enough to satisfy their curiosity, and once we returned to our small place, Joshua was laying down in his usual spot. Mother was stroking his head; his arms and legs were still bound by thin, rough ropes, the soft skin rubbed away beneath them.

"I'm going to see to things," said Mother.

"No. I'll take care of things. Mind the girls."

She sensed the seriousness in my voice and huddled up with my sisters. I waited for them to fall asleep before I woke Joshua. I couldn't understand how he could sleep, all tied up as he was, though he seemed to be making attempts to sleep his way through life. At first he refused to open his eyes, so I held his nose shut until he looked at me. There was something different in his look, a sense of doom I had never seen before. He tried to roll over so as to not face me, but I grabbed his hair to prevent him from doing so. He spit on my shirt and I wiped it on his face.

"I'll cut you free if you listen and do what I say." Joshua shook his head, his stubbornness an act of pure stupidity. My mother should have left him at the gate. "I have a plan, but I need you."

"Your plan's doing nothing for anybody. We're dead and I'm tired of pretending differently," said Joshua.

"Tell me what happened and I'll cut you loose."

"What? With your teeth? This is a coil rope. You can't use your—"

I unveiled my knife and held it closely to his face, proving to him that I was the one with the power in this situation, and he paused. "Free me first and then I'll talk," he said.

"No."

"Then I'm not saying anything," he said.

"I don't care. And I don't care what you did. I'm keeping our family alive with or without your help."

"After today, there's nothing you can do," said Joshua.

With this, I knew I could trick him into telling me what had happened. For most of his life, he'd seen me only as the person who would be impressed with his exploits; he was incapable of remaining silent to me about any of his doings.

"Today's no different than yesterday. We still need food, and you've done nothing to get it for us. That's why I have to take control."

"You're helpless," he said.

"I'm not, actually. Not at all."

"You're not as smart as you think or as great as you think. Just because Dad favored you doesn't mean you're special. He's dead and we will soon be too," he said.

"If we were going to die, it would have happened already. Maybe you don't possess the strength that our family name carries, but your refusal to help us to get food will not in any way diminish us. All you've proven today is that you're weak. Nothing else is different."

Keeping from me the truth of his actions disturbed him so much that he finally came clean with it. "He's coming for us," he said.

"Who?"

"The General. If not tomorrow, then the day after. There's not a thing you can do about it," he said.

"Steppe would have done that years ago. He'd rather let us—"

"Today, they took us out a few miles. This bridge they're constructing over the Gorndon—I think it's for supplies. Something is happening in Hetra. What, I don't know, but it's starting in Timpast. I think they're building the bridge to transport supplies or weapons or something. It's not built yet—that's why they took us out there. And I was working. Honestly I was. I'd refused every other time, but today I said I would work. I would do what I had to do to bring food back for everyone. Even if it was only one potato. I'd labor until my back broke for one potato. I realized that I couldn't refuse anymore. I didn't have the energy. It took all I had to rebel against doing the right thing.

"Then, when I got there, they put me to carrying planks of wood. This was fine for me. I barely had the energy to carry more than one at a time, but I did it. Part of me started to hate myself for not doing it earlier. I know what mom's been through to get us the little bits of food we had. I'm a terrible son. I thought of this as I carried those planks, and then we were signaled to stop. The General had arrived and he needed to see our progress. As he rode through, each of us was supposed to kneel. To prove how small we are and how great he is. I watched as the men dropped to their knees, one by one, as if a king or an emperor or a god rode before them.

"He stopped in front of me and said, 'Give me your knee, Grey,' and I couldn't. So help me Uryston, I could not do it. I stood firmly and looked at the ground. Most days he was alive, I hated Father and wished him dead. Except there was nothing in this world or any other I hated more than the man who killed him. I expected to be strangled or shot, and all Steppe said was, 'Your family has no place in this world— I'll see to that before the week ends.' Then he rode on. Four soldiers beat me down and tied me up. They hanged me from a tree for the rest of the day and pulled me behind a horse for those three or so miles back here. He's going to kill us. Blame me if you wish, but I suspect all I've done is sped things up," said Joshua.

"You could have knelt without him seeing your face."

"That's easy for you to say, Isaac. But I'm guessing that you would have done the same thing as me, especially since you watched him kill

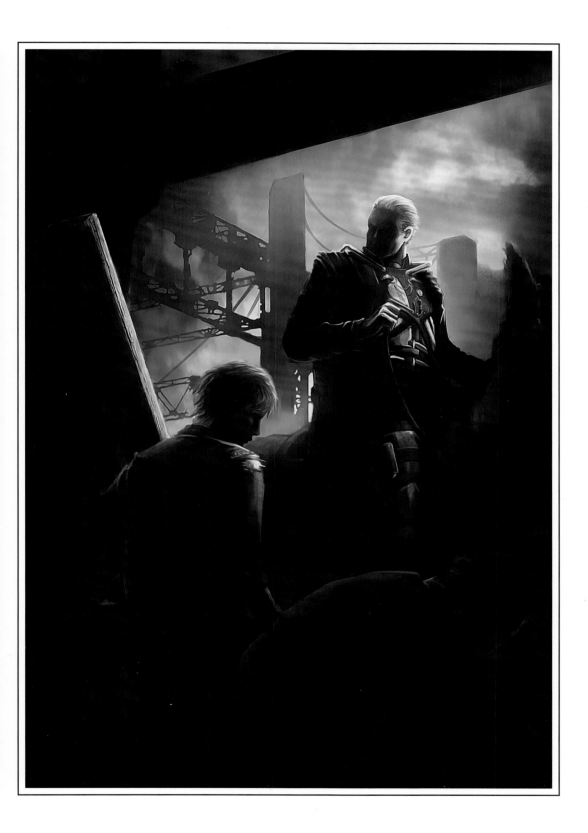

Father," said Joshua.

"Maybe he won't kill us. Part of me believes he is more interested in having us serve him than outright killing us. He had to say something bold in front of everyone so they would not think that they, too, could get away with outright disrespect. Let's not wait for the end. Instead, we are going to bring food to the family tomorrow."

"How? I am now forbidden to work, and they won't allow you to go while I'm still alive. They probably wouldn't let you work anyway. Our family's name is ruined forever," said Joshua.

"We don't need their system to survive. I am going to hunt tomorrow and you must come with me."

"Nobody's allowed to leave," he said.

"I spoke to Lopdan today, and—"

"You did what?" said Joshua.

"These are desperate times. I took the risk and walked away unscathed. He told me a bit of news that we can use to our advantage. Gill allows men to hunt only if they return by the time the gate opens for the workers to return, and if they bring him some of the game they hunt."

"That sounds like a trap," said Joshua.

"It's of no benefit to Lopdan to mislead us. We're no threat to him."

"Even if it is true, we cannot hunt. We have no proper training," said Joshua.

"We're only after small game, like galrabbits."

"A galrabbit can be big if you're trying to kill it," said Joshua.

"But it's not as clever as us."

"I suppose," said Joshua. "That doesn't make sense, though. If people are permitted to leave the camp to hunt, why wouldn't they flee?"

"This isn't a widely known arrangement. And the Steppe Army is sent after anyone who fails to comply with the rules."

"Cut me loose," said Joshua. I did as he requested. "Maybe a hunt will be better than sitting and waiting to die."

Lopdan wasn't inaccurate about the hunting arrangement, but Gill was none too pleased to see me or Joshua early the next morning. He had the bridge work crew lined up for morning inspection. The men were searched thoroughly to assure they had no food or weapons. I pulled Joshua to the back of the line, and the workers—who'd been with Joshua when he refused to salute Steppe—anxiously awaited Gill's reaction.

When he finished with his inspections, Gill stopped in front of Joshua and struck him in the face. Joshua fell and remained on the ground. Gill turned to walk back toward the gate.

"Don't ignore me," I said.

One of the workers snickered. Gill rushed at me and kicked me to the ground. I ignored the pain and stood up to face him.

"I'm not going to fight you. I just need a word with you."

"Your brother's actions were words enough for the General. And that's word enough for me. Get out of my face before I kill you and him," said Gill.

"You trained under my father. Is that what he taught you? To kill children?"

"I do what is necessary to serve the General," said Gill.

"So why does he disrespect you, make you eat the same thing as these men? You are the ruler of this place, yet you eat like a slave."

"The food here is fine," said Gill.

"Any man who trained under my father—"

"A traitor," said Gill.

"Any man who trained under my father knows of Lady Grey's famous galrabbit stew."

"That's just a rumor," said Gill.

"That dish is blessed by Uryston. Let Joshua and me out. We know the arrangement. We'll return before you bring these men back."

"You're not as clever as you think you are," said Gill.

"And you're not as satisfied as you pretend to be."

Gill thought for a moment, grim amusement in his eyes. "Our deal is this, and these men are my witnesses: you will return with five galrabbits before this gate closes tonight. I will keep four. If you return with any less, you will both be shot. In front of your mother. And then I'll kill your sisters, too. After that, I'll let these savages drag your mother off and have their way with her. Understood?" said Gill. I

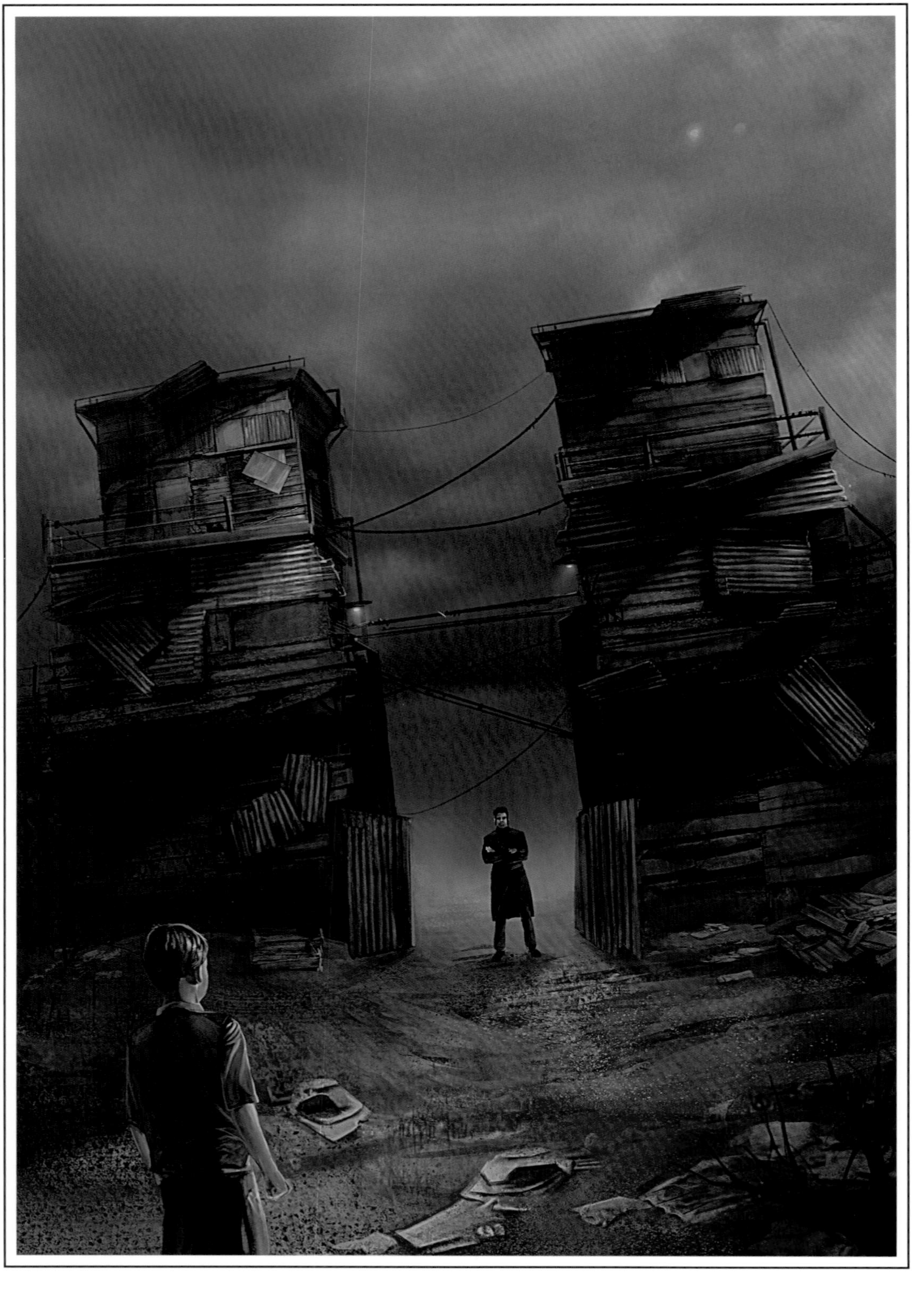

nodded. "This is your death sentence. The most any man has ever trapped is three."

"The Greys are not like any other men."

We left with the workers and headed in the opposite direction.

The person who left Purg that morning, a self I barely recognize now, was not the same person who returned that evening. I'd arrived prior to the work crew's return and I did not feel comfortable waiting near the four guards at the gate. I hid under some Kenning bushes and watched as Gill led the tired crew back to Purg. I joined the back of the line, but one of the soldiers stopped me. I said nothing and waited for Gill to acknowledge my presence. When he finally did, he took his pistol from his holster and approached me. Before he could say a word, I emptied the sack I carried of its nine galrabbits. Gill was speechless.

"I hope you've learned something from this."

"Wha—what? I'm sorry. What did you say?" said Gill.

"This is a lesson."

"And what might that be?" said Gill.

"Grey men are unlike any others."

"Well, if that's what you want to believe. Wait—your brother was with you," he said.

"And he no longer is."

Gill squealed out a few laughs without opening his mouth. "Take these sumptuous little beasts with you. Stop by my tent and see the officer there. Tell him I sent you. Then have them send for your mother. We've got everything she needs. A good pot. Water. Veggies. Potatoes. Kindling. Tonight, I'll see if those stew rumors are true."

"Yes, sir."

"And as far as your brother is concerned, I hope you realize he won't get very far," said Gill.

"I've made sure of that."

At the moment I could not tell if he knew what I had done, yet I sensed that I had a power over him that he no longer had over me. It was a strange thought for a twelve-year-old, certainly, though at that moment I felt more like an adult than a child. Here was a man relegated to an undesirable post who could not help but notice that the young boy in front of him was already greater than he would ever be. I almost pitied him.

I delivered the galrabbits and instructions at Gill's behest, though I did not wait for my mother's arrival to his tent. After what I had done, I was unprepared to face her. She would have questions or she would know, and even though I took responsibility for my actions, she would not understand. There was a chance she would never understand or forgive, but I was set on freeing us from Purg, and I hoped that this would be enough.

Though Purg was big, it was not easy to find a place to hide. Different groups occupied particular areas and they were quite territorial. Eventually, I found a group of workers and their families who allowed me to rest near their camp. I somehow managed to fall asleep.

This sleep was disturbed when I was lifted from the ground and placed in a large sack. I kicked and clawed to try and free myself, but it was useless. I was dragged along the ground for what felt like forever and finally suspended from what I guessed to be a tree. Eventually, a knife cut through the sack and I fell ten feet to the rocky ground.

It took me a few moments to regain my senses, but once I did, I realized the General was standing over me. My mother and sisters were huddled behind him, a small platoon of his best soldiers poised to do Steppe's bidding.

"Where is your knife?" said Steppe. This question surprised me; it was unusual and unexpected. I stood up. "I know you have one. A small, curved blade capable of killing." He smiled, displaying his copper teeth. The man, who many thought was more than man, was already an imposing being, but the dull shine of the artificial teeth made him look more menacing than any other man alive. "Have you cleaned it?"

I stood unwavering, staring straight into the blacks of his eyes. "I've not."

The General looked offended by my tone. He stood so close to me I could hear his breathing. "Look at your mother." I did, and I could see she knew something terrible had happened and something terrible could happen again at any moment. Looking at my mother was awful and uncomfortable. "Tell her what happened. Or at least what I presume happened." I lowered my gaze to my feet. "There must be so much to share with her. You have returned from a great hunt with nine galrabbits. That's impressive for anyone, novice or expert. How is it you came to learn the art of killing so quickly?" I remained silent. "Have I been misinformed? Misled? If so, then I will kill the soldier who told me of your exploits. Say the word and he will suffer just as—"

"It did not take me long to figure out how to trap the galrabbits. Even Joshua found it to be quite simple. Upon catching our ninth, we set out for our return. Both of us were excited. Joshua insisted that we travel south, but I knew that we needed to go west first. Our decision was made for us when three soldiers came up behind us. We ran and outpaced them. They were inexperienced in Blackbin and could not keep up with us. Once we were far enough in the distance, we hid in a hollowed-out tree corpse. The soldiers ran on and we traveled south. It wasn't but a half mile from where we hid that we were ambushed. Two dozen Fortache surrounded us. I had never seen natives before. They were impressive, made up to blend in with Blackbin. Their language was foreign to us. Joshua began to panic, especially when the Fortache leader began to call out and the others responded. Joshua grabbed the sack from me and dumped the galrabbits at the leader's feet. He kept saying, 'Take these, take these,' but I knew our whole family would die if the leader took them. All I could think of was keeping my family alive. Joshua had given up. I refused. The Fortache's cries increased. I began to yell back, and this silenced them momentarily. While I had never seen them before, they hadn't seen me either. They pulled their weapons, clubs and long blades and crossbows, and aimed them at us. I knew I could not fend them off. No one wielding only a knife could.

"Before they could attack me, I did something they did not expect: I walked up behind Joshua, wrapped my arm around his neck, lifted his head by the chin, and dragged my blade across his throat. I held him till he died, then released him. He fell face down. I screamed over and over again, pounding my chest. The Fortache leader approached me and held an unblinking gaze for what felt like an eternity. He grabbed my right arm and held it up, examining the blood dripping from the knife. Then he held my left hand up and forced the blade across my palm till a stream of blood flowed. He wiped the side of the blade, covered with Joshua's blood, into my wound. He rubbed my hands together, the blood mixing, and I restrained myself from wincing in pain. He let go of my hands and spoke. 'First kill. In you. Forever.' He led the Fortache away, and they blended into Blackbin. I watched Joshua for some time, almost expecting him to stand up and join me. The soldiers who had pursued us earlier were nearby. I cut off part of the bottom of Joshua's pants and tied it to my bleeding hand, gathered the galrabbits, and returned. I don't know if that's what you heard, General, but that is exactly what happened."

Mother bawled out a cry and yelled things at me that were true but too painful to write down. The girls said nothing.

"Wasn't it my task to kill your brother? Wasn't it he who publicly insulted me—who, along with you, refused to serve me? Don't you realize that everyone serves me? And by doing my bidding, unbeknownst to me, you have only pledged your loyalty to this great army. You will come with me now and receive the training needed to turn those raw skills into an unbreakable will," he said.

"I cannot serve the man who killed my father."

"You are no different than me. Maybe you're worse. I have done many things other men would flinch at—though I never killed my own family," he said.

"I had no choice. If I didn't kill him, all of us would die."

"Is it that simple?" he said. I looked up at him, trying not to see my mother in my periphery. "Is it?" I did not budge. Steppe grabbed my mother by her hair, dragged her away from Lillian and Mariam, and threw her to the ground. He stepped on the back of her head and pressed her face into the dirt. "Will you let her die like this or join me?"

"Stop." Steppe released her. I tried helping my mother from the dirty ground she lay upon, but she slapped me away and attacked my face. One of the soldiers restrained her. She cursed and yelled at me. I looked at Mariam and Lillian, looks of confusion on their tiny faces. Steppe smiled at me, then signaled to his soldiers. Two of them approached me, forced me to the ground, and bound my arms and legs. They carried me off.

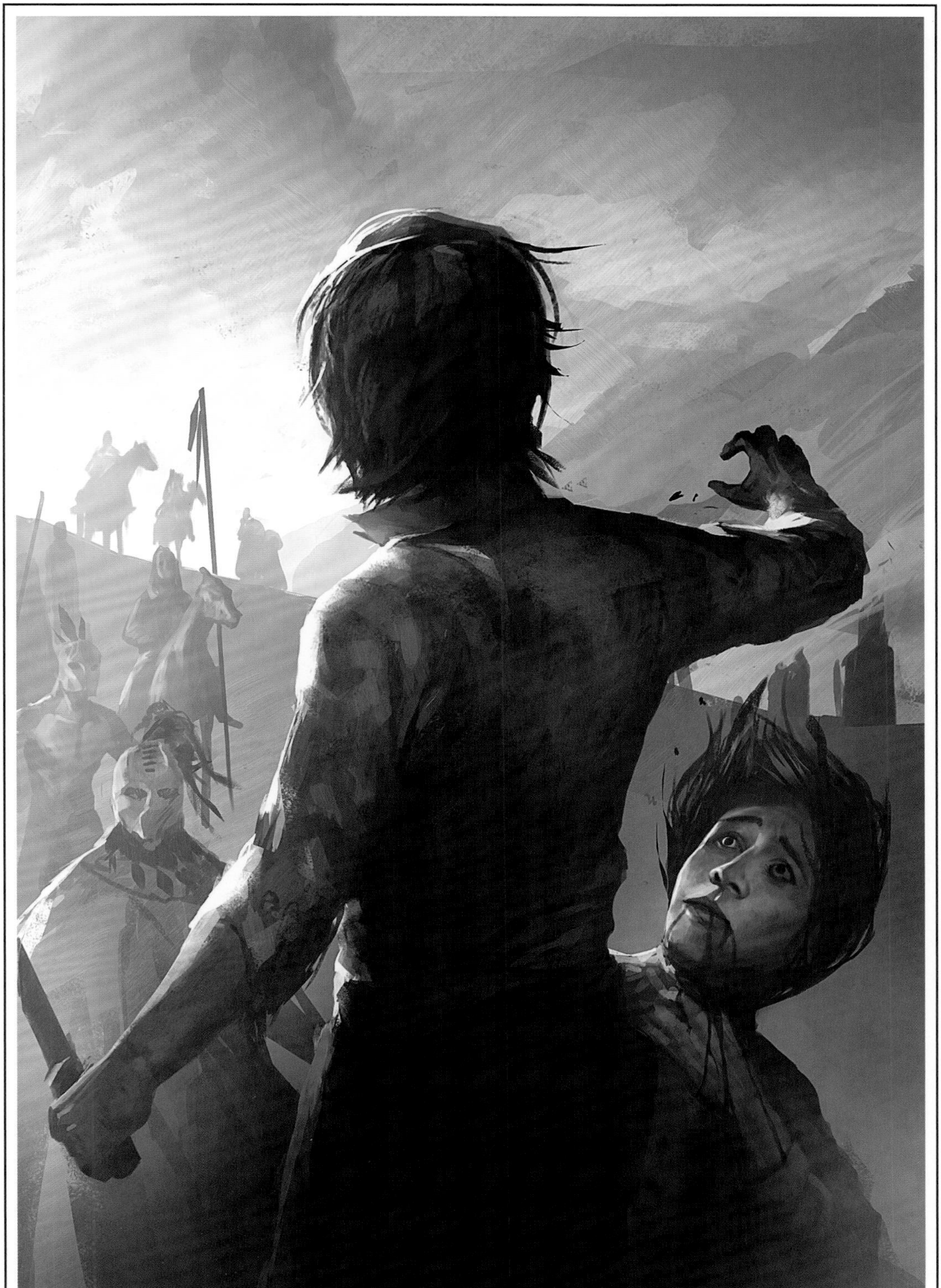

I listened to my mother scream. Even if she rejected me as her son, I vowed to return one day to save her.

There was no more fighting it. In fact, I decided during my breaking period, when I was put through the rigors of army training, to become the best soldier possible. Not because my loyalties had changed in the slightest; rather, because I would only earn revenge on Steppe if I was a product of his system. Adopting the training and doctrine would make me appear like all of his other soldiers. This taught me great patience and restraint. So often I wanted to flee or kill, yet I suppressed these urges in order to learn like everyone else. The main difference between the others and myself was that I was much younger and much quicker to learn. Being promoted in the Steppe Army is close to impossible, for so many young men are forced into service; I'd joined just as the army was growing exponentially. More training grounds were erected, more uniforms stitched, and more weapons constructed. This was no longer the small army intended to protect against invasion—this was an army of conquest and rampage. Steppe was restructuring Hetra in his image, and his army would clear the path for him.

Even though the likelihood of me rising in the ranks was slim, I challenged myself to be a great soldier. This destroyed me every day, for I thought only of how disappointed my father would be to see me as a disciple of Steppe's, though he would have to trust my master plan. In retrospect, it was the only option I had. If I planned to stay alive and avenge my family, I had to become a great soldier in the Steppe Army.

My encounters with Steppe were few and far between. Depending on who was telling, the army had grown to a million strong. Regardless of the fact that I never saw Steppe, my commanding officers would often send word to him that "this Grey boy shows great promise," which Steppe would have viewed with a skeptical eye. He did not seem like a paranoid sort, especially since all of Hetra feared him, but he had to know that I would one day come after him.

It took me four years to rise in rank and sport the title of colonel. Colonel was a respectable position and it offered my first true test, a task that pushed my willingness to stick with my ultimate plan. I was called up by Steppe along with a few other officers. He was voicing publicly what my father had known eight years prior: he was now ready to seize the cities of Hetra. Timpast was already in his control, but the other four cities were not willing participants in his great drama. It surprised me greatly that he attempted diplomatic measures at all; he was not a man of negotiations and treaties. We were gathered to hear of his master plan, and more importantly, the first steps toward achieving it.

Steppe addressed us as a general and motivator.

"The leaders of the free cities of Hetra are blind and ignorant. I have offered a peaceful takeover for each of the four remaining cities. Our men would occupy their streets, but rule from a distance. That is ideal for all of us. My intentions were not to stomp these leaders out, but they leave me with no choice. They see no benefit in a supreme ruler; they live in the past.

"Our first order of business is to take Inim. Its leaders are the most resistant. Whether this is due to its freestanding army or its geographical positioning or learned populace, I do not know, nor do I care. My hope is that once we remove their leadership, the citizens of Inim and all the nearby villages will support us. We are capable of shedding much blood, but I would rather not in this instance. Their ability to ward off invaders is unrivaled. Even we in Timpast, with our Blackbin shield, cannot compete with the Dinorvan Mountains. You who have never been there will reconsider everything you know about warfare as soon as you attempt to pass through those mountains. Their peaks touch the suns and provide no clear routes. Predators are few, unless you believe the legendary stories of the Dinorvan Tigers that stalk men in the mountain's caves. I recognize the improbability of succeeding with a mountain approach, but it is our greatest hope of sending a wave of shock through this nation. Nobody thinks Inim can fall, and we will strike them where they have never been attacked before. I am sending Isaac Foster Grey and a small order of men through the Dinorvans to the capital building. It is there the leaders will fall, and I will march our men through the front gates of Inim."

This was the first I had heard of Steppe's plan for me to lead a group of men through Inim. I didn't know if he felt I was the most qualified for such a treacherous mission, or if he was purposefully sending me to my death. Perhaps it was both, and either result would satisfy him. Regardless, I was charged with leading a team of soldiers, all older than me, on the most important mission in the history of the Steppe Army. If it was a success, as many hoped it would be, the tides would turn for Hetra.

I had never traveled to Inim, for it had always isolated itself from the rest of Hetra. Geographically, it was as far north and west as it could be, making trips burdensome for most travelers and traders. The villages to the south were extremely loyal to the city, providing most of the agriculture and livestock Inim's citizens needed to survive. The leaders of Inim could not promise protection as much as they could promise the potential for protection—Inim had never been sacked by invaders, all thanks to the Dinorvans. It was rumored that the shores of the north side of the Dinorvans were littered with ship carcasses. Besides the protection of the mountains and an isolated location, those who sought refuge in Inim would face a journey rife with danger. The most direct route would be to travel through Blackbin, though the chance of surviving was slim. The other more common option was to go east, cross the Gorndon River, travel north through the untempered east, then cross the Gorndon River yet again. While the Gorndon flows bountifully, it is difficult to cross, and it has stolen the lives of many who have attempted it.

With such a perilous path to Inim, one might wonder why anyone would attempt to reach its gates. The answer to that question was quite obvious to its residents: Inim is the city of science, invention, intellect, and progress. Great minds throughout history faced daunting obstacles to become citizens there, to work freely and do the work that would push the world forward. Steppe understood better than anyone that toppling Inim would be a greater symbolic victory than military victory. It was also his hope to exploit the citizens to his benefit.

After poring over different maps and consulting with Steppe's advisors, I chose the most unconventional route to Inim: I would lead my men west through Blackbin to the Heling River, and from there travel to the southernmost passing of the Dinorvans. From there we would attempt what few men ever had: we would travel through the vast net-

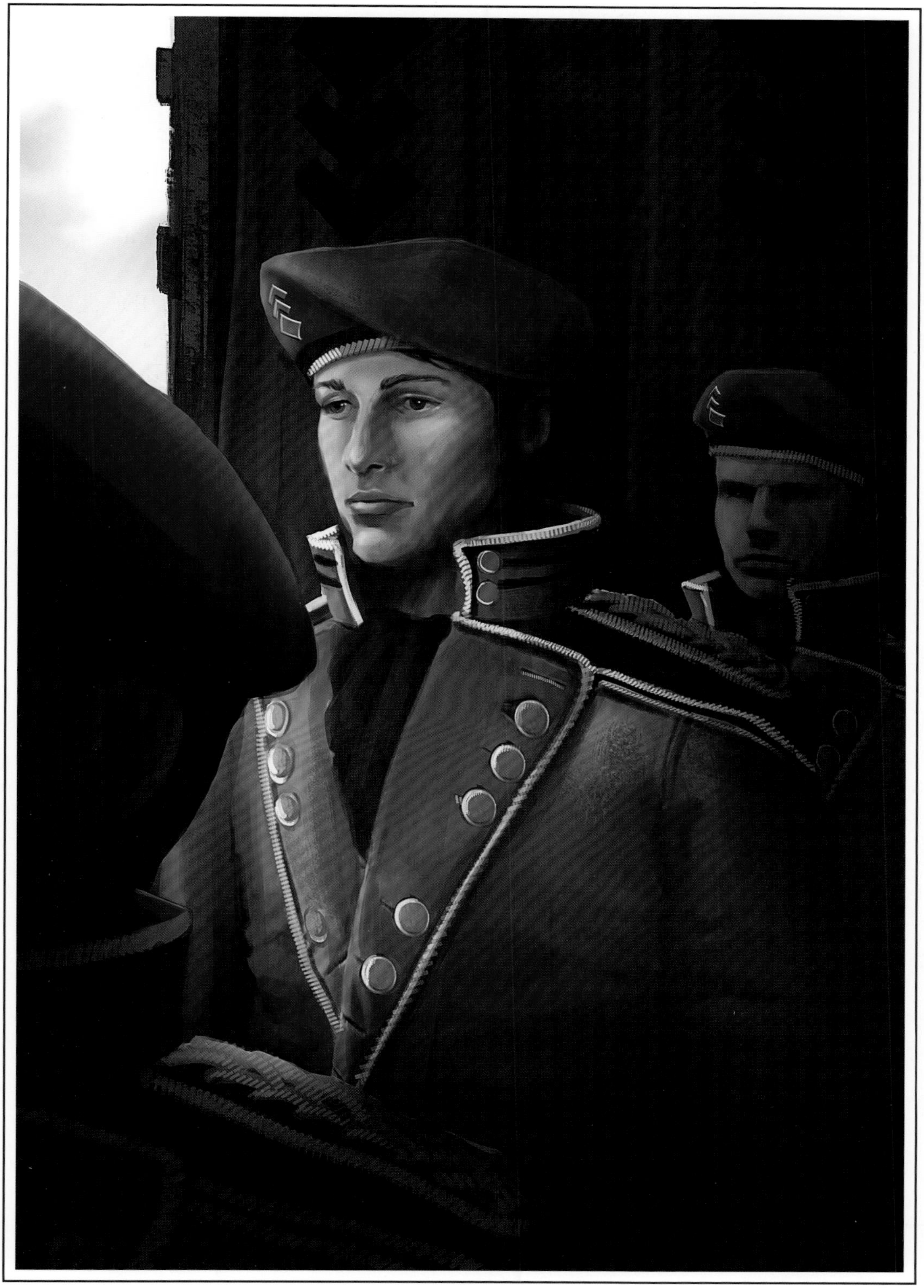

work of caves carved within the great chain of mountains.

Steppe approved my plan and said prior to our departure, "I may be a fool for trusting you."

He wasn't—at least not in this case—because I planned to complete the mission and set into motion his conquering of Hetra. It would have been easy for me to kill him then, but I knew that he had to rise to greater heights before I knocked him down; his fall would be far and the echoes of his screams would reverberate throughout the world. Only then would I be able to save my mother and sisters.

Five men were assigned to me, all qualified for such work, though I was distraught by having such a small platoon. Not all of us could be expected to survive the journey, let alone the specifics of the mission. Steppe argued that he could not afford to send too many men, for he was going to march a few thousand men to Nacht Lake, just eighty miles to the south of Inim. Once our mission of removing the Inim Council was complete, we would send signals to some of his rangers, who would, in turn, inform Steppe. The General would move his men to Inim and take over. The strategy was brilliant, even with the slim possibility that it would actually work. Not only was Steppe changing the course of Hetra, he was rewriting military strategy.

The night before our departure, I met the men assigned to me. At sixteen, I was the youngest, though only by a narrow margin. These five young men, Kresge, Best, Perphin, Lone, and Tavears, were neither the best nor the worst at soldiering, though all of them had a leanness to them that led me to believe they knew how to survive. Survival was the key to our success, for the actual mission of assassinating Inim's leaders would be easy compared to reaching them.

Steppe was concerned that there were spies in his army, so he announced that we were going to travel east, then sent us off in the night. We traveled silently, cautious not to attract the attention of any Fortache or White Wolves. After three days we needed to set up camp, hunt, and rest. Kresge and Tavears volunteered to build a fire and create a cover while the rest of us went off to hunt. The other three weren't very skilled hunters, but they did not get in the way, either. I trapped three galrabbits and the others seemed quite impressed; they shouldn't have been, because they were all gaunt beasts. I was too fatigued to hunt anymore, and the meat from the galrabbits would only sustain us for one day.

Once we returned to camp, skinned the beasts, and cooked them, there was hardly enough meat for even one man to feel satisfied. We divided the food and rested, warmed by the fire. My hope was to sleep for a few hours and use the sunlight to guide us to the Heling River by the next nightfall. Lone had other things on his mind.

"Your dad's the traitor we're all told about," said Lone matter-of-factly, picking his teeth with a galrabbit's leg bone. "Was a hero once, but turned on the General. Ain't I right?"

The others kept their eyes on me in anticipation. Their sudden attention told me they had spoken about this prior to our departure and Lone had been the one elected to elicit such a sordid topic. Before responding, I finished my meager portions. "It's what we've all been taught."

"Don't take that line with me," said Lone.

"Must I remind you that I am your commanding officer? That it is the great General Steppe who values my expertise in Blackbin navigation and covert strategies and chose you to follow? That if I were to disappear this very moment you would be lost to your loved ones forever? That you would be killed by a Fortache warrior, or feasted on by a White Wolf, or—and I wish this upon no man—a Korbear?"

"All that talk don't scare me off. I could kill you easy. I'm a lot better soldier than you think. And I don't think you're much of a commanding officer," said Lone.

"Then you should not have picked this mission," I said.

"I had no choice," said Lone.

"Leave it," said Kresge. "He's in charge and we have to trust he knows what he's doing."

"You're dumber than I thought, Kresge, if you trust him," said Lone.

"He's gotten us this far," said Tavears.

"We ain't nowhere yet," said Lone.

"In a day's time we'll be at the Heling," said Perphin.

"I say we can't trust him," said Lone. "His father's a traitor and that makes him a traitor."

Best stood up. He was short in height, but he had broad shoulders and the demeanor of a wild dog. Of the five young men with me, he was the only one I couldn't take for certain in a hand-to-hand fight. He was probably a kid from the slums of Timpast who would never lose that lean look of hunger that haunted his eyes. "Why don't you keep quiet, Lone, so we can rest."

"We're being led by a traitor right to our deaths," said Lone.

"Maybe we'll kill you if you don't shut up," said Tavears.

"I'd like to see any of you try," said Lone.

I spoke calmly, holding my rage at bay. "I was eight years old when I watched the General kill my father. He deserved it. Steppe is the only man who can govern Hetra. And after my brother refused to pledge his loyalty to the General, I killed him myself. Did you hear that part of the story? Or did you only listen when they mentioned my father was a traitor? If anyone here knows what becomes of traitors, it is me. I don't give a damn if you want to be led by me or not. A Fortache could sneak up behind you and slit your throat and it would mean nothing to me. So if it bothers you so much that my father, who even as a traitor was still more of a soldier than you, betrayed the General and this nation, I suggest you find your way back to Steppe and explain that to the General."

Best smiled and sat down. Not another word was spoken that night.

By the time the first sun began to rise, the fire had died out and Tavears was missing. Nobody had seen him wander off, and he'd been gone too long to simply be freeing his bowels or bladder. Lone studied me, convincing himself that I was somehow responsible. I reminded everyone that we needed to move onward if we were going to reach the Heling River before the suns set. The men looked very uneasy about this. I knew they would protest, but as the commanding officer, I had to take action.

"The General has high expectations of us. None of us know what happened to Tavears, but we must assume that he fled willingly. Now pack up and move out."

They did so. We started south and only made it a few hundred yards before we discovered Tavears. His head, severed and pierced through with a pike, hovered at eye-level atop a spear planted in the earth. His body was nowhere to be seen. My first concern was that we would quickly be surrounded by those that committed this horrific act, and as I turned toward my platoon I was faced with the end of a rifle. Lone aimed between my eyes. The other soldiers were too shocked to rationalize with him. Lone did not waver.

"Put the gun down."

"You did this! I tried to tell you he would do this!" said Lone. The others were lost in their imaginations, piecing together the gruesome details of what had happened to Tavears, each undoubtedly grateful it had not happened to him.

"Do not listen to him!"

"I'm the only one they should listen to!" said Lone.

"If you kill me, you are killing yourself. You cannot get out of here without me." I tried to make eye contact with the other three, but they were transfixed by Tavears's head.

"I'll try!" said Lone. I watched as his finger, firmly gripping the trigger, started to contract. I moved my head to the right and brought my right arm up, connecting with the gun just as it fired. I punched Lone in the jaw, knocking him down. Perphin reached for his gun, and I realized that, in his confusion, he too thought I had killed Tavears. So I fled, using Blackbin as my shield. Perphin unloaded his gun, though no bullet reached me. I needed to move north, deeper into Blackbin, where I'd find refuge from my own men. It was impossible to know what the men thought about the incident; the only logical move I could make involved me fending for myself.

Days passed, and I had to move slowly to the north. Each move I made was the result of great analysis. My greatest allies were the natural hiding places Blackbin provided. In all that time, with nothing but my thoughts, I decided that Uryston was providing me with the opportunity to flee. My life was not one of revenge. I would either avoid or kill the remaining four soldiers, move north through Blackbin, and upon freedom from the great forest, work my way east and find a ship sailing from Hetra. Fate would have me elsewhere. Yet the more I tried to convince myself that this was true, the more I knew it would not be—

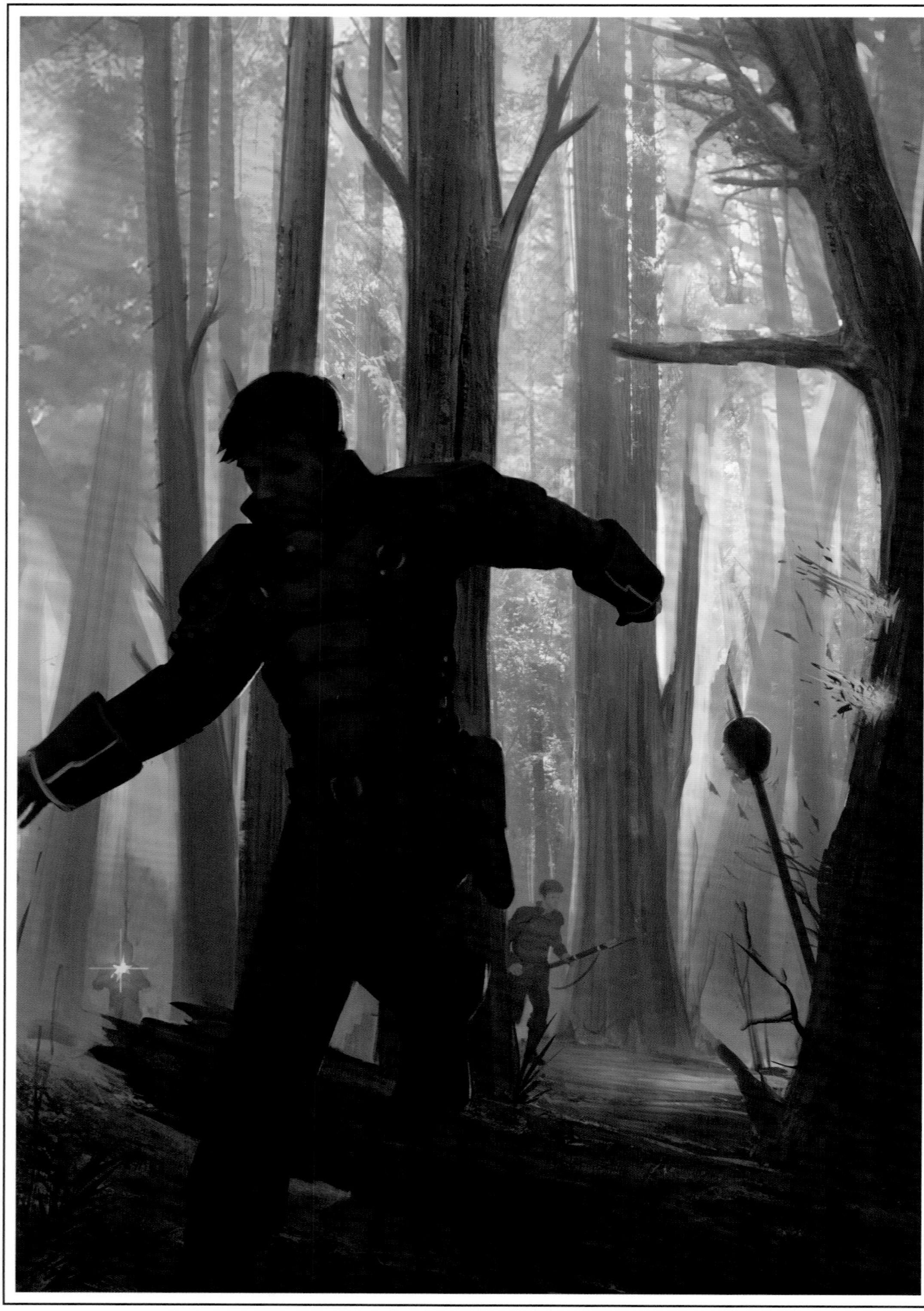

for what greater purpose could be in store for me other than killing Steppe and freeing my family from Purg?

Hunger set in, and the more I tried to ignore it or fight it, the more my senses betrayed me. I heard noises that nothing in Blackbin could produce, smelled the wonders held by warm yellowberry tarts, and realized I needed to rest.

Perching in the embrace of two branches, I tried to rest when I looked out to a clearing just behind some Wild Kenning bushes. Eniam, in her black garbs and scythe posture, stood and watched me. What did she see? Was this some message from Uryston or Wareis? I pressed upward on my eyelids to omit as much light as possible, needing to see her more clearly. She was gone before I understood her purpose, though I strained to see her and fell from my nest. The fall was broken by the pistol strapped to my waist; it broke into four pieces, and I did not have the tools to repair it. I cursed the gods and tossed the remnants of the pistol into the Wild Kenning bushes. The only option I had was to hunt and feed, although I knew that I could not waste time building a fire. Galrabbits, my easiest prey to obtain, would kill me if eaten raw. This left me in a troubling position: the only animal meat that could be eaten raw, at least as far as I had heard, was that of the Korbear. But this could have been nothing more than a myth, for the Korbears were almost legendary—they barely left their dens, and they were impossible for one man to kill.

I gathered a few thick branches of varying sizes and found refuge underneath a cluster of fallen Brown Oak trees. The trunks were turning to ash, and some beast had once burrowed underneath the natural protection. I lay on my back to relieve the pain of my right side; the ugly effects of the fall had been hidden, at least immediately afterwards, but soon my right leg began to feel as if it was being pierced by pins. The pain grew worse the longer I remained stagnant.

I worked the knife with quick precision to fashion the branches into sharp points; so far I lacked a strategy, though having proper weapons provided some assurance. I thought of what Kelman had told me back in Purg: never hunt with your knife. I secured my knife in my boot and crawled out from under the trees. I limped to the nearest Wild Kenning bush and broke off one of its nimble branches to bind my five spears together. Climbing the tall Brown Oak was murder on my leg, but I could not hunt anything on the ground. Every creature I was likely to encounter would be too fast and cunning and would either tear out my throat out or flee. Any chance I had of killing anything would start with me attacking from above.

Sitting and waiting was something any hunter needed to learn, though I was not able to think of anything but my hunger. I must have waited for three hours before I witnessed the artful work of my enemy. A female White Wolf, distinguishable from the males by the grey streak along her back, stalked out of the shadows with two lifeless galrabbits in its mouth. I'd always heard that White Wolves ate their kills on the spot, leaving no trail of dead-beast scent to their dwellings, so seeing that White Wolf with two galrabbits in its mouth struck me as odd; I could have, of course, been misinformed about the habits of the White Wolves, though the reasoning seemed logical. I watched as the White Wolf placed the galrabbits atop one of the fallen Brown Oak trees, then retreated to the hiding place I had used just a few hours earlier. I understood the reasoning behind her actions: she was luring something to her, but who? The only creature with a taste for galrabbit, at least as far as I knew, was the White Wolf, but I could not imagine one White Wolf hunting another.

The reason I could not imagine it was because it was not her intention to catch a White Wolf after all, but rather a much bigger game. Out of the east came a Korbear, a golden-haired behemoth, a beast that ruled Blackbin by sheer size, force, and aggression. It was one thing to have read about them and studied sketches in old books, but seeing one was something altogether frightening. I could not breathe in its presence. All I could look at was its long, powerful jaw that protruded far from its face, and its claws that looked like curved knives. From what I read, the Korbears had a keen sense of smell, and I prayed to Uryston that the scent of the dead galrabbits was stronger than mine.

Something in the Brown Oak across from the one in which I was perched caught the Korbear's attention. It stood on its legs and swatted at one of the branches. A flock of Hamil Jays exploded into the sky, trying to reach the heavens before being snatched by the Korbear. On its hind legs, the Korbear exceeded twenty feet in height, but even more impressive was how he climbed the tree and swatted two Jays to the ground. The birds were dead before they hit the ground, and the Korbear dropped and hit with such force that my tree shook.

The Korbear tore both Jays to shreds for just that hint of meat, then continued on to the fallen trees. It spotted the galrabbits and picked them up in its mouth. This was exactly what the White Wolf had planned; she sprang from her hiding spot and clenched her teeth around the Korbear's throat. The Korbear spun to his right and collapsed atop the fallen trees, rolling backwards. The White Wolf held on, even as the Korbear rolled onto his belly. I could not believe that I was witnessing something so profound, and this amazement kept me from doing what I should have done: escaped. Without realizing it, I was standing up to procure a better view of the struggle between these two magnificent beasts. The Korbear, swinging both arms at a furious rate, finally freed himself from the White Wolf's lock.

My sense of logic returned, and I grabbed the spears I had just fashioned. Thinking clearly was to my advantage, although I'd lost my opportunity to flee—I should have dropped and ran while the Korbear struggled to loosen the White Wolf from his throat. Now the Korbear was backing toward me, the golden fur around its neck caked in blood. The White Wolf licked the wounds near her ribs. Tasting her own blood brought about a newfound sense of purpose and viciousness. The Korbear sensed this too and stood up, his head within reach of my grasp. The White Wolf lurched around, and I could not understand why the Korbear did not attack.

The White Wolf leapt and knocked into the Korbear's belly. The Korbear stumbled into my Brown Oak, and I had but two choices to make: fall to the ground, susceptible to attacks from both, or cling to the Korbear's back. I could not remain in the tree, for the Korbear hit it with such force that the tree shook violently. I chose the second option and grabbed onto the Korbear's fur with my right hand as I held onto my spears with my left hand. The Korbear sensed my presence immediately and tried to grab me, but my position was such that he could not. He concentrated on the White Wolf instead and collapsed onto his belly to crush her.

I flew off the Korbear's back and scrambled toward the Wild

Kennings. I was knocked to the floor by the corpse of the White Wolf, whose spine was snapped in half and jaw jutted forty-five degrees to the left. The females average five feet in height and eight feet in length, and I could not guess how much they weighed, knowing only that it was far too much weight for me to lift upward and free myself.

I pushed the White Wolf's belly toward my feet and tried to dig into the ground with my heels to roll her off me. The Korbear spotted my struggle and charged toward me. Instead of making one last attempt to move the White Wolf, I held fast to my spears and prepared to give a good fight before dying. I sat up as far as I could, and the Korbear knocked the White Wolf off of me, scraping his claw across my arm in the process. Ignoring the pain was impossible, although I was driven by instinct. I raised my spears just as the Korbear tried to bite down on my torso. The Korbear's hot breath engulfed my arms and I released my hands from the spears.

Before I could grasp what was happening, I rolled away from the Korbear's thrashing arms. He swung with the sole purpose of killing me, but he was choking on the spears and could not connect. I gathered my strength and sprinted toward the nearest Brown Oak and climbed, ignoring the pain that flowed rapidly through my body. The higher I climbed, the safer I thought I was, but the Korbear finally realized where I had escaped to and attacked the tree. I clung to a branch with my arms and legs, but once the Korbear realized I would not fall, he climbed toward me. I took the knife from my boot and took a leap of faith. I planted my knife in the Korbear's shoulder and it dragged down to his neck as we fell together.

The Korbear landed on his back and I atop his chest. Before the Korbear could react again, I pulled the knife across his throat and rolled off, crawling toward the base of the tree. The Korbear turned over with its last gasp of life, and I watched with profound relief as he died.

My wound looked worse than it felt, though I knew the pain would set in momentarily. There was no use worrying about the profuse bleeding or not having any bandages. To maintain any semblance of energy, I needed to eat. I had to cut into the Korbear. I crawled over to him and worked as quickly as I could, never having managed such a task

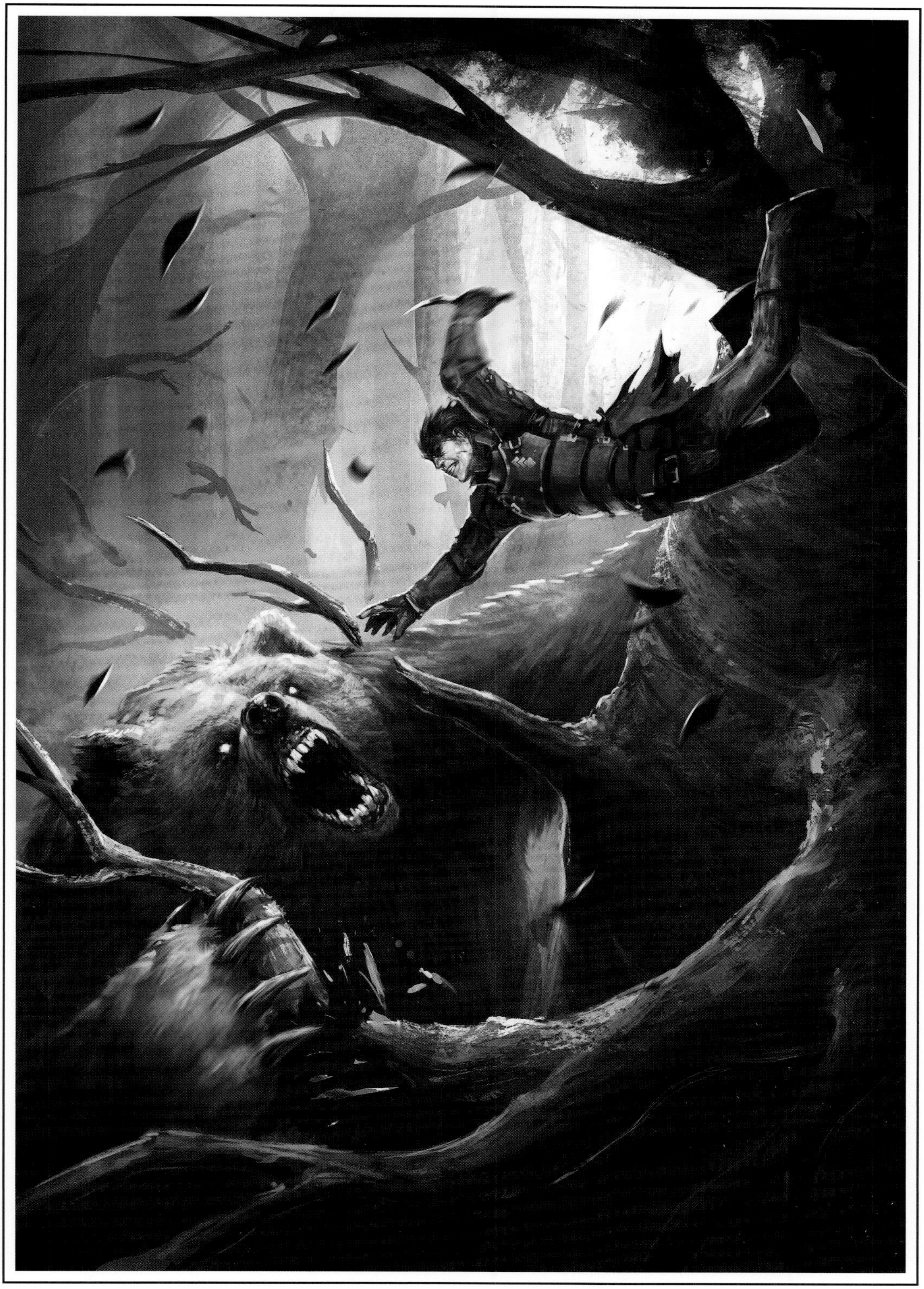

before. My butchering was worse than amateur, though I only needed to get any meat I could. Having never tasted Korbear before, I nearly vomited, yet I choked it down. My mouth filled with the taste of the raw flesh and I ignored how vile it was. I cut and ate, cut and ate, until my stomach was full. The Korbear, dead and dissected, still looked like a fierce creature. All of the pain in my body rushed to my knees and I collapsed on top of the Korbear; I turned and rested my back against him, wanting nothing more than to sleep. I fought against it, amusing myself with the thought of how I must have looked.

Kresge's voice carried over the trees. I didn't have the energy or will to move from my spot and hoped that the soldiers wouldn't have the nerve to approach the dead beasts, believing they'd encroached on a den. The soldiers whispered among themselves until they spotted me. Lone kept his distance, though the others formed around me quickly. My appearance must have been quite frightening, with the blood seeping from my arm and my face stained with Korbear blood—perhaps they assumed that I had killed the fierce beast with my own teeth!

Best removed his jacket and cut the arm from it; he wrapped it around my arm and fastened it with the strap from his holster. The tightening of the strap amplified the pain and I clenched my teeth to suppress a scream. Once the pain subsided, I thanked Best and he simply nodded his head. He continued to view me as his commanding officer, and this alone told me that the indiscretion from a few days prior no longer swayed their judgment. At least not for Kresge, Best, and Perphin—Lone, I knew, would prefer swallowing hot stones to saluting me.

"You killed a White Wolf and a Korbear?" said Best.

"I didn't think Korbears were real," said Kresge.

"They are. And I only killed the Korbear."

"How?" said Perphin.

"By forgetting I was only a man for a minute."

"I didn't hear any gunshots," said Lone.

"That's because I didn't use a gun."

Silence hung over our rough-looking crew for a minute as the other four tried to decide if I was lying or not. They seemed to realize quickly that the truth did not matter at the moment.

"We're lost," said Kresge.

"We're not."

"We stopped trying to find you yesterday. Maybe before that. And we tried to leave. I think we walked for eighteen hours straight and can't find our way out. We're not even that deep into Blackbin," said Perphin.

"The gods designed it as their own field of play. Men are supposed to wander off and die in here. But I assure you we are not lost."

"Then why don't you lead us out. Isn't that what you're to do? Lead?" said Lone.

I stood, using more strength than I ought to have, just to prove to him that I wasn't weak. "I'll do that as soon as you four eat."

"We don't have food," said Lone.

"We do." I cut into the Korbear's flank and held out a chunk of meat for anyone to grab. They looked at it with suspicion. "It's either this or you starve. We're moving out soon whether you eat or not, but don't expect to make it far on an empty stomach."

"Can't we build a fire, cook the meat, and rest awhile?" said Kresge.

"Korbear meat is best eaten raw."

"We'll get—"

"You won't. I just ate about a pound. It tastes miserable, but it will keep us going till we get to the Heling. There we can get some fish, maybe some vegetables too. There will be some traders there."

"It won't take but a few minutes to build a fire," said Best.

"Look there." I hobbled over to a nearby Brown Oak. It was marked with holes from crossbow target practice. "Nothing in nature burrows like that. The Fortache made those. If we start a fire, we'll be inviting our own deaths. And as far as resting is concerned, we won't have a speck of it till after we get back from killing the Inim Council. To make that happen, we all need to work together. So forget about everything that's bothering you and start eating."

Best took the first hunk of meat and chewed through it with a look of disgust on his face. The others waited for his reaction before taking their own share. Once he swallowed the food, he held his hand out for a second serving. I cut him a piece, handed it to him, and carved again into the Korbear. Everyone, even Lone, ate till they were full. Instead of resting, which all of us wanted to do, we pressed on, moving our way to the south and the west.

We were a few days behind schedule, and it would have been easier to move further north and west till we found a good entryway to the Dinorvans, but I was concerned that we had already caused enough chaos in Blackbin and that if we made it out of Blackbin on its northwest front, we would certainly encounter Inim loyalists that would send word of our journey. Paradoxically, traveling through the Dinorvans was both the safest and most treacherous route we could take; there would be no spies or enemies to greet us at any turn, but few men had ever attempted to travel its rough course, leaving no word of safe routes.

We arrived in a small makeshift village at the mouth of the Dinorvans early the next morning. There were about two dozen families camped on either side of the Heling. Word of our sudden arrival spread quickly, and the residents expected that we were there to pillage. Two gentlemen dutifully approached us and I explained that we were there only to buy some goods and potentially learn the best route to Inim. I showed my purse to prove that we were truly there to pay for our goods, and this eased the demeanors of both men. I told my men to wander about until they found certain things we needed, especially weapons, ammunition, and foods that would last for more than a few days, as I went off with the gentlemen. They led me to Daryus and Dovive, an elderly couple whose wrinkled faces told the stories of many generations.

It was custom to formally introduce visitors to the elders of a village, even one less established and unnamed as this one. The couple had grown old together and, strangely enough, resembled each other. Dovive, in her long white dress and rope of hair hanging down to the floor, offered me Wrostlet petals in warm water from the Heling. I knew to take the drink as a sign of respect, ignoring the bitter taste. I finished in one gulp and handed her the clay bowl.

"Eat these," she said, removing the petals with her right pointer finger. The orange remnants of the flowers, typically only found in the north, were best swallowed without chewing—the taste would remain in your mouth for months, tainting everything you ate. Without my permission, she unwrapped the bandage on my left arm and ran her fingers across my wounds. "Korbear." I nodded and she smiled. "It's dead." I nodded again. "You are now part Korbear."

"What do you mean?"

"You have killed it? Yourself?" she said.

"Yes. Yesterday."

"Any man who is cut by the Korbear and kills the Korbear carries the spirit of the Korbear. Forever. You are a special young man," said Dovive.

"I ate its flesh."

"Your spirit is mixed. Let the wound breathe. It is contained and will heal," she said.

"The pain has not subsided."

"It takes days for the spirits to join. The mark will be there till long after you die," she said.

"I'm concerned about infection."

"It is you who infected the Korbear," she said.

"You confuse our guest," said Daryus. "First you offer him the Wrostlet tea, and then you offer him your interpretations. Let him be. Let him feast on our salted Terma. Let him drink the Cuday wine. Let him enjoy the company of our daughters. And more than anything, let him tell us why he brings the ravagers to our home."

"My men and I mean no harm with our intrusion. We are representatives of the Steppe Army. I cannot tell you why we are traveling, but I can say that we are headed to Inim. We were hoping to buy some supplies and learn of possible routes."

"You travel from Timpast?" said Daryus. I nodded my head. "Then you know the route to Inim. It's clear north of where you were. This has been drawn in the maps for centuries. If you cannot follow the stars north, I suggest hiring a man that can."

"We need new routes. Blackbin is too dangerous and it will take too long to cross the Gorndon twice."

"What will work best for you is to tell your General to not establish a base in Timpast or have relations with Inim. Or perhaps he can bring wreckage to Blackbin, if that is the greatest obstacle to your journey," said Daryus.

"That's impossible."

"That might also be true of finding a new route. Especially if you wish to stay on land. Are you and your men sea-ready?" said Daryus.

"I can't speak for them."

"You're their commander, are you not?" he said.

"Yes, but—"

"Then you are expected to speak for them," said Daryus.

"Then yes."

"The Vundallia Ocean is plentiful and calm on our western shores. There are men here who could take you to the north. If you have money to pay them," said Daryus.

"We do."

"The General's riches know no bounds," said Daryus. "Remain with us today. Eat and rest. We are an agreeable lot. In the night you will leave. One of our men will sail you to the north. Pay him double what he charges. None of us will forget that."

"You can see the Korbear in him already," said Dovive.

I had not seen my reflection, yet I believed every word she had spoken. I was not the same person.

With our departure from that small village, I did not expect to alter the course of Hetra's future in quite the way that I did. Our mission, of course, was to alter the power dynamics of the nation, removing the leadership council from Inim and sending a message to the other cities that the General was going to be the absolute ruler whether they agreed or disagreed. My participation in this plan was selfish, because I was simply making as many attempts as possible for the General to trust me, to allow me into his fold of closest advisors, so that I could ultimately kill him. With the benefit of hindsight, I see how narrow this thinking was, because though I planned on his murder and my immediate departure, I did not have any details worked out. Which is exactly why Uryston intervened.

We chartered a small boat to sail north along the western coast of Hetra. This was a view unfamiliar to most inhabitants of the country, since Hetra did not produce great explorers or traders, its inhabitants instead mostly isolationists. Our captain was a young man with little experience on the unforgiving oceans, though he was capable enough to set our course and maintain it. He spoke little, and I don't know if I ever knew his name. My soldiers were in a state of absolute discomfort while on that boat. Sailors and the sort might be born with seawater in their veins, but men who have never graced the sea do not have a natural inclination for it, and it is quite apparent whether or not a man has only stood upon dry land. The ocean is not so much cruel or punishing as it is indifferent. At times it tossed our boat with viciousness, while other times it gently rocked us with the care of a new mother.

It was difficult to know if we were making progress, for our view of Hetra was of the unfamiliar side of the Dinorvans. The mountains were majestic, but it would require an expert or cartographer to distinguish the differences between one pass and another. I asked our captain on many occasions how many days our voyage would take, and he never gave a clear answer. This seemed like ignorance at the time, yet in his defense I would now argue that he did not know because we did not have a specific destination in mind; we were not traveling to a port, and I believed that we would know the best place to begin our climb once we laid eyes upon it. The young captain did not seem to mind, since he was being compensated handsomely.

Our foolish plan was thwarted on the fifth day of our voyage. The specificity and details could never be removed from my memory, even long after I perish from this world. Lone and Kresge were attempting to catch fish with some rods they had purchased from the villagers—and as to not blame the craftsmanship of the rods, it should be noted that neither had any prior fishing experience, nor had they purchased any suitable bait to be used with their rods. They busied themselves with their task for a few hours as Perphin and Best attempted to rest. Sleeping on the boat was another matter entirely. The vessel was too small for six men to fit comfortably, let alone lay down for sleep at once. We had to sleep in shifts, and anyone who drew the daytime hours could hardly sleep at all with the two suns shining brightly overhead. The captain claimed that the suns, while punishing with their warmth and brightness, were the best guides and indicators for a perilous-free journey. Once black clouds blocked the suns, a storm would soon follow and our tiny vessel would certainly be destroyed. I wondered how often a terrible storm came through on the western shores and our captain replied with, "It's unpredictable." This was not the assurance that I was looking for, although I should not have expected so much from such an inexperienced captain.

As it turned out, weather was not what I should have been concerned with anyway. At the exact moment that Lone started to make a great fuss about something at the end of his line, my attention was drawn further out to sea—not on the water, mind you, but in the sky. The rest of the men on the boat were making great attempts to lure in whatever creature had hooked itself onto Lone's line. I stared as a vessel floated in the air toward us.

Not only did the sight of this strange flying object render me speechless, but I could not even form reasonable thoughts. My initial instinct was that I was imagining it, something my mind had conjured from sleep and food deprivation. I settled on this explanation for a few moments, incapable of reacting rationally. Then the vessel coursed in front of the first sun, creating a great shadow over our small boat. Best turned and bumped into me, nearly knocking me into the sea.

"What?" said Best, the only word he or anyone else could conjure.

As the vessel neared, my eyes, if not my comprehension, could absorb its awesomeness. It was a spectacle of innovation and design. To describe it is not to do it justice, though the first airship I ever witnessed has branded itself upon my memory. Its basic shape was similar to that of a massive sailing ship, though it did not seem to be made of wood. The hull was painted a greyish-black with thin red strips that ran the middle; there were black circles across the bottoms and sides, all sealed; the top sides of the hull flared out in the gesture of a bird displaying its wings; the interior was impossible to see, though what kept it afloat was not—extending out from either sides of the wings and from the tall poles atop the vessel were massive cylindrical-shaped containers, brimming with fire. It was not a thing I ever expected to see in my lifetime, nor had I ever imagined that such a thing could exist.

Perphin fell from the boat. Nobody helped him back inside. The captain began praying, and his mutterings triggered something in Lone. Lone picked up his rifle and fired at the airship while emptying

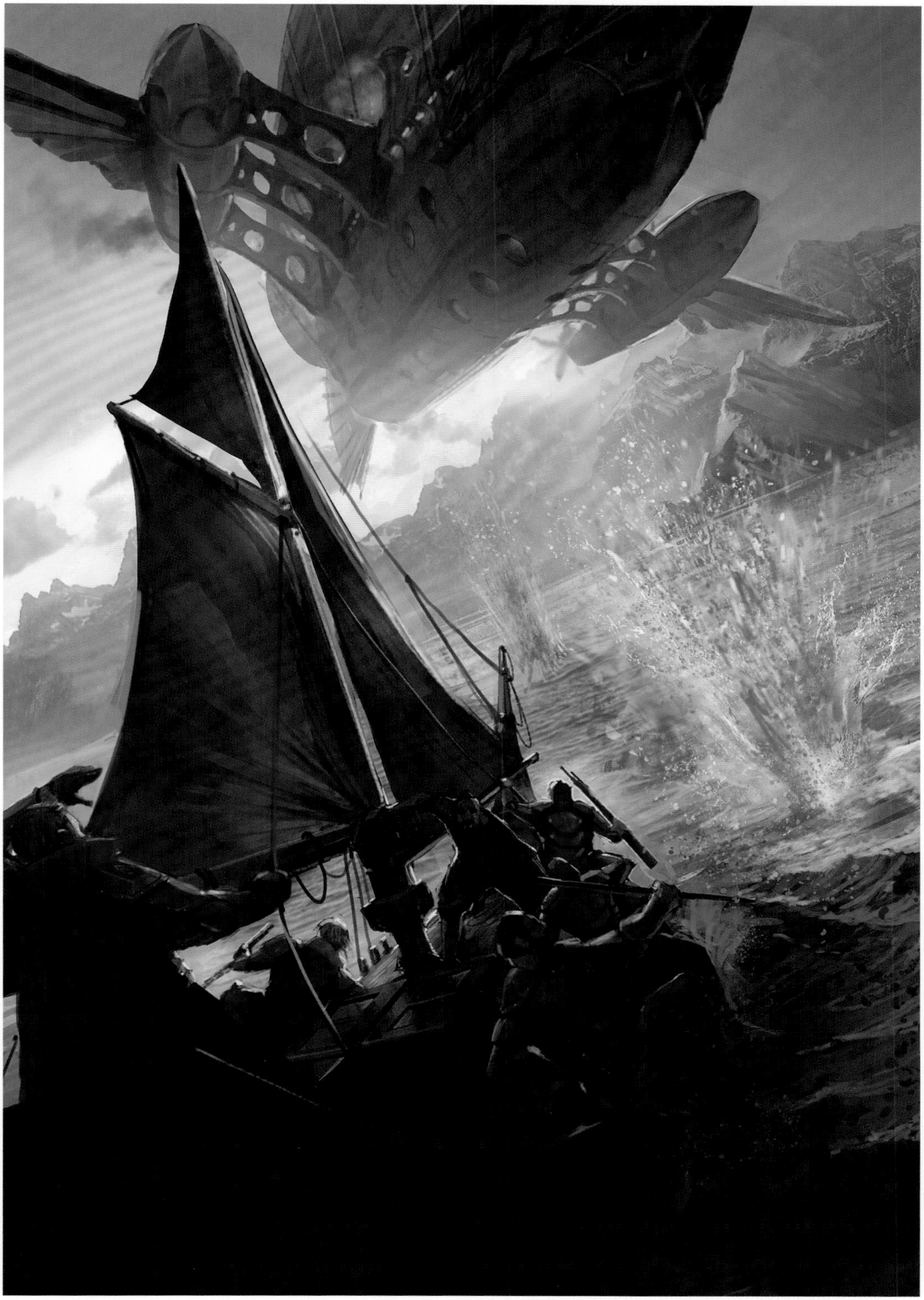

his lungs with a great scream. He continued to pull the trigger even after his rifle was emptied. The next thing that occurred was both unbelievable and fitting. One of the black circles on the side of the airship opened up and a speck appeared from within it. Lone continued to aim his gun at the ship while the rest of us were frozen in place. A particular sound, akin to a fly speeding around an ear, cut through the air and ended as a three-pronged spear ripped through Lone's chest and sent him overboard. His body sank quickly.

"This is the end this is the end this is the end this is the end this is the end this is the end," said the captain as he dived into the ocean and swam toward the shore. Perphin pulled himself back into the boat. The men were waiting for my reply.

"We're men of the Steppe Army. We do not flee."

Four more circle ports opened, and with that came a barrage of bombs. The explosions sent streams of water hundreds of feet into the air. The boat capsized and it was impossible to hold onto anything. The waves created by the bombs tossed us about, then dragged us back underneath. There was no reprieve until a bomb hit our small boat and splintered it into the ocean. I grabbed two planks and held on with every ounce of my being. When the ocean tried to pull me to its bottom, the planks, squeezed between my arms, forbade it. It felt as though I swallowed half of the ocean, and I could not throw it up fast enough. My nose, eyes, and chest burned from the salty water, yet I held on till I was washed ashore. The beach had never seemed so safe, even though my legs betrayed me when I attempted to stand. Collapsing was my only option, and it was far more welcome than being abused by the sea.

When I had the energy to look up, I could only turn my head to the left. For the third time, I saw Eniam, standing next to a boulder—she neither said nor signaled a thing to me, though her presence was a gift, for I knew that it was not yet my time to perish. The only thing I could do after Eniam disappeared was black out.

My slumber was disrupted when a strong hand turned me over on my back. With the two suns glaring with an atypical fierceness, I could see only a shadow of a figure standing over me. He was a massive shape, blurred until he leaned in closely.

"You're a stubborn one, aren't you?" said the shadow. His bright green eyes peered at me, waiting for my response. White teeth beamed from his smile; I knew then that he had no intention of killing me.

"I . . . guess . . . I . . . might . . . be."

"It's a good quality, my friend. What's your name?" he said and pulled me to my feet. He towered over me and I noticed his unusual garb: a dark purple shirt, pants that only reached to his knees with pockets on the outside, and a leather satchel across his shoulders. His hat's brim covered his neck and there was a strange symbol stitched onto the front—it appeared that his head was as bald as his face. His leather boots were painted with mud.

"Isaac Foster Grey."

"Sounds like you might be royalty. Are you?" he said.

"No."

"Maybe you are and don't know it yet. You're young," he said. I looked beyond him and noticed that his great airship was hovering just above the ocean's surface. "It's something else, isn't it? Impressive as all hell. I've flown some beautiful machines in my time, but nothing like this. And I don't regret for a second that I stole it," he said.

"Who are you?"

"There I go again. Running my mouth without properly introducing myself. I've gotten into the worst habits since I've been here," he said, taking a moment to consider something I could not weigh upon. "The name's Gordon Spruce. Colonel Gordon Spruce, actually, not that that insignia means anything here."

"I'm a colonel too. Are you with the Steppe Army?"

"Kid, you look too smart to ask stupid questions," said Spruce.

"I—"

"I look like something spit out of a Salvation Army. I can't really blame the clothes I've been wearing, because they are not my clothes. To be honest, I'm typically in a uniform not so different from yours. But why are we talking about fashion? We should be talking about a lot of other things, including her," said Spruce, pointing with his thumb to the great flying ship.

"I've never seen one before."

"Me neither. I've flown helicopters and airplanes and even hot air balloons, but this is something altogether different. The guy who designed these things is more than a genius. Beyond Einstein and Newton. I've almost got the whole thing figured out. Along with some of these other things I've got on board. The key thing is, I can fly it and just about land it. Am I making sense to you? Probably not," said Spruce. He took a few steps toward the Dinorvans, then sat down. "Why don't you take a load off?" He patted the ground next to him. He was a strange being, and I could not follow what he was saying, but he was certainly fascinating and no longer a threat. I joined him on the sand and enjoyed the view of the airship. He opened up his leather satchel and offered me a shriveled, yellowish-brown food. I did not know what to make of it. "It's an evel. Kind of like an apple."

"What's an apple?"

"It's like an evel," said Spruce, and he laughed uproariously. "Fruit. You've got fruit here, don't you?"

"Yellowberries, mostly."

"For some reason they dry 'em out before they eat 'em, but they're pretty good," said Spruce. I took the fruit from him and took a bite—its texture was like soft leather, but its taste rivaled the sweetness of yellowberries. "Told you it was good. I got more if you want. No offense, but you look a little hungry."

"We were trying to catch fish."

"Using a gun?" he said.

"No. That was one of my men who deserved what you did."

"I'm sorry about that. It's kind of tricky to figure out who's your friend and who's your enemy around here. I never used to be a shoot-first-ask-questions-later kind of guy. I wasn't trained that way. No one in the Air Force is. It seems around here it's good to send a message. I hope you understand," said Spruce.

"Our training teaches us not to fear death."

"I guess that's true for militaries everywhere. Makes sense," he said. "So how is it a kid so young is leading a platoon? No offense, but you can't trust most kids with chores, let alone all it takes to be a colonel."

"I was told that I was advanced. My story is a little bit complicated and probably too long to tell."

"I've got a little bit of time. Not much, because I'm not exactly a free man in this world. If you get my drift. But I'd like to hear your story, and maybe you'd like to hear mine. What I'm really hoping is that we can help each other out," said Spruce.

"I'm not in a position of power."

"Don't sell yourself short there, Grey. Why don't you tell me your story and I'll determine if we're good for each other," he said.

And I did. He was fascinated throughout the duration of my stories. When I brought him up to the exact moment of when he and I met, he said simply, "We can definitely help each other. Now I'd love to tell you my story, but I need some food. Join me up there and we'll find a good place to land. Unless you're staying here. Staking your claim on some beachfront property." I shook my head. "Then let's get out of here."

For such a grand ship, Spruce had a small crew, about a dozen in total. In retrospect, it is quite surprising that he convinced any men at all to join him. This, of course, had nothing to do with his personality, for he was quite intelligent and amicable, though an association with him would, fairly or not, brand such an acquaintance as a traitor and fugitive. He explained this to me as we toured the top deck of the ship, which I assumed was similar to that of a great ocean vessel. I heard very little of what he was saying because I was so enamored by the ship. The contraptions that kept us hovering raged with a controlled fire, and it is difficult to express my absolute wonderment that such a thing could have kept us afloat.

And flying is exactly what we did as soon as we boarded—or perhaps "floating" is the more accurate description, for we hovered above the same spot in which Spruce had landed. We were higher than the nearest Dinorvan peaks, and I couldn't help but question whether man was meant to be so high. My initial thoughts dissipated rather quickly, for Spruce insisted on giving me a tour of the airship. He pointed out things on the top deck, mostly emphasizing that the weapons that looked like cannons were not in fact traditional cannons at all, but rather harpoon cannons, whose harpoons were intended to be fired into solid surfaces while the connecting chains helped to steady the ship. This could be used either when the airship was docked, or to allow the crew a quick escape. Next to each cannon was a small pouch of leather bands that the men would to use to slide down the chains, which to me at the moment sounded like great fun. Other than the cannons, Spruce was excited by the eighteen escape ships mounted to the exterior of the airship; he mentioned how he had only flown an escape vessel once, but that it was the greatest thrill of his life, something "straight out of a movie." It was unclear to me how they would fly. Spruce then became distracted and started describing how the ship was steered, which was managed from the bridge below.

When Spruce said "bridge," I thought of Joshua and his refusal to kneel before the General near the bridge construction project, which had led to all of this. This thought quickly transitioned into thinking how unstoppable I would be if I had an airship. I could destroy Steppe and his army in a matter of hours, bombing them until they surrendered; even if they were spread out across the whole of Hetra, I could travel across the entire country in seemingly no time at all. Not only would the ship rage for war, but it could also help me raid Purg.

These thoughts elapsed as soon as we reached the bridge—for it was not the type of bridge that I was accustomed to. It was, instead, where the ship was controlled, and the very sight of it forced me to freeze. The bridge, layered with various levels, was as big as the ship's perimeter, with windows encasing it throughout, providing a view in every direction. We walked toward the bow and I tried to imagine what all of the sophisticated equipment did: the gears and levers and switches and lights that somehow blinked and flashed. It seemed as if it would take a lifetime to learn how to operate the airship. My expression must have reflected my thoughts, because Spruce said, "It's not as tough to learn as you think." Near the bow, which provided quite a view of Hetra just beyond the Dinorvans, were three wheels, and beneath each wheel an enclosed compass that displayed directions and numbers. All three compass needles held a southeast position.

"This is all you really need to know when you're captain. Where to point this thing," said Spruce. "And the best thing about it is, if you go off course a little bit, you probably won't crash."

"This seems like something out of a dream."

"For me, too. Things like this aren't in my world either," he said.

That comment confused me—he seemed to insinuate that he was from someplace that I had never heard of. I had never traveled outside of Hetra, but I was aware that other nations existed. Hetra's position on the globe was quite isolated from every other nation, save for a few islands within a hundred-mile radius. All the great nations, like Chimio, North Peimer, South Peimer, and Lound, never bothered with Hetra because we offered nothing to them: our natural resources barely sustained us and our position was not vital to anyone, for we were far from bountiful trade routes and strategic military positioning. Hetra was, in a sense, a world unto its own. Yet Spruce did not look or sound like he was from one of the other nations on Jalta.

"What do you—"

"Let me show you the rest of the ship first," said Spruce.

We toured all the levels of the ship, from the weapons room in the bottom to the crew's quarters to the mess hall and kitchen to the very spacious captain's quarters. Spruce seemed to know how egotistical and illogical it appeared for one man to have such a vast space, and he was quick to explain himself.

"I know what you're thinking, kid. But in my defense, I didn't design this ship here. I just stole it," he said.

"How could you possibly steal this?"

"I like your tone, Grey. I mean, for a kid who's had a lot of bad shit happen to him, you're still a kid. Well, I can't avoid a question like that, can I?" he said. I assumed his question was rhetorical, but I shook my head anyway. "Why don't you grab a seat in one of those comfy chairs over there and I'll tell you how I got here. Not the whole thing, of course, because not everything's important, but I'll give you the juicy parts."

I went to the egg-shaped chair he had indicated but couldn't figure out how to sit down in it. Not until after Spruce ordered one of his crewmen to bring a feast for us and he plopped down in the egg-shaped chair opposite mine did I understand how to properly sit. The back of the chair was curved, and the base was bolted to the floor but allowed for rotating. My feet did not reach the ground and I could not help but feel that I would tip back at any moment.

"It's fine, kid. I know it's no La-Z-Boy—not that you know what the hell a La-Z-Boy is anyway. You can't miss something if you never knew it existed, right?" he said.

"Sometimes my mother would call my brother and me lazy boys."

"I think that's fine, just as long as she didn't try to sit on you," said Spruce.

"No. She was always a gentle woman. Even in Purg."

"It was a bad joke, Grey. We have very different reference points," said Spruce.

"If you don't mind me saying this, I have always known that I would travel far beyond Hetra and encounter people from the other nations of Jalta, but I never expected them to be as queer as you."

"That's because you always expected to meet someone from Jalta. I'm from a little bit further out than that," said Spruce.

"That's impossible. Jalta is the world."

"We-ell . . ." he said, extending the word.

"Yes, I know that at night, with certain sophisticated instruments, you can see into the sky beyond the suns. And there very well could be other places like Jalta out there. Based on some of the reading I've done—although this is not necessarily the work of scientists and more the recorded output of men with vivid imaginations and a penchant for speculation—I still allow myself to believe in the possibility of another place like this in the heavens. But even in a marvelous machine like this, I do not think you could fly beyond our world."

"You're right. The air's too thin, and I don't think anyone here has invented the spaceship. Don't get me wrong, though—there is some really cool shit here. This amazing thing we're sitting in right now doesn't exist where I'm from. Someone could invent it and make it work, but not like this. It's like a submarine and pirate ship and airplane all in one. It just doesn't make sense. And I have blueprints for all this stuff! It's just that I'm not an engineer or architect. I'm a pilot. Air Force test pilot, actually. I fly all the machines people dream up. Which is no small hill of beans, mind you. I'd argue it's more impressive, actually—but you don't care, because none of this means anything to you anyway," he said.

"Where are you from?"

"Southern Colorado. About twenty miles from the New Mexico

border," he said.

"Is that in North Peimer?"

"More like North America," said Spruce.

Three crewmen entered the captain's quarters carrying large silver plates of food. I hadn't seen a feast like this since the last officer's feast my father attended; he'd always taken me to prepare me for what he thought my future held.

The crewmen placed the trays on a nearby table and I thought I would pass into a coma from the brilliant aromas. Spruce saluted and thanked his men and stood up, and the men departed. "Don't be shy, Grey. Dig in." Most of the foods were exotic and unfamiliar, so I watched how Spruce filled his plate. He ripped a leg from a golden-cooked bird and bit into it immediately. "I can't remember the name of this bird, but it's a lot like chicken. At least, it looks a lot like chicken, but it kind of has a steak taste to it. We can call it sticken. Or cheak. It's the best of both worlds. I'd eat it baked, fried, or grilled." I grabbed a leg and tore into it with my teeth—it was tender, juicy, and perfect. "If you grabbed up a couple of these birds and brought them back to your country, they'd start multiplying real quick. Grab up some of those veggies and fruits and breads too. You look like you've never eaten. You've got to put on some pounds soon. Nobody trusts a skinny ruler."

"I'm not a ruler."

"Yet," said Spruce. His comment confused me, but I didn't press him further on it. "I apologize that there's no dessert. There seems to be an overall lack of sugar around here."

"The food is enough."

"It's always nice to end with dessert though, isn't it?" said Spruce.

We sat down and I ate my food slowly, savoring every bite. Spruce ate intermittently, only finishing half his food—he was too concerned with getting to his story. He looked at me with the same seriousness that my father had before he told my family we had to leave Timpast. I stopped eating to show that I was listening.

"I can't get into everything. That's only because it'll take you too long to understand. Because I don't understand. I'm starting to get what your world's about, but I haven't been here for that long. And I'm not trying to stay for too long," he said.

"I don't understand how you could be from somewhere else."

"Me neither. Not a hundred percent, at least. And I made the trip from my world to yours. Let me at least tell you the important stuff. I was working out of Kirtland on a few projects. All classified. I wasn't flying as much as I wanted to. Coming off all those missions in Laos and Cambodia, nothing would seem like a lot of flying. The thing is, when you're trained to fly, you need to fly, in war or in peace. My ex-wife was trying to convince me to settle down somewhere and fly for one of the big airlines. Yeah, that would've been flying, but not the kind I was looking for. I'm not saying I wanted another war. Vietnam was—well, it's only been three years and I can't wrap my head around it. Part of me can't believe it's already 1978. In my world, at least. What year is it here?" he said.

"It's 6030."

"Chalk up one more difference between my world and your world," said Spruce.

"I don't—"

"I'm getting there. So as I was saying, I wasn't doing much flying. New things were being designed and built, and it was all hush-hush, of course, but it don't mean a damn to a pilot when it's a blueprint or a drawing. It's not in me to sit around and wait, either. But still, I couldn't take my ex's advice and go fly people to their vacations. I figured the Air Force would come through for me," said Spruce.

"What's the Air Force?"

"That's the Army. In the air," he said.

"Using machines like this?"

"Kind of sort of. Well anyway, I started to get a little restless, and if I don't do something with myself, I can get mean. I had enough down-time to leave base and do as I pleased. If I was still a drinking man, I would have blown my paycheck on whiskey, but I quit that cold turkey in seventy-five. But I had to do something with my time, so I took up hiking. Seems like everywhere you go in New Mexico there's a place to go hiking. I grew up just north of there and I'd never bothered to check anything out in my southern neighbor. You know, one of the reasons I joined the Air Force was to go all over the world. I pictured myself living in Japan or Germany, but life, in its twisted little way, brought me right back home. I could fly anywhere in the world and the farthest I got was a hundred miles from where I grew up. So much for my plan.

"Anyhow, I took to spending my time out by myself. Just walking trails, trying to get lost just so I could find my way back. One day I drove out about halfway between Albuquerque and Santa Fe. Just to drive, really. That land makes you feel a little bit like a cowboy in a Western. Even when you're raised on John Wayne and Gunsmoke there's not much chance of being a cowboy. I'd take roads that led me further out from the world and never find much but a cluster of trailers. Then I decided one day just to park and walk. I'd go out a few miles and circle back. Really just to stretch my legs. I walked until my truck was a speck in the distance. Foolishly, I forgot to bring my canteen, and I walked on to a trailer that I used as a marker. As I got closer, I thought it was abandoned. Looked like it was, anyway. Most of the windows were broken out. There were a couple of dead cars parked around it, too."

"What's a car?"

"It's like a horse and buggy without the horse. Though the place looked deserted, I decided to see if anybody had left something behind to drink. Even a warm can of Coke would have done me fine at that point. Well, Grey, it turns out that place wasn't abandoned. And this is where our stories intersect—at least, our worlds do. There was a guy in there with a look I recognized. I'd seen enough POWs to know how they looked when they weren't POWs anymore. A lot of these guys don't trust the light or they like to keep to corners. The guy in that trailer was hiding from the world. I knew something was off with him because of how he was dressed. He had a funny black and green uniform on. Not the kind of thing you'd see in 1978," said Spruce.

"That's impossible."

"What is?" he said.

"Green and black are the colors of the No-Side Army."

"So I found out," said Spruce.

"But they're a myth."

"Oh yeah? Who do you think I got this ship from?" he said.

"But if they were real—"

"They're as real as real gets. Let me finish the story quick and then

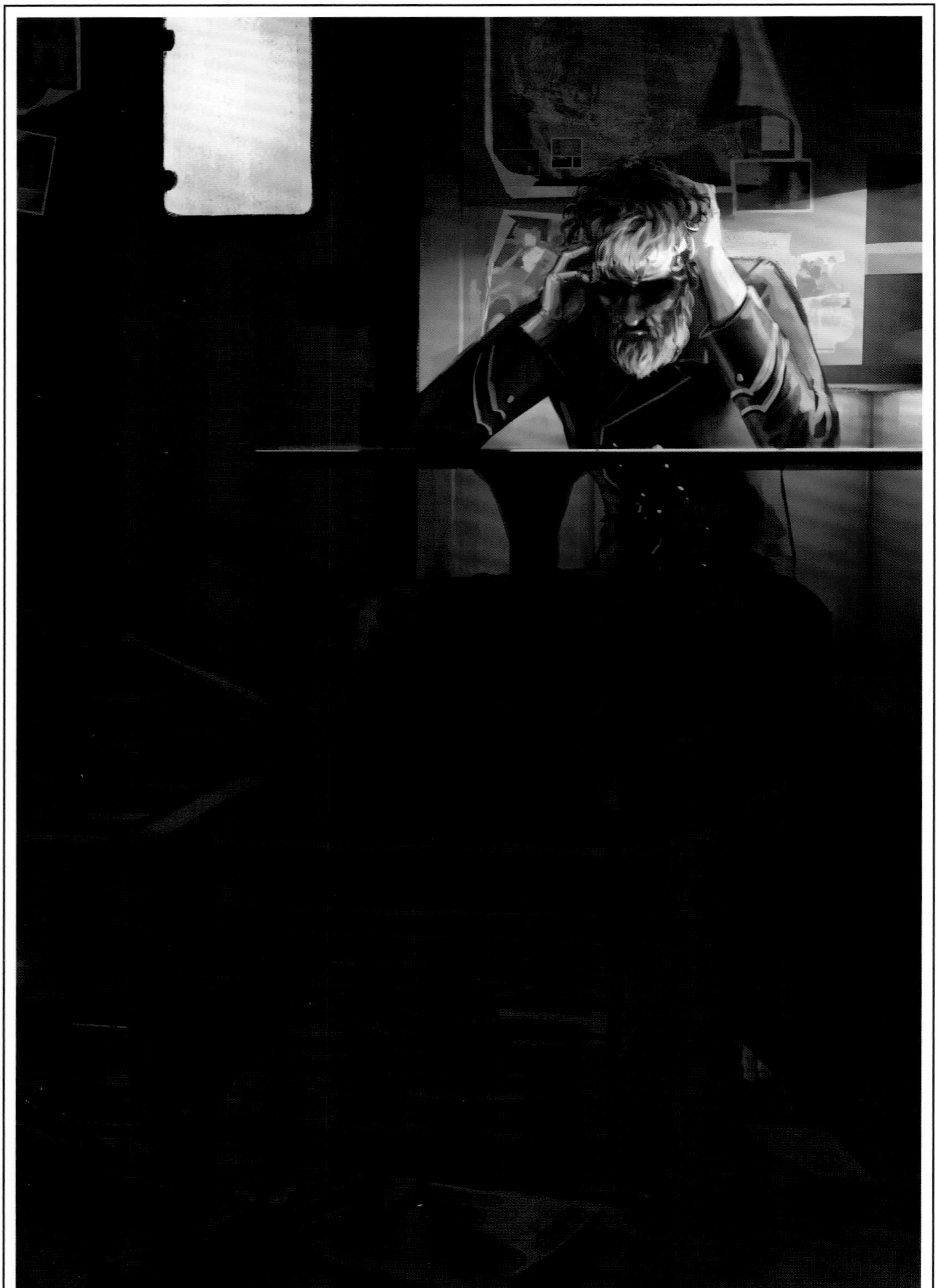

we can talk all about the No-Side Army if you want. So the guy in the trailer probably thought I was there to kill him, but I assured him I wasn't. He looked really hungry and I felt bad I had nothing to give him. Not even a stick of gum. I just knew he was lost and I wanted to help him. He wasn't in any condition to follow me back to my truck and he was too big for me to carry. I told him to sit tight, knowing he wasn't going anywhere. It took me hours before I got back—well, with the walking back to the truck and driving till I found a store open, you'd think it would have taken longer.

"The guy was grateful for sure. Once he knew he could trust me, he asked for some paper and ink. I happened to have a couple of notebooks and a pack of pens in my truck; a couple of the doctors I saw after the war told me to write down my thoughts about what happened, and as far as I ever got was buying notebooks and pens. The guy never saw pens before, and I never saw someone so fascinated with something so simple. I showed him how to use it and he took to drawing. I sat and snacked on some chips while he just drew and drew. When he finished he showed me the drawings. I wasn't sure what I was looking at, but the artwork was impressive. Then he spoke his first words to me. He said, 'I need to build it.' I asked him what 'it' was, and that got him telling his whole story," said Spruce.

"What was it?"

"The drawings were for something he called a lantern. I got him everything he said he needed to build it, and when he needed more, I got it for him. It was great to see him go from a drawing to the real thing. But besides that, he told me his whole story. His name was Bartleby Quinn. And he wasn't from my world. He was from yours. Typically I wouldn't believe some science fiction like that, but I enjoyed his stories. About North Peimer and being captured by the No-Side Army and designing and building all sorts of wonderful things. I listened for days. I told him to write it all down, but he said there wasn't time. He had to finish the lantern before he died. He wanted to get back so he could destroy the other lantern he'd built. He wanted to destroy most everything he built, but especially the lantern. Quinn knew the worst thing that could happen was the No-Side Army getting that lantern," said Spruce.

"Why did he build it, then?"

"He built it in secret. Yes, he was building them better weapons and flying machines and god knows what else, but he'd figured out a way to escape. He just couldn't control it. He thought he'd end up somewhere else in Jalta. But he found a portal or something from your world to mine. Now if that's not crazy, I don't know what is. That's the greatest discovery ever. Really, that beats anything else," he said.

"I can't believe that all he'd want to do is find a way back to Jalta and destroy the lantern."

"Right. I was onto that too. One of the things I thought was, maybe he was trying to build a lantern in my world so that this No-Side Army could pass back and forth and take over both worlds. He claimed that wasn't true. In fact, he claimed he wanted to come here. To Hetra," said Spruce.

"Why would he do that?"

"He said there was a great city in Hetra," he said.

"Inim."

"No," said Spruce.

"Timpast?"

"No. Selbrout," said Spruce.

"He couldn't have said that."

"He did," said Spruce.

"Selbrout is a miserable place."

"He thought otherwise. He said it was the only place in all of Jalta that was 'impervious' to attacks from the No-Side Army. I don't know if it's true. But it's one of the reasons I'm here now," he said.

"So the lantern he built in your world works."

"I usually went out to see him every day. But then I had a few missions to fly and I couldn't get out there for three days. Before I met Quinn, all I could think about was flying and how miserable I was because I wasn't. When I was flying again, all I could think about was that lantern. As soon as I could leave base I drove out to the trailer. When I got there, I had the same feeling I did the first time I saw it: this place is abandoned. And it was. All that was left were the notebooks and the finished lantern. My heart raced because I knew it had worked. Quinn didn't wander off somewhere. He went back home. I took the things, put them in the truck, and drove north.

"My ex-wife had told me about some sights I had to see in Santa Fe, and I figured it was finally time to listen to her. It was nighttime and the drive was quite peaceful. She'd told me about a state park up off of Old Santa Fe Road. According to the signs it was closed, but there was no ranger there. I followed a trail just a mile or so and found a perfect view. If I hadn't been reminded enough of how beautiful it was, that view really did it. I set the lantern down about fifty feet from the base of some cliffs. I figured if this thing was going to work, I might as well project it onto something special. And that was the first time I really looked at the lantern. It was incredible. Kind of like a projector. It looked like it should have been in a museum. The artistic details, which didn't seem to have anything to do with whether it worked or not, were amazing. It was like latticework designed with interconnected gears. There was a lock on the rear side that was comprised of three seemingly random shapes. I dialed them around until they connected properly and made this interesting emblem. That's what unlocked the lantern. Like it was a safe. Its top split and fell open. Inside, it was very simple. There was a lens, a slot for the glass slide, and a thick wick which, when lit, would provide the light to project the image. I was too excited to work my hands. I wasted three matches before lighting the wick with my final match; it burned much brighter than I expected. I closed the lantern and looked in awe at the image. Two grand mountain ranges intersected, like two roads. And atop the intersection was—"

"A village."

"How do you know?" said Spruce.

"Those are the Trelvnir and Curnist Mountains. In North Peimer. I have seen sketches before in a book my mother gave me. Her grandfather was from North Peimer. That village is called—"

"Lase," said Spruce. "The image struck me as so amazing that I walked toward the light. As soon as I did, I was sucked into the light. It felt like I was being pulled and pushed in a hundred directions at the same time. The light was too bright for me to keep my eyes open. When it stopped, I was in Lase."

"I still don't understand how you got there."

"Me neither. If anyone does, it would be Quinn," said Spruce.

"Or maybe the No-Side Army."

"Exactly. You guys might be a bit backwards in Hetra, but the rest of this world isn't so advanced either. Except for the No-Side Army. They have been slowly building themselves up for generations, developing the best minds and weapons that can help them complete their master plan," said Spruce.

"What might that be?"

"Domination of this world," said Spruce. He stood up and accidentally kicked over his plate of food. He cursed under his breath and waved his hand as if brushing crumbs from a table. "I have to show you something else."

We walked to the opposite end of the quarters and Spruce produced a key with which to unlock a door. The door opened, revealing a strange laboratory. Spruce guided me inside and locked the door behind us. The lab was no bigger than our apartment in Timpast, yet it was crammed with blueprints, maps, sketches, and prototypes for all types of wondrous things; some appeared to be weapons, others navigation tools, while others were indescribable. "Look at any of the drawings or blueprints. You'll notice something." I doubted Spruce, for I had little experience with such documents, though as I thumbed through the intricately detailed designs, I recognized what they all had in common. Written in the bottom right corner of each document was the name "B. Quinn."

"It's him."

"There's no other explanation," said Spruce.

"It's all very fascinating, Gordon, but I can't help you. This has nothing to do with me."

"It might," he said.

"It doesn't in the least. I am a colonel in the Steppe Army, and I have a mission. While I am bothered by the fact that I must kill the Inim Council, which is comprised as far as I know of innocent men and women, that is exactly what I must do in order to save my family."

"Inim's a waste of your time," said Spruce.

"It is where I must go to see my plan through."

"It won't exist much longer—it's going to be destroyed," said Spruce.

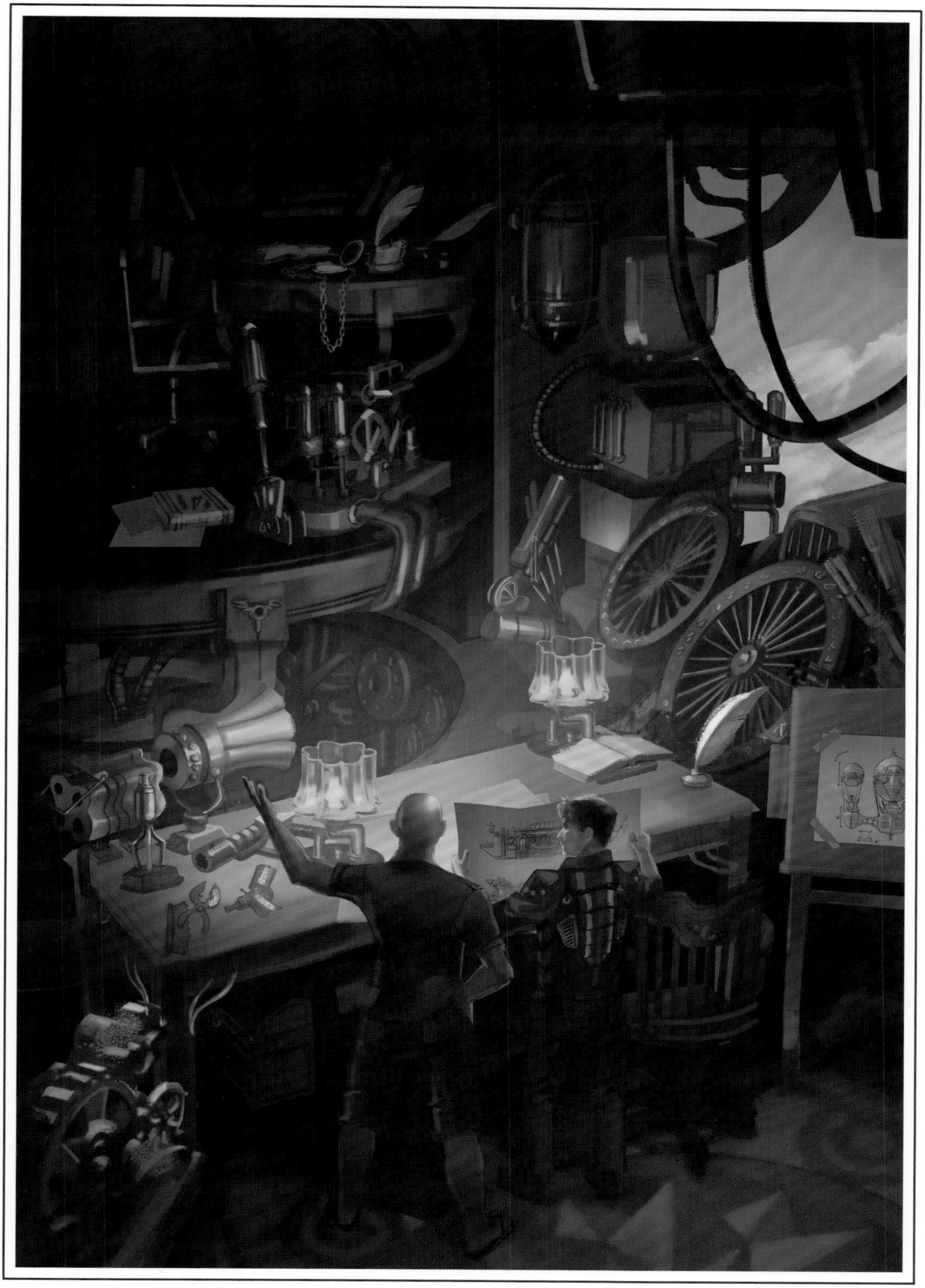

"Yes. I told you this myself. The General's plan includes destroying Inim and every other city but Timpast. He will destroy them to control them."

"No, kid, you're wrong. The No-Side Army is coming. To invade Inim, kidnap its best minds, and blow up all the rest. It's basically target practice for them. Steppe has nothing on the No-Sides. Trust me," said Spruce.

"What makes you such an expert? And how would you know anything of their plans?"

"I was their prisoner. For about two months. They captured me as I was wandering North Peimer. My smarts impressed them a bit, but it didn't take long for me to figure out that they wouldn't keep me alive for long. I knew my military training would help me out one day. So I escaped and stole this ship. Their best ship. But before I left, I bombed their main hangar. They only have a few transport ships left. But they'll build their airships again. It'll only take them a few months. And then they'll come after me. Because I have all of Quinn's work. They will destroy Inim as soon as they're ready," said Spruce.

"That doesn't mean they'll destroy the rest of Hetra."

"Of course they will. They need a place for target practice. And they're not going to blow up a place with good resources or good positioning on a map. No offense to your home, kid, but it means nothing to them," said Spruce.

"It means something to me. It means something to everyone who lives here. It's our home."

"Well, your General friend is about to muck things up anyway—with your help. If this place means so much to you, why are you doing what you're doing?" he said.

"Because I want to kill Steppe."

"Then kill him and not your country," said Spruce.

"Yes, but if what you're saying is true, then we have no hope against the No-Side Army."

"They have power. They have force. They have some pretty impressive weapons. But they aren't the smartest guys on the block. Think of this—it only took one guy to steal their best ship. If you have good weapons and smart people using them, you can beat them. If there's a place that doesn't seem like it's worth taking, they'll leave it alone. And most importantly, if you have a smart leader, you can't be stopped. Quinn said Selbrout was the only city that could survive against the No-Side Army. Let's go there. Warn the people. Give them Quinn's documents. Help them build. What do you say, Grey?" said Spruce.

Spruce was right that we were the only two men that could possibly save Hetra, illogical as that sounded—yet I couldn't just put aside my personal agenda.

"I want to save my family first."

"I get that. It's just that I don't know how much time we have," said Spruce.

"Explain to me why you're doing this. Shouldn't I be the one trying to save my country?"

"That's what I'm trying to get you to do," he said.

"And why is it your concern?"

"It's what I'm trained for. Also, I need a place that's safe from the No-Side Army. So another one of these can be built," he said and produced a blueprint for the lantern. "I'm going to get back home. I can't do it without this. And I can't build it myself," said Spruce.

"Nobody in Selbrout can either. It's a wayward place. Although I'm confident that if these sketches are accurate, there will be men in Inim that can construct it for you."

"The problem is, your boss is about to ransack the place," said Spruce.

"Take me to my family, and I promise I will help you."

"Let's get to the bridge," he said.

The view from the bridge's windows was spectacular, though I was preoccupied with thoughts of my family. My concern was that my mother would not join me and my sisters would not recognize me. I wondered what effect four years had had on their appearances. I tried to convince myself that they would be so overjoyed with their freedom that they would forgive me for murdering Joshua.

None of my fears mattered—for when we sailed over eastern Blackbin, I sensed the worst, and my instincts were accurate. Purg had been abandoned. Not a soul remained inside that terrible place. Whether people had been killed or had escaped and moved elsewhere, I did not know, though I held out hope that my mother and sisters

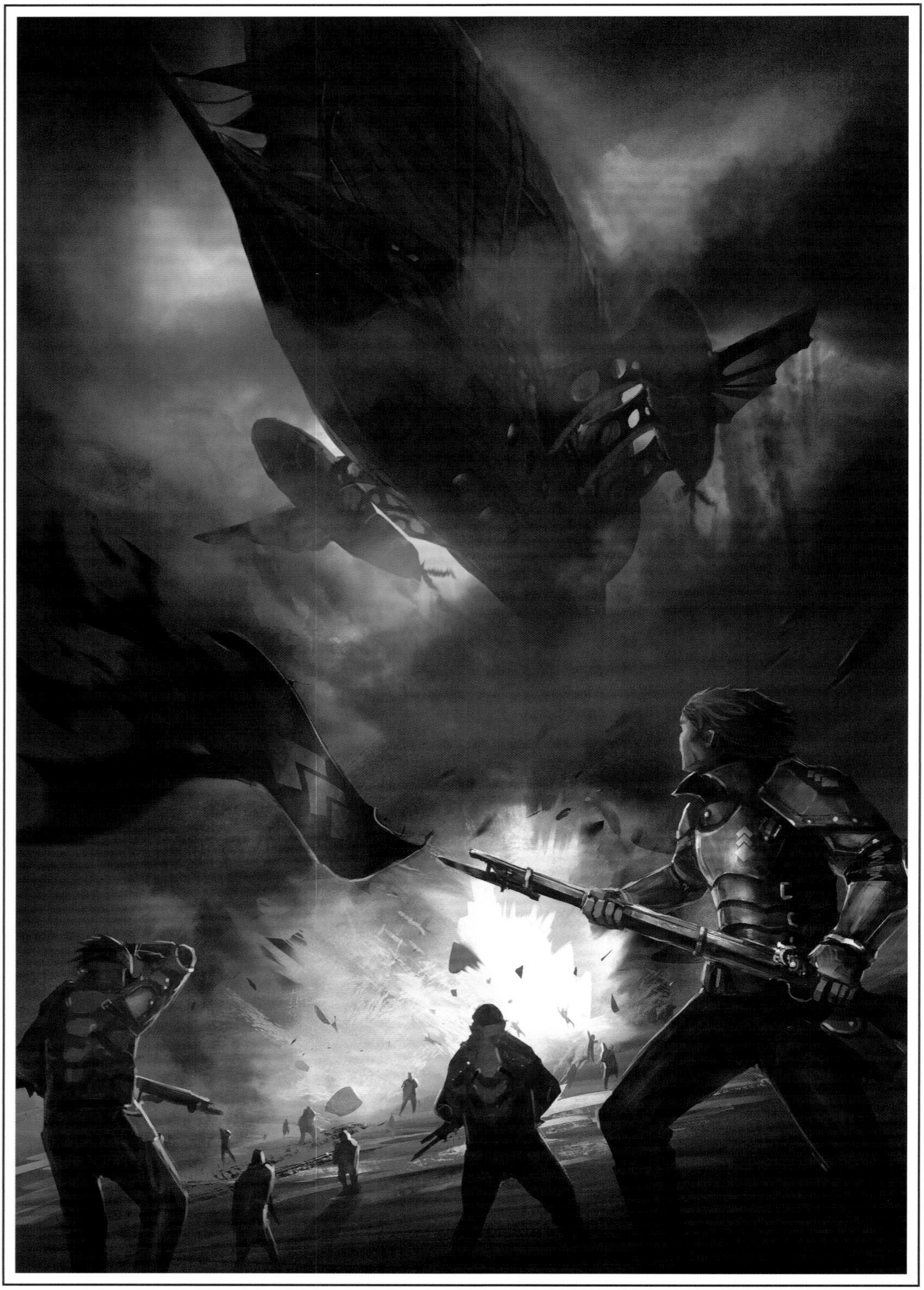

were still alive. I could not imagine them dead. Even if they rejected me, I would scour all of Hetra to find them and save them, but in order to do so, I had to stop Steppe. Not only would I have to end Steppe's reign—I needed to become the leader that Hetra needed. If circumstances had left me as the last remaining Grey, I had to prove to the world the worth that name had held for many generations previous and would for many more to come.

I turned to Gordon.

"Sorry, kid," he said.

"There's no reason for you to apologize. I failed my family and I have to amend things. Right now, I want to do more than kill Steppe. I want to erase him from history."

"The best revenge you could get would be to become what he wants to be," said Spruce. "When you save this country from the No-Side Army, nobody will remember the General."

"We fly north."

"Yes, sir," he said.

Lake Lian, Hetra's largest lake, was transformed into a reflection pool as we flew over it. The underbelly of the ship was a sight to behold, and I could only imagine what the thousands of soldiers below us, who were supposed to be marching toward Inim, thought as they stared above. The young men were featureless specks moving in a giant swarm.

Spruce took the airship past the entire Steppe Army, then slowly turned the ship around to face the soldiers. "You ready?" he said.

"Drop a few bombs from the back."

"We might need those," said Spruce.

"Not as much as we'll need them." I pointed below to the Steppe Army.

"Four bombs! Stern side!" said Spruce. Two men scrambled around the bridge to the weapons dock.

"Four bombs a-go, captain!" replied one of them.

Each bomb that hit sent quivers through my body. I watched only how the army reacted. They did not flee, for soldiers must stand their

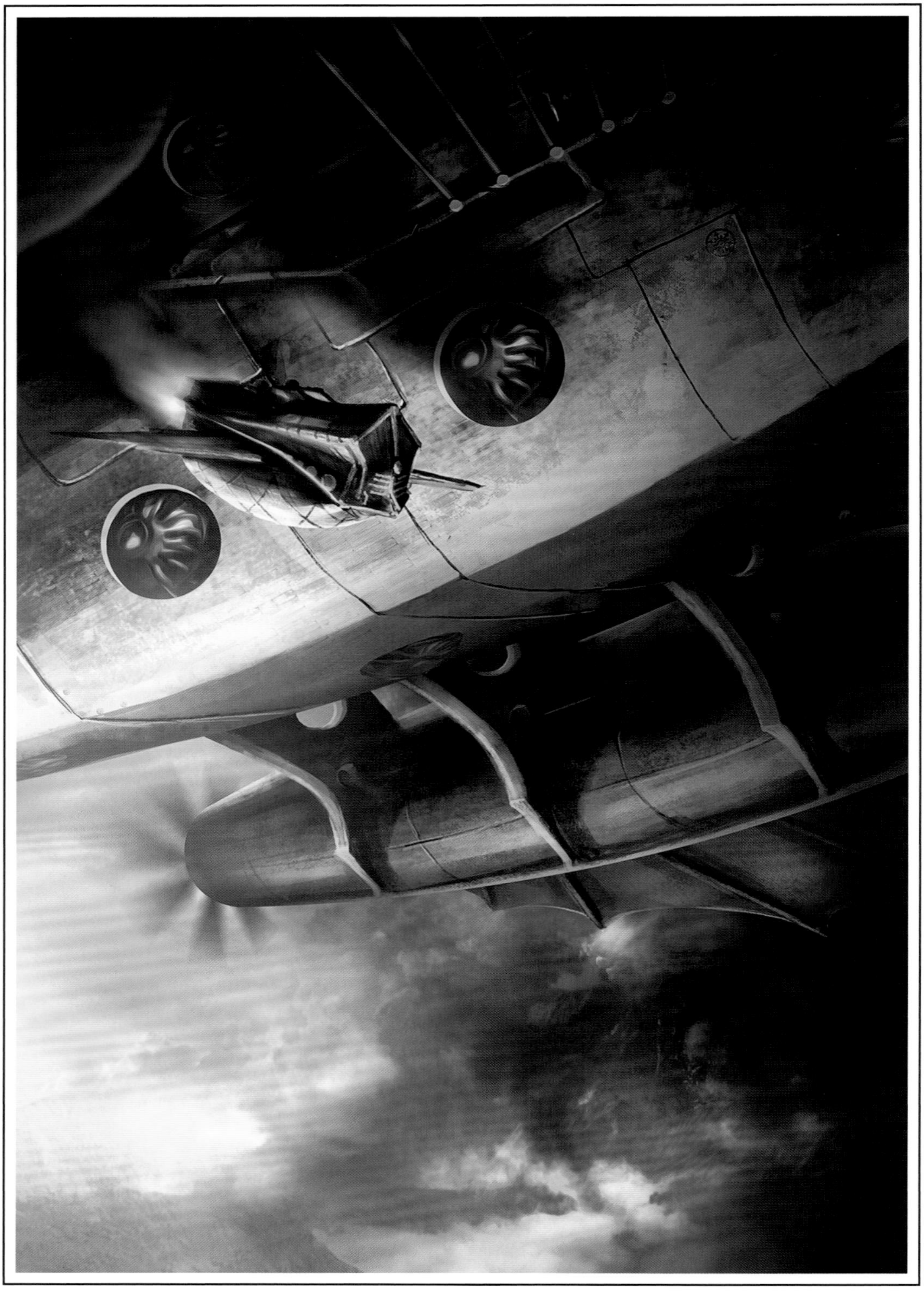

ground regardless of the enemy, though I knew they were scared.

"This is going to blow your mind, kid. Up on the deck," said Spruce.

The deck was abandoned, the entire crew on the bridge. Balancing was difficult with a harsh wind whipping about. I gripped the railing and looked overboard. For a brief instant, I forgot where I was and expected to see water. The view from the heavens was majestic and humbling. Spruce grabbed my arm and pulled me along. I climbed aboard the two-seater airship, sat in the front, and studied the controls. After ten seconds I realized that I'd need months of training to fly one myself; I hoped that Spruce's one test flight was enough training for him. A pair of goggles hung to my right, held by a small hook; I put them on, knowing they were there for a reason.

Spruce yelled out instructions, so I followed; I gripped the round handle to my left, pulled it, and turned it clockwise. This simple gesture released us from the grips of the main airship, plummeting me in a scream of faith. I looked behind me to assure myself that Spruce was still there. His face was filled with delight. Just as I expected to crash into the field, metallic wings shot out on either side, each wing ten feet in its span. The airship did not fly as I expected, though the descent slowed slightly. Then, a fire roared out from the back of the airship, and we stopped dropping vertically and ripped through the sky horizontally. The airship flew over the heads of the soldiers and they dived to save their lives. It was an absolute thrill to be gliding through the air, boundless as a bird. We circled round to the front of the army and hovered.

It only took a few moments for Steppe to emerge from the crowd. He was wearing the same gun suit he'd donned on the day he killed my father and very nearly killed me. He approached the airship fearlessly, the rifles of the gun suit pointed at the airship.

"You're nothing, whoever you are," said Steppe. "This is the greatest army in the world, and I am its commander. Show your face before I kill you!" I did not budge, for I wanted an ire reaction from him, and I was searching for a button that might control the airship's weapons. Bullets ricocheted off the airship, all fired from Steppe. Just as the General yelled, "Men!" indicating that they should open fire, I found the weapon controls, conjectured how to aim, and fired. A harpoon

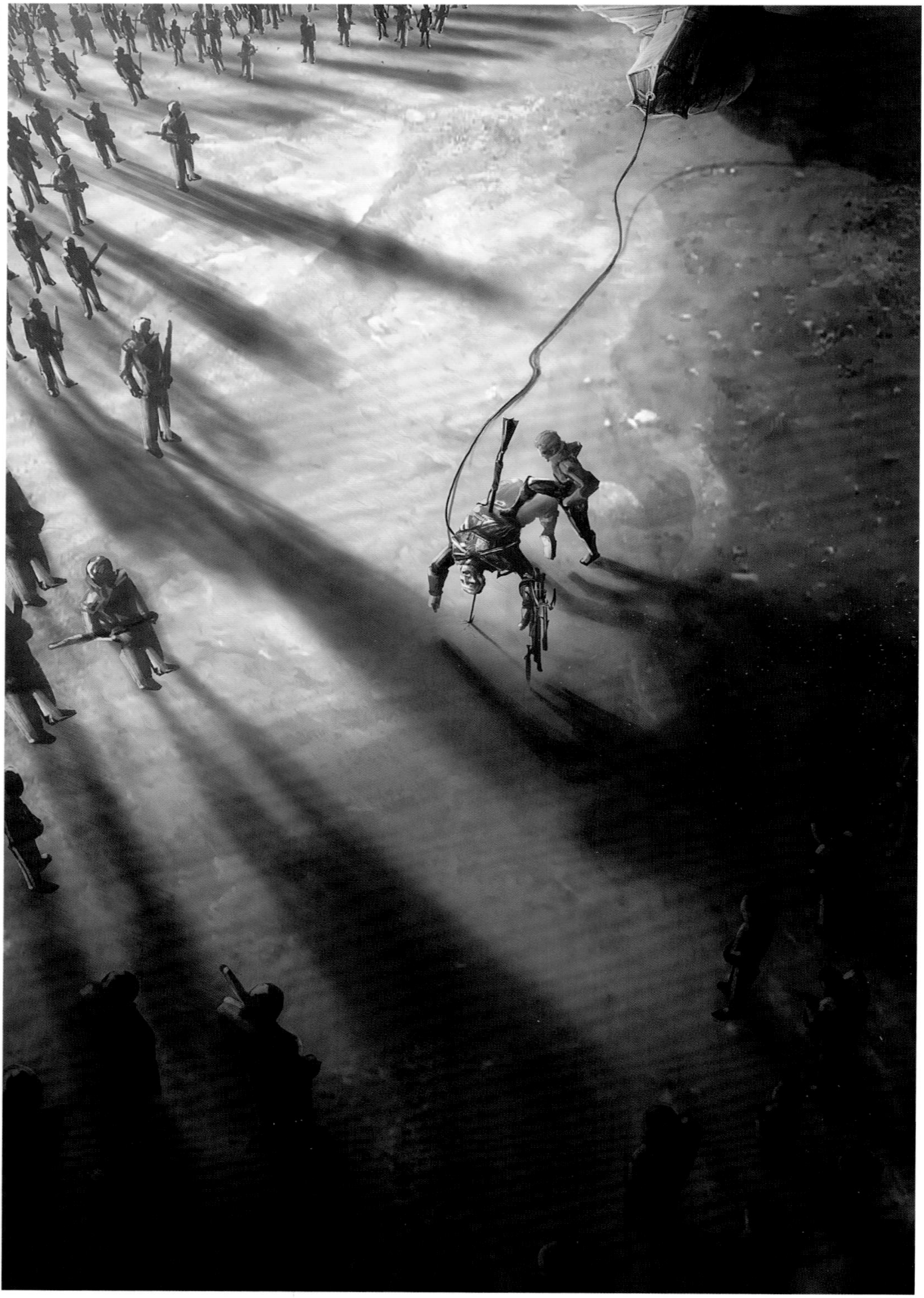

raced through Steppe's belly, burying itself in the ground, pulling him backwards; he looked as if he were in a state of suspension, frozen in mid-fall.

I expected it to rain rifle shots, yet it did not happen. The soldiers were in a state of shock. Spruce lowered the airship and I jumped out. The men in the front started moving backwards and I raised my hands to show that I was unarmed. The goggles masked my identity, and the men watched in wonder as the stranger who had shot their leader approached the dying man. I stood over Steppe and lifted my goggles onto my forehead. Steppe's eyes were an equal mix of terror and anger. He tried to speak, but could not. I quickly looked to see what held him in midair. One of the harpoon's prongs had hooked itself into the back plates of the gun suit.

I leaned in close to his ear and whispered, "When we meet in the next world, tell me what your final thoughts were."

I placed my boot upon his chest and pressed him into the ground. The sound of his last breath gasping from his lungs lifted a weight off my shoulders. I looked out at the men. My men. They stretched for as far as I could see, and I was not bothered that they would not all hear my words as I spoke them then, because I knew they would hear them very soon.

"The General's plan could only have be designed by someone as sick and foolish as him. He is dead because he would have been incapable of protecting you or leading you. He wanted to rule Hetra for the sake of ruling, for a small sliver of power. And he convinced us all that this was the way of the future. How wrong he was. The airship above you, which I assure you is very real, belonged to the No-Side Army. They intend to use ships like this to take over the world. I know this, because I've stolen it from them. The General knew nothing of their plans or their capabilities because he could only think on a small scale. The No-Side Army thinks in grand terms. So do I. Except I do not want to take over the world; I want to protect our world. Our country. Our cities. Our people. Let us use the enemy's weapons against them. Let us come together not to terrorize our citizens, but to unify our nation. Let us unify our nation to build the greatest city in the world. A city that will protect our people against any threat. A city against which every other city will be judged. A city that will be a model of hope and promise. A city that all of Hetra will call home."

With this, the men who could hear me erupted in applause; this, like a wave, rolled to the back lines. Thousands of men were cheering and clapping.

I raised my hands for silence and continued. "The No-Side Army plans to attack your city of Inim. You will march there, and I will lead you—not to overtake them and kill their Council like the General planned, but to liberate them. We will lead them out. As we will do with the people of Timpast, and Evdow, and Guland. It could take us years, but we will march our people to the city you once knew as Selbrout. It is Selbrout that we will transform into our home. It is there we will be safe. It is there we will thrive. Yet we will no longer refer to it as Selbrout. For it must die like our other cities in order for Hetra to have her new dawn. And in their place, one city will rise to the heavens and be known the world over. This, your city, will forever be known as Lantern City."

The destruction of Inim occurred, though not before we freed the citizens. This was true for all of Hetra's cities and villages. Details of the great migration, or the years and labor required to build both Lantern City and its impressive Underground, or the gradual erecting of the city's surrounding wall, will have to wait. I grow tired and must rest before this tale continues. It is my hope that I live long enough to tell it. Understand that the wall was constructed to withstand outside threats, never to imprison the citizens; the Underground was meant for all citizens to inhabit, truly any time they please, though its initial purpose was to provide a safe haven for all Lantern City citizens during an aerial attack. And even though I was the ruler, I relied on the help of the millions who also believed in the city's purpose. My only regret is that Spruce did not stay for long—but he left behind Quinn's work, which guided us toward our advancements. I know not if Gordon found his way back to his world or wanders yet.

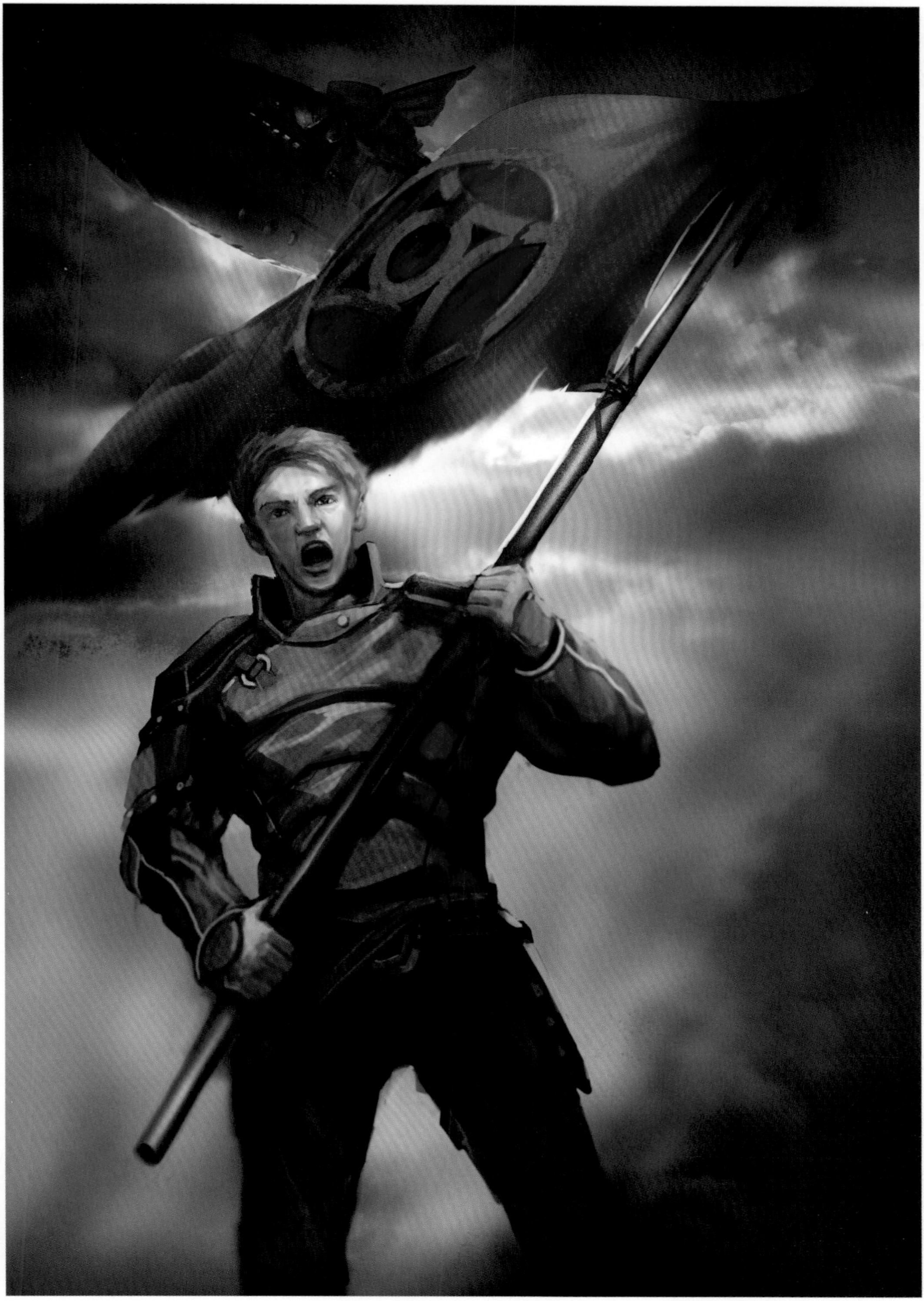

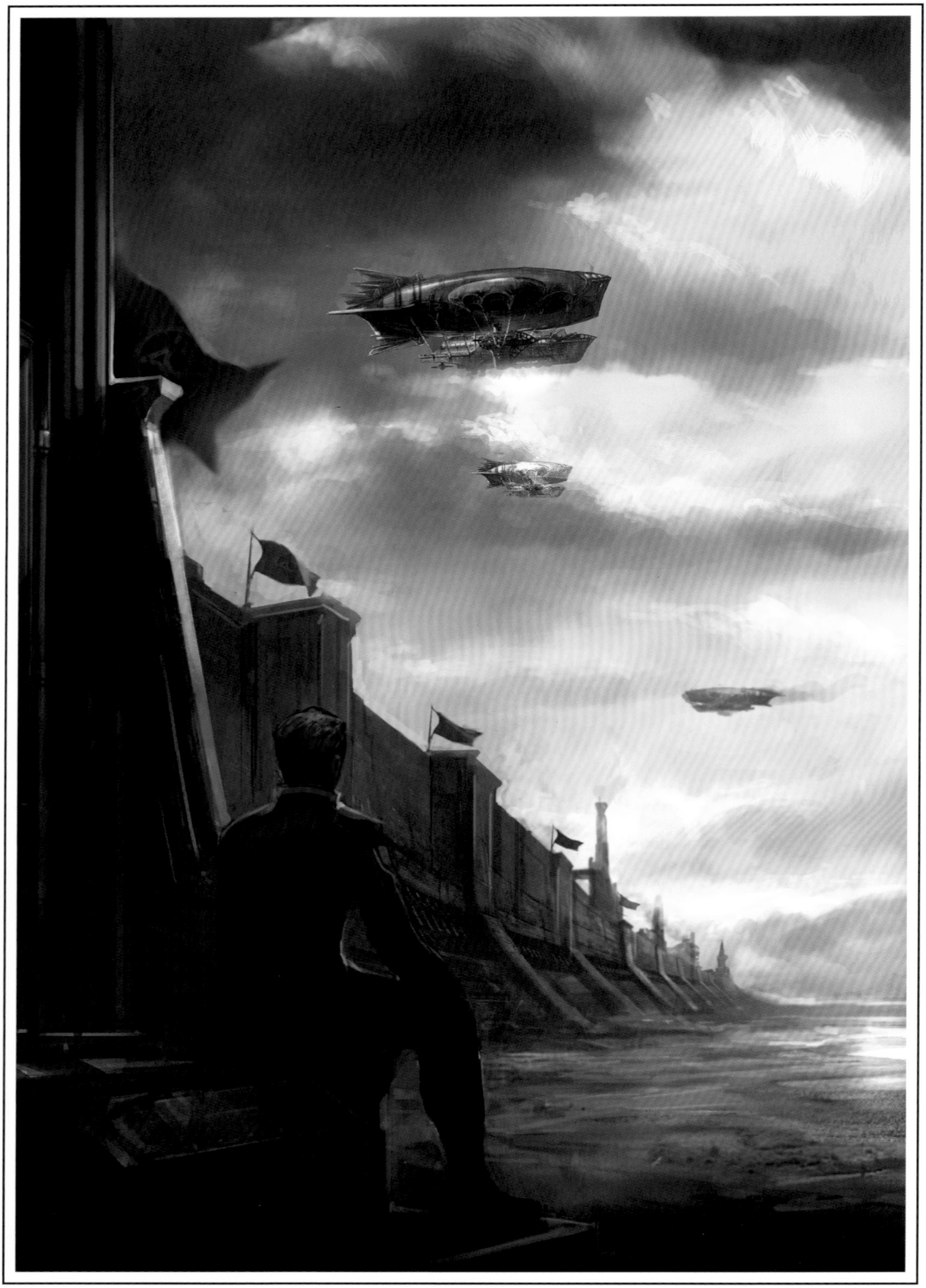

These were the varied thoughts I took with me every day to the perch, built for me and me alone, on the northern side of the wall, just east of the gates. It was there I would retreat to watch the suns set and sit proudly under the flags that bore my emblem.

I know the city, now out of my control, has lost its way. Perhaps the citizens grow frustrated and restless. Perhaps they feel they have been so wronged that they riot in the streets. Perhaps the city has succumbed to many ills born from within. My son has charted a destructive path of corruption and greed. Perhaps his successors have as well. Perhaps you are one of them. If you are, remember why this city was built. Remember, it is never too late to save the city. If you do not, there may not be anyone else. I leave things in your hands.

Epilogue

Killian closed the book and glanced at Hugh, who was reading a book of his own. Hugh removed the glasses from the tip of his nose.

"So?" said Hugh.

"There has to be more," said Killian.

"That's the only writing your grandfather left behind," said Hugh.

"You don't know that," said Killian.

"I do," said Hugh.

"How?" said Killian.

"Because your great-grandfather was a busy man. Even when he was ninety. And if it wasn't for me writing that journal for him, we wouldn't have anything," said Hugh.

"So it's not real?" said Killian.

"Every word of it came from his lips. I merely scribbled them down," said Hugh.

"I'm going to do something about this right now. I'll take this to my father so he can see that—"

"Is that a very wise idea?" said Hugh.

"It's the truth," said Killian.

"And in all your years, how interested in the truth would you say your father is?" said Hugh.

"Not very, I guess," said Killian.

"Tell me what you think your father would do with this book, whether he read it or not," said Hugh.

"Burn it. Discard it. I don't know," said Killian.

"Both, probably," said Hugh. He took the book from Killian and slipped it into his pocket.

"I want to keep it," said Killian.

"It's much safer here. For now," said Hugh.

"But if I keep it, I can read it any time I want," said Killian.

"You can read it any time you want," said Hugh. "Understand this to its utmost, Lord Grey: if you intend on fulfilling your great-grand-father's promise, you have a tremendous amount of reading and work ahead of you. That library is yours. This entire city will be yours. In the meantime, you must always maintain loyalty to your parents—especially your father. Your time will come soon enough and you don't want to jeopardize it."

"How often can I come here? And how will I know how to get back?" said Killian.

"You may come every day if you wish, as long as you are by yourself. And you will know how to get here, because this is the place where you are meant to be."

The Creators of RISE

The creator of Lantern City, **Trevor Crafts** is no stranger to building worlds. Winner of the LATV Festival and numerous industry awards, including an Emmy®, Trevor has spent his career creating dynamic stories with striking visuals featuring strong characters. His love of all things fantastic was nurtured by his dad, who opened Trevor's mind to science fiction literature and film at an incredibly young age. Trevor, now CEO of Macrocosm Entertainment, has acted as producer, writer, and director and seems to work best on little to no sleep, fulfilling multiple roles at a time. Trevor lives in Los Angeles with his amazing wife Ellen and his hilarious dog Audrey Hepburn.

When asked by his grandparents at age ten what he wanted to be when he grew up, **Matthew James Daley** answered confidently, "A writer, historian, or comedian." He wasn't too far off, finding himself in adulthood writing for film and television (winning an Emmy® along the way). He has always been attracted to genres (especially sci-fi and horror) and all things comic books (even when they weren't cool). Matthew resides in New Jersey with his incredible wife and two children, both of whom are destined to be comedians. *RISE* is his first novel.

Bruce Boxleitner, an accomplished film and television actor, producer, and author, has had a love of alternate worlds since he read *20,000 Leagues Under the Sea* as a boy growing up on a farm in Illinois. Starring in some of the greatest genre TV and film productions of our time has garnered him sci-fi fans worldwide. From the title role in Disney's cult film *TRON* to John Sheridan in the popular television series *Babylon 5*, Bruce has an acute understanding of what makes a great epic story and wields these skills as co-creator of *Lantern City*. In addition to his work onscreen, Bruce has authored *Frontier Earth* and its sequel, *Frontier Earth: Searcher*, published by the Berkley Publishing Group. Bruce Boxleitner currently resides in Los Angeles and has three sons: Sam, Lee, and Michael.

The Illustrators of RISE

Section Studios is a Multi-Disciplinary Media Solutions company based out of Los Angeles CA. We specialize in Concept Art, Game development, VFX, Web Design and Full service Publishing. — *www.sectionstudios.com*

Cecil Kim has been working as a concept artist and illustrator in the entertainment industry for the past 17 years. Cecil received his BFA in Illustration from Art Center College of Design. He has worked on projects such as *Parasite Eve*, *Final Fantasy IX*, and the *God of War* franchise. Cecil also teaches at various institutions such as Gnomon School of Visual Effects, Art Center College of Design and Otis College of Art and Design where he serves as Concept Art Area Head. In early 2011, Cecil was awarded the British Academy of Film and Television Arts' Artistic Achievement Award. Cecil then joined Jimmy Yun and Justin Yun at Bluecanvas, Inc. and together they launched Section Studios, Inc. He currently resides as Creative Director/CCO for both companies.

Justin Yun has been working as an art director, concept artist and illustrator in the entertainment industry since he received his BFA in Illustration from Art Center College of Design. His work has ranged from television commercials, video games, music videos and film. Justin also teaches at various institutions such as Gnomon School of Visual Effects and Otis College of Art and Design. In 2008 Justin co-founded Bluecanvas, Inc. with Jimmy Yun (CEO). Soon after, Cecil Kim joined Jimmy and Justin to launch Section Studios, Inc. Justin currently resides as Creative Director/CCO for both companies.

Contributing Illustrators:

Theo Aretos theoaretos.com	**Daniel Kim** danielkimart.com
Max Cederroth maxced.blogspot.com	**Joe Kim** theartofjoekim.blogspot.com
Os Kolarp Em www.osfolio.com	**Leslie J. Lee** lesliejlee.com
Colas Gauthier colasgauthier.com	**Shelby Peterson** shelbypeterson.com
Jason Kang cargocollective.com/artofjasonkang	**Amber Sanders** ambersandart.com
Brian Kim oneminutelifespan.blogspot.com	**Gabriel Yeganyan** gyeganyan.com

WWW.LANTERNCITYTV.COM